CONSUMER REPORTS
MONEY-SAVING GUIDE TO ENERGY IN THE HOME

CONSUMER REPORTS
MONEY-SAVING GUIDE TO ENERGY IN THE HOME

by the Editors of Consumer Reports Books

Consumers Union, Mount Vernon, New York

Copyright © 1978 by Consumers Union of United States, Inc.
Mount Vernon, New York 10550
All rights reserved including the right of reproduction in whole or in part in any form.
Library of Congress Catalog Card Number: 78-72145
International Standard Book Number: 0-89043-011-X
Manufactured in the United States of America

Drawings in this book are by Robert Byrd, page 59; Durell Godfrey, page 44; Walter Hortens, pages 8, 9, 10, 54, and 63; Seymour Nydorf, pages 23, 24, and 25; Whitman Studio, Inc., pages 18, 26, 48, 50, and 52.

Consumer Reports Money-Saving Guide to Energy in the Home is a Consumer Reports Book published by Consumers Union, the nonprofit organization that publishes *Consumer Reports*, the monthly magazine of test reports, product Ratings, and buying guidance. Established in 1936, Consumers Union is chartered under the Not-For-Profit Corporation Law of the State of New York.

The purposes of Consumers Union, as stated in its charter, are to provide consumers with information and counsel on consumer goods and services, to give information and assistance on all matters relating to the expenditure of the family income, and to initiate and to cooperate with individual and group efforts seeking to create and maintain decent living standards.

Consumers Union derives its income solely from the sale of *Consumer Reports* and other publications. Consumers Union accepts no advertising or product samples and is not beholden in any way to any commercial interest. Its Ratings and reports are solely for the information and use of the readers of its publications.

Neither the Ratings nor the reports nor any other Consumers Union publications, including this book, may be used in advertising or for any commercial purpose of any nature. Consumers Union will take all steps open to it to prevent or to prosecute any such uses of its material, its name, or the name of *Consumer Reports*.

Contents

1 **The house as "energy system"** 7

2 **Ways to "tighten" the house against winter weather** 17
    Exterior caulking compounds 17
    Weather stripping 23
    Windows: Escape routes for heat 26
    Insulation: When enough is enough in the wintertime 32
    Cellulose insulation: Handle with care 38

3 **Getting the most from the heating system** 40
    Energy-saving thermostats 40
    Getting more from your fuel 47
    Recovering heat at the flue 49
    The flue damper: Pros and cons of an energy-saver 53

4 **Keeping cool** 57
    Can insulation lower your air-conditioning costs? 57
    Whole-house attic fans 60
    Room air conditioners: How to match the equipment to your needs 66

5 **Saving energy in the home's water system** 68
    Reducing energy usage in the water heater 68
    Restricting the flow in the shower 70
    Conserving water in the toilet 74

6 **Saving energy on a small scale** 79
    Some gadgets to avoid 79
    Igniters for gas ranges 81

7 **If you must seek professional help** 84

8 **Government response to conservation** 88
    Federal conservation programs 88
    State conservation programs 89
    State offices of economic opportunity 95
    Regional community services administration offices 97
    State energy offices 97

Index 101

1
The house as "energy system"

One of Jimmy Carter's campaign pledges, and one of his first major actions as President, was the creation of what he termed a "comprehensive energy policy" for the nation. In an effort to gain support for that policy, President Carter has used some rather strong words.

When he first presented his National Energy Plan to the public, he called energy conservation "the moral equivalent of war." A few months later he said, "America faces the most serious domestic challenge that it is likely to face in our lifetimes —the energy challenge." By saving energy, he added, "we can protect jobs, the environment, and the basic American standard of living, not only for ourselves, but also for our children and grandchildren. We must succeed."

Although Congress may have taken the President's words to heart, it was not a totally receptive audience. In months of deliberations (which were still going on as this book went to press in August 1978) Congress made drastic changes in the President's program.

However, National Energy Plan or no, energy conservation is already a prime concern of millions of Americans. A 1977 survey by Predicasts, Inc., a private market research firm, estimated that nearly half the homeowners in this country planned "specific, substantive work on their homes within the next year or so for the purpose of saving energy." Some homeowners said they were willing to spend $1000 or more to save energy, according to the survey.

Many homeowners have already begun spending. The market for insulation, storm windows, and other products that can help save energy has been booming for months, and it's not hard to understand why. Saving energy is the same as saving money.

No one has yet developed the ultimate weapon to wage this moral equivalent of war, but there are dozens of steps you can consider to save energy in the home. Some will yield a dramatic saving; others will have far more modest results; and still others simply won't work in certain cases.

In order to know which energy-saving measures will be the most effective in your house, it's first necessary to understand something about energy and the way it is used in the home.

Supplying energy

Strictly speaking, energy can't be created or destroyed. But energy can be converted from one form to another, and some forms of energy are much easier to use than others. That is, they are forms of *available* energy—electricity or the energy contained in fuel oil or natural gas— which can be used to turn on lights or run appliances, or to heat a house.

A quick (and somewhat simplified) look at a water heater will show what we mean by available energy and how that energy can be put to use in the home. Suppose, for the moment, that the heater operates on natural gas. The gas is a source of energy. Burning the gas converts its chemical energy into heat, which is transferred to the water in the tank, raising the water's temperature. (For simplicity's sake we'll assume that all the heat is transferred to the water.)

Say the hot water is drawn out of the tank and into the shower. What happens to the energy now? As the hot water travels through the pipes, some of that heat (energy, in other words) escapes through the walls of the pipes and into the air and some of the heat remains in the pipes. And, when the water rushes from the shower head, it loses more energy as heat leaves it and warms the air, the tub, and the person taking the shower. What's left goes down the drain. The energy hasn't been destroyed, but it has been scattered so widely that, for all practical purposes, it cannot be reclaimed. If you want more hot water you have to use more natural gas to supply the heat for it.

Suppose, now, that the water heater runs on electricity. Unlike natural gas, which is a fuel or matter that contains energy, electricity is pure energy. It has been generated at a plant (usually by burning fuel but sometimes by converting the mechanical energy in moving water) and then transmitted to the house. Thereafter, an electric heater works in the same general way as a gas-fired heater does. Electricity, passing through a heating element, is converted to heat which is transferred to the water in the tank.

Since it's not possible to keep heat in the house forever, it's necessary to acquire more natural gas, oil, or electricity for use in the house. That, of course, is what costs you money.

When you buy electricity from the

7

local utility company, you pay directly for the energy you get. When you buy natural gas, fuel oil, or propane, you're paying for some quantity of fuel—a cubic foot or gallon. But what you're really looking for is the energy available in those fuels. The units to measure energy are somewhat less known than those units of quantity. The most common units (and the ones we will use repeatedly in this book) are the British thermal unit and the kilowatt-hour.

British thermal unit (Btu) is a measure of heat. Specifically, it is the amount of heat required to raise the temperature of one pound of water one degree Fahrenheit. (Heat, remember, is one form of energy.) One Btu may seem to be a large amount of energy, but it's not. One gallon of fuel oil would yield about 140,000 Btu if it were burned completely, and 100 cubic feet of natural gas would yield about 100,000 Btu.

Kilowatt-hour (kwh) is a measure of electrical energy. Specifically, it is the amount of electricity required to operate a 1000-watt appliance for one hour, or a one-watt appliance for 1000 hours, or any combination of watts and hours which, multiplied together, total 1000. A 100-watt light bulb burned for 10 hours would consume 1 kwh.

While electricity is most often used to provide light or motion, it is also used to supply heat. Just as it's possible to compute the number of Btu in a gallon of fuel oil or a cubic foot of natural gas, it's also possible to compute the number of Btu in 1 kwh of electricity. One kwh is the equivalent of 3413 Btu.

Inside the "energy system"

A house contains dozens of devices that use energy—light bulbs, kitchen appliances, televisions and radios, heating systems, and more. One way or another, they all use energy, releasing it in the form of heat or light.

According to the Department of Energy, heating and cooling for the living area constitute around 70 percent of a typical household's en-

HEATING CYCLE

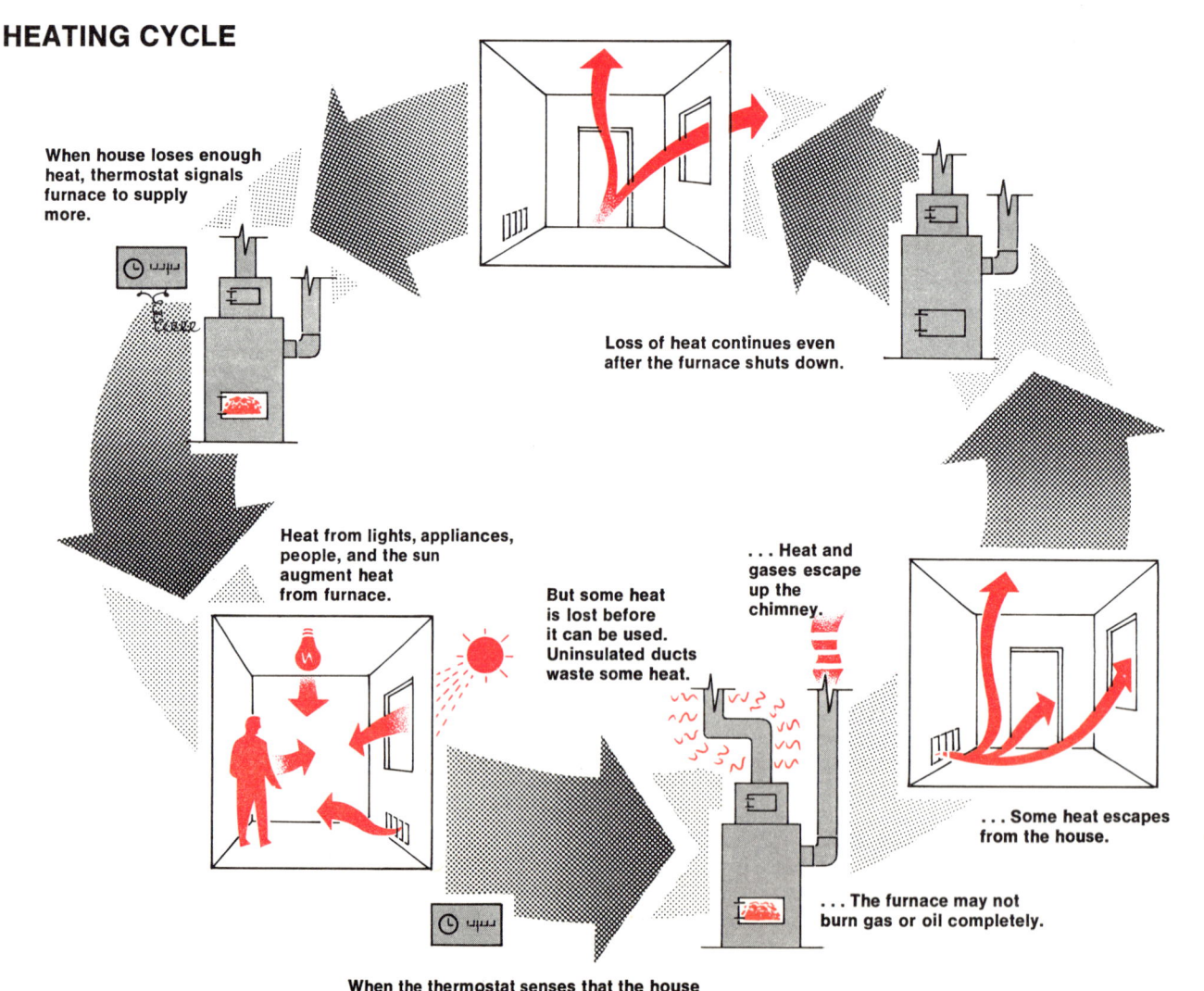

When house loses enough heat, thermostat signals furnace to supply more.

Loss of heat continues even after the furnace shuts down.

Heat from lights, appliances, people, and the sun augment heat from furnace.

But some heat is lost before it can be used. Uninsulated ducts waste some heat.

...Heat and gases escape up the chimney.

...Some heat escapes from the house.

...The furnace may not burn gas or oil completely.

When the thermostat senses that the house is warm enough, it signals the furnace to stop.

8 The house as "energy system"

ergy needs. Heat for hot water (raising the water temperature and maintaining that temperature) accounts for another 20 percent of a household's energy needs; and lighting, cooking, and other uses account for the remaining 10 percent.

In order to understand how energy is used in the home, you should look beyond a specific task (heating, cooking, or whatever) to see how that single task relates to all other energy-consuming equipment in the home. In short, you have to think of the house as an energy system.

To see how the system works, consider a hypothetical family at home in the middle of the afternoon on a cold winter's day. The windows are shut, of course, and the furnace is running. Lights are on in several rooms, there's a load of clothes in the dryer, and dinner is baking in the oven. One member of the family is taking a shower while the others are watching television. The system is hard at work using energy. Oil is burned in the furnace to supply heat for the rooms; fuel is burned in the water heater so there is hot water for the shower. Electricity is providing heat to dry clothes and cook dinner. Electricity is also providing light and running the television set.

While the furnace provides much of the heat in our hypothetical house, it's not the only heat source. All the activities—showering, cooking, laundering, and so on—are contributing some heat to the system. Even the people themselves are supplying some heat.

But not all of the energy you buy is effectively used in the house. Some of the heat from the furnace travels up the flue and out the chimney, carrying with it the products of combustion. And even if the furnace is operating at peak efficiency, some of the fuel will not be burned, going off in smoke instead of heat. (Here and throughout the book, we'll use the word *furnace* to stand for all types of oil-fired or gas-fired heating systems. Electric heating systems convert virtually all the electricity into heat for the house, but there's a different kind of energy loss associated with electric heat. For every three units of energy that enter a generating plant, only one reaches customers' homes as electricity; the other two units are dissipated when the electricity is generated or along the transmission lines.)

At some point, the house will warm up sufficiently. (For practical purposes, that point is the thermostat setting selected by the family.) When the thermostat senses that the desired temperature has been achieved, it signals the heating system to shut down until heat is needed again. The house will stay comfortable, but only for a while because the heat inside the house will escape. One source of heat loss is *conduction*—the flow of heat through solid substances, such as ceilings, walls, floors, and windows. A second source of heat loss is *air leakage*—the movement of heated air out through cracks around doors, windows, and other gaps in the house.

Some appliances can also contribute to air leakage. A kitchen exhaust fan, for example, will remove heated air as well as cooking odors. The heating system, in turn, is then forced to work longer (or more often) to replace the heat removed by the fan. Also, the draft created in the chimney when the furnace is on pulls warm air up and out of the house—even after the furnace shuts down. Cool air from outdoors replaces the warm air.

When the house cools down sufficiently, the thermostat will signal the furnace to replenish the heat that's been lost.

During a warm summer's day, the cycle essentially changes direction. Let's assume our hypothetical house has an air conditioner. When the house has warmed up because heat has flowed into the house, and because lamps, sunlight, appliances, and people have warmed the air inside, the air conditioner provides cooling by forcing unwanted heat out of the house.

Influences on the system

There are three factors that have the greatest effect on the amount of energy used in your house.

1. Temperature—specifically, the difference between outdoor and indoor temperatures. Heat, as we've noted, will flow through solid materials. Heat can move in any direction, and will always move to an area of lower temperature. The greater the *difference* in tempera-

TWO WAYS TO LOSE HEAT

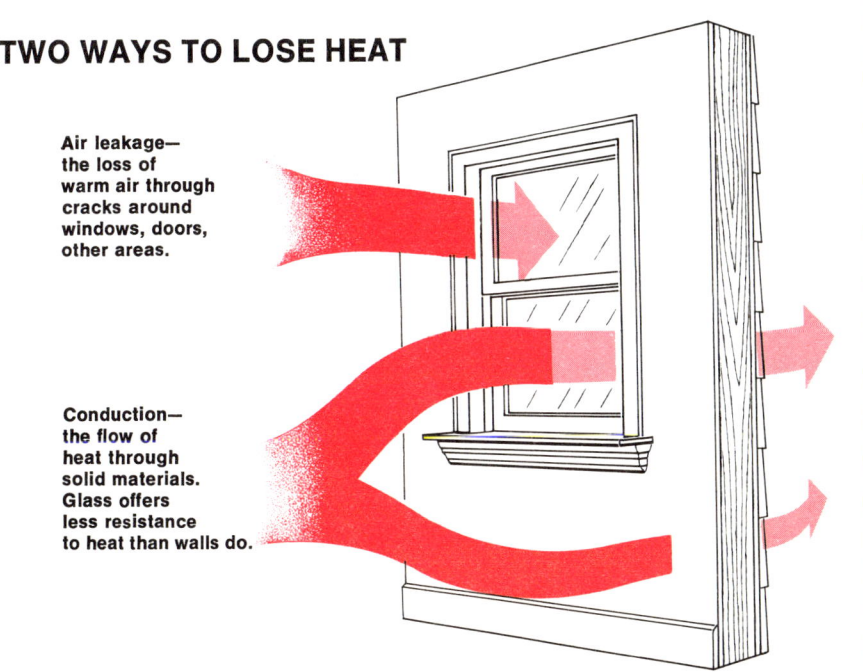

Air leakage—the loss of warm air through cracks around windows, doors, other areas.

Conduction—the flow of heat through solid materials. Glass offers less resistance to heat than walls do.

ture, and the less resistance a material offers to the flow of heat, the faster heat will move.

R-value is the term used to express a material's ability to retard the flow of heat. Every part of a house has its own R-value: Window glass has a low R-value, walls have higher R-values depending on, among other things, whether or not they are insulated. The insulation itself has an R-value. Doubling the R-value (by adding insulation to a wall, for example) cuts the flow of heat in half. Some building codes, including the Minimum Property Standards prepared by the Federal Housing Administration and the Farmers Home Administration, use the term *U-value* to prescribe how effective an insulated wall, ceiling, or floor must be in retarding the flow of heat. The U-value is a measure of heat flow and is the reciprocal of a material's R-value; that is, $R=1/U$ and $U=1/R$.

While it's often said that heat rises, it's more accurate to say that hot air rises. Heating a given amount of air causes it to rise because it expands and becomes less dense. (The Montgolfier brothers demonstrated this principle dramatically in France in 1783. As a crowd looked on, the brothers put together an immense bag with a basket attached to it, and suspended the works over a fire. The king's historian climbed into the basket and waited. When heat from the fire had expanded the air inside the bag, it was cut loose from its moorings—launching the first manned balloon flight.) In the home, warm air will rise to the ceiling. Unless the ceiling is insulated, a good deal of the heat in the air will flow through the ceiling and escape from the house.

Temperature is measured in degrees; *degree-day* is a term that combines both temperature and time and serves as an index of the energy required to heat or cool a house. During the winter, the greater the number of heating degree-days in your area, the more heat your house will require to maintain a given temperature. Heating degree-days won't tell you precisely how many Btu your furnace will have to produce, but they can give you a measure by which you can predict the amount of heat you'll need and allow you to compare heating requirements from one winter to the next. In general, if the number of degree-days drops from one winter to the next, the amount of energy you use for heating should be smaller. During the summer, the greater the number of cooling degree-days, the more air conditioning would be required to maintain a given temperature in a house. (Note, however, that cooling degree-days are a far less useful index than heating degree-days, for reasons explained in Chapter 4.)

Heating degree-days (often included in weather reports) are calculated by taking the high and low temperatures for the day, adding them, and dividing the sum by two. That number is subtracted from 65. For cooling degree-days, the day's high and low temperatures are added and the result divided by two; 65 is then subtracted from that number. Why 65? It has been shown that a house generally needs neither heating nor cooling to maintain a comfortable indoor temperature when the temperature outside is 65°. As a result, 65° becomes a useful starting point for determining the demand that will be placed on the heating and cooling systems.

2. The condition of the house. The house may be what builders call "loose"—that is, there may be cracks around the door or window frames, or around the foundation; the windows and doors themselves may also be loose or warped. All contribute to air-leakage losses. Conversely, a "tight" house, one that's relatively free of leakage, will permit heated air to escape relatively slowly. But, as indicated previously, even a "tight" house can lose heat rapidly (by conduction) through the roof, walls, windows, and floor—that is, unless the house has adequate insulation, thermal windows, or storm windows.

3. The condition of the heating and cooling systems. The insides of the furnace may be covered with soot, which can reduce the amount of heat delivered to the rooms. The oil-burner nozzles or gas orifices may be clogged, air inlets may be improperly adjusted, and the chimney may be obstructed. The furnace controls may need adjustment so that the furnace will fire when it should and shut off when it should. Filters on the air conditioner or furnace may need cleaning or changing. Whatever the

HEAT FLOW

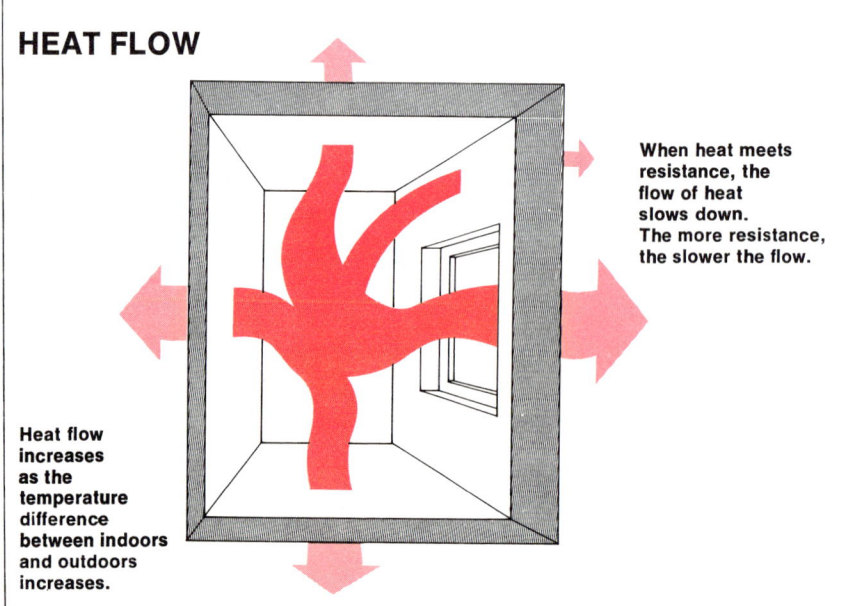

When heat meets resistance, the flow of heat slows down. The more resistance, the slower the flow.

Heat flow increases as the temperature difference between indoors and outdoors increases.

10   The house as "energy system"

problem, it means you're getting less heating or cooling than you're paying for.

It should be noted, however, that other variables affect the interplay among temperature, the condition of the house, and the heating/cooling systems. Humidity, house size, the number of windows—even the location and color of the house—influence the working of the household energy system.

Rapidly rising energy prices, along with the increasingly widespread realization that oil and natural gas supplies are limited, have both emphasized the fact that more needs to be known about exactly how energy is used in the home. Government agencies and private research laboratories are now trying to determine just how a house uses energy, how much energy is used, and what could be done to reduce the level of consumption. Experiments in actual houses, as well as complex computer simulations of heating and cooling needs, are testing traditional engineering techniques used to determine a home's heating or cooling requirements. Those standard methods, devised years ago, were based on assumptions that may no longer be valid. For instance, when fuel was inexpensive and plentiful, architects and engineers would often "oversize" a furnace or an air conditioner. That is, they would specify a unit big enough to handle the worst weather possible —and then some—because doing so was the simplest approach to take. Now that fuel prices have skyrocketed, more attention is being paid to the optimum size (and operating cost) of heating and cooling equipment.

In preparing the material for this book, Consumers Union has often relied on the traditional methods of calculating energy consumption, including those developed by the American Society of Heating, Refrigerating, and Air-Conditioning Engineers (ASHRAE). We recognize that the standard methods may have their shortcomings, and we have modified them where we felt it was necessary to do so. Still, the conventional methods are frequently the best way (sometimes the only way) available for calculating energy consumption and energy saving.

What saving energy means— ways to do it

At the most elementary level, saving energy in your home means using gas, oil, and electricity sensibly to minimize waste: turning off the lamps when you leave a room, for example; or keeping the doors and windows closed when the furnace or air conditioner is running. But there are three broad goals to saving energy, each of which incorporates the sensible use of fuel and electricity.

First, saving energy means getting the maximum amount of energy out of the fuels you buy. Your furnance should be set up and maintained to deliver as much heat as is possible from the fuel it burns. That, in turn, will reduce the total amount of fuel burned over the course of a heating season.

Second, saving energy also means keeping heat locked inside the house —or, in the summer, locked out—for the longest possible time so that less energy will be required to keep your house at the desired temperature.

Third, saving energy means tailoring the equipment to the task. In other words, you should choose and use appliances sensibly so that they give you the results you want without using too much energy. In selecting a room air conditioner, for example, look for brands with a high Energy Efficiency Ratio (EER): The higher the EER, the more Btu of cooling you'll get per watt of electricity consumed. Using an appliance wisely can also save energy. If you lower the thermostat setting on your water heater from, say, 150° to 120°, you'll also lower your gas or electric bill since the heater will use fewer Btu to raise the temperature of the water and keep it hot.

There is more than one way to achieve those goals. To find out what conservation measures will work best for your house, take a close look at your household energy system.

Begin with the structure of the house itself to see if windows and doors are tight and that there are no drafts, and if there is adequate insulation in the walls, ceiling, floors, and crawl space. Consider whether installing storm windows and storm doors could help reduce air leakage—and your heating bills.

Next, look to the heating and cooling equipment and the way you use it. The furnace may be supplying heat when it's not really needed— late at night or during the day if no one is at home. Changing the thermostat setting, or replacing the thermostat, may be a useful way to reduce the amount of heating (and cooling, if you have central air conditioning) you require. Of course, if the furnace is operating at less than peak efficiency, you're spending more than you need to heat your house. A tune-up (by a qualified technician) might save you money. Or, there may be devices you could have installed that could extract a bit more heat from the system or keep some heat inside the house for longer periods.

Finally, look to the water heater and the plumbing. There are simple steps you can take to reduce the expense of heating the water you and your family use.

In dealing with these three areas— the house itself, the heating and cooling systems, and the hot-water equipment—you will be covering 90 percent of the energy consumed in your home. You may well decide that there are steps you can take to save energy in all three areas. But which steps should you take first?

There's no single set of conservation measures that will work for every house. And there's no single step to take that will always result in a significant saving. You will obviously want to give special consideration to those measures that will yield the greatest saving per dollar of cost. Unfortunately, the saving must be calculated on an individual basis. Businesses, government agencies, and trade associations, however, often offer general and less precise guidance. For example, the Federal Government's booklet, "Tips for Energy Savers," maintains that "you can reduce the load on your heating and cooling equipment by as much as 20 to 30 percent by investing a few hundred dollars in insulation." And, according to an engineering society, lowering the thermostat setting on the water heater will produce a broad range of savings—from $10 to $90 per year. But such generalizations are apt to be of little help to the individual homeowner.

The point to remember is this: Since energy consumption varies widely from one house to the next, and since electricity and fuel prices vary widely from locality to locality, the amount of energy and money to be saved will also vary. Investing in insulation may well cut your heating and cooling requirements by 30 percent, as the Government suggests. But the saving could also be far less. You'll have to work it out for yourself.

One approach is to weigh the saving from a conservation measure against its cost, in order to determine the payback period—that is, how long it will take that measure (insulation, storm windows, or whatever) to pay for itself through lower utility bills. Generally speaking, the shorter the payback period, the more attractive specific conservation measures become in relation to others. Let's say a contractor has offered to blow insulation into your walls for $1000. By using the work sheet on page 36, you can estimate how much money the insulation will save during the heating season. If the saving will be about $200, then the insulation has a five-year payback. But if your calculations show that the same amount of insulation would save only around $50, then you're facing a twenty-year payback. At that point, you might want to look for ways to save $50 a year (or more if possible) for less than a $1000 initial cost. We can't tell you how short a payback period will be right for you; that's your decision to make.

How this book can help

You may already have taken some steps toward saving energy in your home—by buying storm windows, say, or by having the heating system tuned. Even so, you're still faced with rising fuel costs and a bewildering choice of other steps to take to save energy. To help you get started, the table on pages 13 to 16 summarizes the conservation measures we cover in this book, outlining advantages and disadvantages of each. A careful reading of the table can steer you toward the measures that would make the most sense (in terms of energy conserved or dollars saved) for your house. The table also includes some no-cost or low-cost steps you can take that should save some energy without bringing on a major sacrifice of comfort or a great change in daily routine. The reports in ensuing chapters give detailed information on each measure. In many cases, the reports include Ratings of specific products tested by Consumers Union.

The reports on windows and insulation also include work sheets to help you estimate how much money a specific conservation measure will save in your home. Other reports ("Recovering Heat at the Flue," for example) will give the range of fuel savings found by CU, based on our laboratory tests. Those tests are reasonable simulations of conditions in many homes, we believe. We have also tried to explain conditions you may encounter that would yield smaller or greater savings than those we found. Still other measures, such as caulking, are generally regarded as worthwhile ways to save energy, although it's impossible to say what the precise saving will be for a specific house.

In discussing ways to save energy —and money—in this book, we'll base our estimates of possible monetary saving on the nationwide average costs for energy in 1977, as computed by the Federal Government:

Fuel Oil: 46 cents per gallon.
Natural Gas: 21 cents per "therm" (a therm equals 100,000 Btu, which is equivalent to the energy content of approximately 100 cubic feet of gas).
Electricity: 3.8 cents per kwh.
Propane: 30 cents per gallon.

Chances are, the prices you pay are different from the Government's average prices. So, in sizing up the energy-saving products and procedures we discuss, keep in mind that the dollar savings we give are only examples; the more you actually pay for energy, the more money you stand to save.

While we're concerned primarily with saving energy, we also discuss ways to conserve water—a resource that's as vital as oil or natural gas.

Most of the reports in this book originally appeared in *Consumer Reports*; that material has been reviewed and revised by CU's technical staff and by the Editors of Consumer Reports Books.

Missing from this book is a report on solar energy. The solar marketplace—most immediately, solar-powered equipment for heating water for home use—is expanding rapidly and there are many unanswered questions about the economy, durability, and effectiveness of these products. CU has begun a test project on solar home water-heating systems and ongoing reports on its progress will be published in the pages of *Consumer Reports*. CU has also planned projects that will test woodburning stoves for space heating and devices to make fireplaces more efficient.

Finally, a few words about the Ratings of products and the prices we quote for those products. The Ratings are based on CU's laboratory tests, controlled use tests, and/or expert judgments of products purchased in the regular marketplace. Products are rated, for the most part, in order of estimated overall quality, without regard to price. (Note that some products may have changed slightly since we ran our tests.) The Ratings are not an infallible guide, but they do offer comparative buying information that should greatly increase the chance that a consumer's money will be well spent.

When you get to the Ratings, there may be a strong temptation to look first at which brand is listed at the top of the Ratings order. Resist the impulse if you can. The first thing to look at is the paragraph that introduces each set of Ratings. Among other things, the paragraph may tell you which features, qualities, or deficiencies all the rated products have in common. Or it may tell you what *most* had in common, in a sentence starting with or including the words: "Unless otherwise indicated" or "Except as noted."

By far the most important bit of information in the paragraph, however, is right at the beginning, in a sentence that tells you how the products are listed. Most often, it will say: "Listed in order of estimated overall quality." That means we judged the brand listed first to be the best, the one listed next, second best, and so on. If the paragraph says, for instance, "Listed, *except as noted*, in order of estimated overall quality," it means that somewhere in the Ratings lurk one or more groups of products that are about equal to each other and are therefore listed in a special fashion: "Listed in order of estimated overall quality; closely ranked models differed little in overall quality" indicates that, while the first is best, it isn't all that much better than the second or third.

When a number of products are judged just about equal to each other, the introductory paragraph might then say, "Listed alphabetically" or "Listed in order of increasing price." So, sometimes a brand can land at the top of the Ratings simply because it starts with the letter A, or because it lists at a slightly lower price than the next model. A product is given a BEST BUY designation when it combines a high rating in overall quality with a list price that's low in comparison to other products tested.

For the most part, prices given in the Ratings are list prices, dating from the time the original report was published in *Consumer Reports*. (Those dates are given in each set of Ratings.) Prices of mail-order items, which normally do not include shipping costs, are from catalogues available to CU when the original report was prepared. Prices for same products at mail-order company retail stores may vary somewhat.

AN OVERVIEW OF CONSERVATION MEASURES

Conservation measure	Advantages	Disadvantages	Comments
Caulking and weather stripping (pages 17-25)	Relatively low cost; "tightens" house to help retain heated or cooled air.		Effective measures to take in any region, with any type of heating/cooling system.
Storm windows (pages 26-31)	Sharply reduce heat flow through windows.	Possibly high initial cost, depending on type used.	Effective measure to take in any region, with any type of heating system. For greatest saving, windows should also be caulked and weather stripped.
Insulation (pages 32-37)	Reduces heat loss and heat gain through ceilings, walls, floors.	Can be relatively expensive. Scarcity of some types (as of early 1978). Possible safety hazards with other types.	First few inches of insulation yield the largest saving. Saving diminishes as more insulation is installed. Amount needed for optimum saving varies, depending on region and type of heating/cooling system.
"Energy-saving" thermostat (pages 40-46)	Changes house temperature regularly and dependably so heating/cooling system operates only at preset times. Lowering house temperature in winter puts less demand on heating system; raising temperature in summer puts less demand on cooling system.	Difficult to adapt to electric room-heating systems. May not be effective with heat pumps (devices that supply both heating and cooling). Large number of samples CU tested proved to be defective.	Can be effective in any region. Saves greatest amount of money in very cold or very hot regions; saves greatest percentage of fuel bill in relatively mild climates. Saving depends on normal setting and number of degrees of "setback." The greater the setback, the greater the saving.

The house as "energy system"

Conservation measure	Advantages	Disadvantages	Comments
Furnace tune-up (pages 47-49)	Can bring furnace up to peak efficiency, thus delivering more heat. Also a good way to spot safety hazards.		Saving per $100 spent on fuel ranges from about $6 to $37 per year, based on experiences of CU staffers whose homes have oil burners. Not applicable to homes with individual-room electric heat.
Flue heat recovery device (pages 49-53)	Reclaims heat that would otherwise be lost when furnace is on.	Cost of devices may not be offset by saving. Most effective on very inefficient furnaces; heat can be used only in areas near furnace. Device may not meet some local building codes.	Likely to yield small saving. Not applicable to homes with electric heat, or new gas furnaces.
Flue damper (pages 53-56)	Prevents warm air from escaping when furnace is off.		Can yield saving of roughly 10 to 20 percent on many fuel bills. Devices must be certified by recognized testing agencies, installed by trained technicians, and inspected regularly. Not applicable to homes with electric heat.
Whole-house attic fan (pages 60-65)	Cools house less expensively than air conditioning.	High initial cost; can be difficult to install. Will not cool house as well as air conditioning; will not dehumidify air.	Can be effective measure in any region. Most effective in regions with low relative humidity and relatively cool nights.
Lower thermostat setting on water heater (pages 68-69)	No cost. Reduces amount of energy needed to heat water and maintain its temperature.	In effect, reduces amount of hot water available for bathing or washing. Dishwasher performance may suffer.	Amount of hot water used for bathing and showering may increase, since more hot water will be used to achieve desired temperature at tap. But will result in saving with dishwasher, which uses fixed amount of hot water.
Insulation for water heater (pages 69-70)	Helps tank retain heat, reducing amount of energy needed to maintain hot water. Insulation inexpensive and easy to install.		Yields saving of roughly $10 to $25 per year.
Insulate hot-water pipes and heating ducts that pass through unheated areas. (page 70)	Can sharply reduce loss of heat to unheated areas of house.		Increases amount of heat available to living area, thus reducing heating costs. Saving depends on how much duct is insulated, type of heating system, and other factors.

Conservation measure	Advantages	Disadvantages	Comments
Water-saving devices for showers (pages 70-73)	Some devices very inexpensive. Can substantially reduce amount of water used for bathing, and energy used to heat that water.	Reducing water flow rate can also adversely affect quality of spray from shower head.	Saving will vary, depending on water temperature, duration of shower, number of showers family takes.
Water-saving devices for toilets (pages 74-77)	Low cost. Can substantially reduce amount of water used in home.	Any modification, if carried too far, can impair ability of toilet to clear solid waste or to refill trap after a flush.	Commercial devices have no advantage over home-made variety. Saves some money, but also reduces load on sewage-treatment plants, need for new reservoirs, pumping facilities, etc.
Turning off range-top pilot lights (see "Igniters for Gas Ranges," pages 81-83)	Will reduce need for cooling during summer.	Inconvenient; requires other means for lighting burners.	Saves very small amount of gas. Not applicable to homes with electric appliances. Pilots on cook tops can be turned off. Pilots on ovens, water heaters, or other appliances will require installation of other ignition devices.

No-cost (or very low cost) measures

Close off unused rooms; do not heat or cool them.	No cost. Reduces amount of heating/cooling required.	May result in frozen pipes in extremely cold areas, unless pipes are drained.	Saving can be considerable but will depend on number of rooms closed off, local weather, and type of heating/cooling system.
Close fireplace damper when fire is out; use exhaust fans in kitchen and bathroom sparingly.	No cost. Closes off escape routes for warm air in winter.		Saving can be considerable but will vary.
Clean filter on air conditioner and lint screen on dryer; clean and replace furnace filters regularly.	Allows appliances to work at higher efficiency.		Saving will vary, depending on how clogged filters become.
Clean condenser coils on refrigerator.	Allows appliance to work at higher efficiency.		
Be sure door gaskets on refrigerators and freezers are airtight; replace or adjust loose-fitting ones.	Cuts operating costs because appliances run for shorter periods to maintain temperature.		To test tightness of gaskets, close door on dollar bill; if bill can easily be slipped out, gasket is too loose.
Fill dishwasher, washing machine, and dryer to capacity but do not overload.	No cost. Enhances operating efficiency of appliances.		

The house as "energy system"

Conservation measure	Advantages	Disadvantages	Comments
Set dishwasher to skip "dry" cycle.	No cost.		Saving will be small.
Use "warm" or "cold" wash settings and "cold" rinse settings on washing machines.	No cost.		Can save $10 to $30 per year.
Use major appliances early in the morning or late at night.	No cost.		Will save on electric bill only if local utility offers a discount for "off-peak" usage.
Use window shades or draperies to control house temperature.	Can help reduce drafts somewhat; allows use of free sunlight to warm house when needed. In summer, keeps out some of the sun's heat.		In winter, open draperies but leave windows closed to collect heat from sun. Close draperies at night to prevent heat loss. In summer, close draperies in daytime to prevent sunlight from entering; open windows and draperies at night to allow heat to escape.

2 Ways to "tighten" the house against winter weather

It's long been known that caulking, weather stripping, storm windows, and insulation can save energy during the heating season. Those products seal off drafts and retard the flow of heat out of the house. Until recently, however, little systematic research had been done to find out just how effective an energy-saver a heat-tight weatherized house could be. Two studies published in 1977 indicate that sealing the house can be quite effective, indeed.

The National Bureau of Standards conducted a three-stage weatherization test on a fairly large, one-story ranch house near Washington, D.C. NBS engineers began by applying caulk around window frames and along cracks in the siding and foundation. (Weather stripping had been installed when the house was built.) Next, the engineers installed storm windows. Finally, insulation was put in place in the crawl space and blown into the walls. Thick layers of insulation were added to the insulation already in place in the attic. The result: Energy consumption for that house was slashed by 58.5 percent per year, the NBS reported.

The second study, sponsored by Chevron USA and the Chevron Research Company, assessed the energy-saving potential of various measures on three homes in the Pacific Northwest. In one house in Seattle, adding insulation, storm windows, and weather stripping around storm doors resulted in an overall energy saving of 24 percent during the heating season. (In the other two homes, insulation plus modifications to the heating system yielded a larger overall saving.)

Those figures are quite impressive, overall, but they do merit a closer look. In the NBS study, storm windows alone accounted for nearly half the saving, and the extra layer of attic insulation contributed the least, accounting for only a 6 percent energy saving. Caulking had no measurable effect since the house was tightly built in the first place. In the Chevron study, too, storm windows saved more energy than an extra layer of insulation.

Of course, installing storm windows on your house may not save more money than adding insulation, and caulking may not be an ineffective energy-saver for you.

The point is, when it comes to "tightening" the house, improvements are cumulative. That is, every crack you fill with caulk, every inch of weather stripping you apply, every square foot of insulation you install helps retain more heat, thus adding to the saving. Even though the improvements are cumulative, however, there does come a point where each improvement will add smaller and smaller amounts to the saving. The NBS study, remember, showed that adding more insulation to the attic in its test house yielded only a 6 percent reduction in energy use. As a consequence, a balanced program for saving energy involves careful consideration of the kinds of improvements—caulking, weather stripping, storm windows, insulation—most needed in your house.

How much—if anything—can you save? To show the kind of saving possible, Consumers Union's engineers have calculated the saving for a hypothetical house in Columbus, Ohio, to which weather stripping, storm windows, and insulation had been added; the reports that follow give the specifics. More important, we've included work sheets that you can use to estimate your saving from weather stripping, storm windows, and insulation. The reports also explain what to look for in caulking compounds, how and where to apply caulk, and where different types of weather stripping can best be used.

Exterior caulking compounds

Spring and fall are the best times to caulk your house. Don't wait until cold winter winds remind you that the gaps are still there. During May, June, and September, temperatures are warm enough to make caulking compounds easy to apply but not so warm that the job becomes downright unpleasant. At its best, caulking is a tedious chore. At its worst, it is muscle-straining and, occasionally, hazardous—as when you're teetering on a ladder with your hands over your head trying to exert slow, steady pressure on the trigger of your caulking gun. It is not a task you'll want to repeat very soon. The more durable the caulk, the longer you'll be spared.

The first caulking compounds were probably mud or clay. Later, someone discovered that mixing the clay with oil staved off the time when the caulk dried and fell out. The direct descendant of that early caulk is with us today, in the form of oil-based caulking compounds, still the cheapest type, by and large. A lot of newer formulations are around, too—many touted as superior to oil-based caulks in one way or another. In 1976, CU tested seven oil-based compounds, along with nine butyl-rubber, fifteen latex, and six expensive, "high-performance," special-purpose caulks. (Three of the special purpose caulks are silicone-rubber-based and cannot be painted over. They're discussed in detail on page 20.) We also subjected seven of the more durable caulks to a long-term outdoor aging test.

All the caulks we tested came in standard, nozzle-equipped cartridges that fit common caulking guns. All delivered roughly 25 feet of caulking in a ¼-inch-wide bead.

As things turned out, the advantages claimed for the various formulations didn't always hold up under close scrutiny. Oil-based compounds are reputed to have a relatively short life, but the oil-based *M-D Speed Load Caulking Compound* was judged to match the most durable of the other products tested—and we paid less than a dollar a cartridge for that brand. Butyl compounds, on the other hand, often make claims of long service life, yet our tests indicated that most of those tested wouldn't last any longer than other types. And latex products aren't supposed to bleed through paints or to stain nearby surfaces, but we found one that's likely to.

Durability—the major factor

Since some brands of caulk perform better than others, regardless of the type of compound, you should use our Ratings to guide your choice. We've listed the brands primarily according to the way they held up in our tests for durability, which were based on two considerations.

1. Flexibility. Almost every joint in a house moves a bit. Winds make structures sway slightly, and shifts in the ground make them settle. The opening and closing of windows and doors cause vibrations. And structural materials expand and contract with changes in temperature or humidity. All those movements require that a caulk be flexible if joints are to keep their integrity.

2. Resistance to weather. Resistance to the ravages of the elements is obviously important in an outdoor product. Accordingly, we ran laboratory tests to check each caulk's ability to stand up to high-intensity ultraviolet light and an intermittent water spray.

A number of caulks took the worst we dished out. Others suffered greatly from the exposure tests and so were severely downgraded. By and large, the tests showed that the useful life of almost any caulk will be improved if joints are primed before caulking and the caulk is painted over afterward.

Our outdoor aging test was designed to be a severe test of a caulk's performance in actual use. We installed the caulks in cracks ⅝-inch wide (an extremely wide crack) on test panels, and left the panels on CU's roof for sixteen months. Some of the caulks held up extremely well, showing almost no evidence of cracking or separating; others fared less well. The Ratings note the

The obvious places to caulk—around door and window frames, and at the corners of the house (A). But there are other important, if less visible, places that may need to be sealed. Check first for gaps between the house framing and the foundation (B). To spot cracks here, stand inside the basement and look along the top of the basement wall; if you can see light, you need caulk. Another place to check is the space between the siding and the sheathing (C). A bead of caulk behind the siding helps block the flow of cool air, allowing the house to retain heat longer.

18   Ways to "tighten" the house

caulks that performed better or worse than the norm in this test.

(We would hope that your house doesn't have cracks wider than ¼- to ⅜-inch. If your house does have cracks more than ¼-inch wide or deep, pack them with wood strips, oakum, or other filler before you apply caulk. For some hints on how to use caulk, see below.)

Together, our flexing and weathering tests told us how well caulk would resist aging. We looked in particular for caulks that remained elastic or plastic after our tests; they would withstand joint movements better than those that turned crumbly or hard with age. We also looked for compounds tough enough to resist penetration or cuts.

Other factors to consider

Though durability is important, a number of other considerations may affect your choice of caulk.

Shrinkage. Whether shrinkage in a caulk is a boon or a bane depends on the type of joint you're sealing. A

THERE'S A KNACK TO WORKING WITH CAULK—THESE TIPS SHOULD HELP

Remove old caulk. Be sure joints are dry (only latex caulks can be used in damp joints). Prime raw wood, masonry, other porous surfaces. Latex can be cleaned up with water; with other caulks, masking tape next to crack can aid cleanup. Don't caulk if it's colder than 45° F.

Cut the cartridge nozzle on an angle, so you can slant the cartridge for better visibility and control. The nozzle cut should just span the joint you're trying to fill (⅛- to ¼-inch diameter is usually enough). You can fill extra-large gaps by moving the tip from side to side.

Poke the nozzle into joints wider than the nozzle so that the caulking fills the gap from the bottom up. Rough-fill the bottom of a really deep, wide gap with oakum, wood strips, cotton or glass wool, or other inert filler to within ½-inch of the surface.

Press the nozzle firmly over joints and move it so that the caulk is pushed ahead of the tip, rather than released behind the tip. That way, you will force the caulk deeper into the crevice and reduce the nozzle's tendency to pull the caulk up and out of the joint.

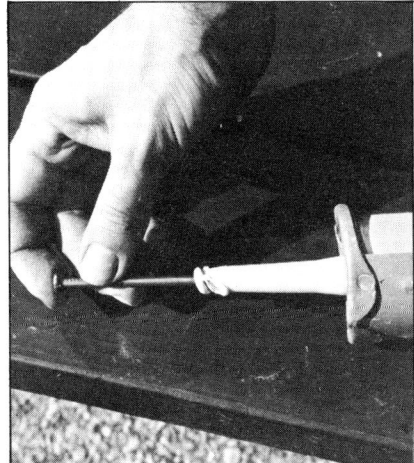

Before you level and trim the caulking, close off the cartridge. Push a large, headed nail (a common 10-penny nail serves well) into the nozzle and wipe away the excess that oozes out. Cover the nail and nozzle end with aluminum foil. Use up the cartridge in one season.

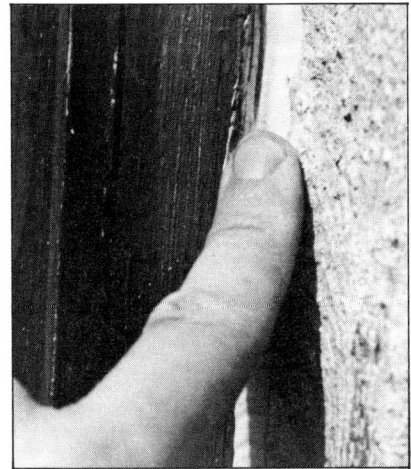

Remove excess caulk and smooth the joint by running a wetted finger, putty knife, or stick along the surface of the joint. Remove excess caulk at the sides immediately with a cloth wetted with water (or recommended solvent). Remove masking tape before caulk sets.

Caulking 19

high-shrinkage caulk works well on an inside corner, where shrinkage will make the caulk particularly unobtrusive. It will also serve perfectly well in cracks less than 1/16-inch wide, since shrinkage there won't be noticeable. High-shrinkage caulks should not, however, be used in cracks wider than 1/16-inch, where concavities may cast shadows and catch dirt. And if the caulks continue to shrink, they're apt to crack any protective paint that is applied over them.

Mildew resistance. Even after three months in a shaded, high-humidity tank that had been inoculated with mildew spores, half the caulks we tested supported virtually no mildew growth. They were graded good. Products scored as fair showed only minor areas of growth. The poor products ended up covered with mildew. If you're caulking dry areas that are regularly exposed to the sun and have had no history of mildew problems, you can ignore those differences. Otherwise, they're worth considering.

Dirt resistance. A product with a tacky surface will trap whatever dust, dirt, leaf fragments, and grit are blown its way. Tackiness may develop as the caulk ages, even in a product that at first seemed to be dry to the touch. Of course, if you plan to paint over the caulk, as CU recommends, this characteristic need not affect your choice.

Whiteness after aging. All the caulks we tested started out nominally white, but most darkened as they aged. Only four ended up white enough to be graded good in that respect; even unpainted, they wouldn't stand out as a contrasting line on a white house. If you paint over your caulk, however, its color is unimportant.

Staining. To assess any tendency on the part of a caulk to stain surfaces or to bleed through paint, we applied each caulk to stacks of absorbent paper. After seventy-two hours, we measured how far any discoloration had penetrated. We judged one (*Rely-On*) particularly apt to cause stains or to bleed; seven others, noted in the Ratings, including the top-rated *M-D Speed Load*, offended to a lesser degree. But you'd be wise to avoid all eight caulks if you wanted to seal light-colored brick or masonry joints. Priming would help to control the problem on raw wood and other porous surfaces.

Application and after

More than half the caulks gave us application problems in some respect. One was uneven in consistency. Others were too thin to gun easily and uniformly into joints. Still others tended to adhere to new caulk flowing from the cartridge nozzle—they often pulled out of joints as we caulked along. And some were also hard to tool, or level off, after being gunned into a joint.

If you caulk in warm weather, you may well be working on sunlit surfaces whose temperatures exceed 100°F. It would be frustrating to have your caulk ooze out of a joint after you had leveled it. Happily, our tests indicated that only three caulks (see Ratings) seemed likely to present the problem of sagging.

In addition, three other caulks—*Sears Polyurethane, M-D Perma-Calk*, and *G.E. White Modified Silicone Paintable*—demand a bit of special care in handling, for reasons noted in the Ratings. The other caulks tested present no special hazards if used with common sense. In general, it's not a good idea to expose caulking compounds to flame or to high heat; they might not burn, but they could produce unpleasant fumes. Don't smoke while you caulk. Read and follow label instructions and cautions. Use caulking compounds with adequate ventilation (some have a disagreeable odor). Store them out of children's reach. Wash your hands after caulking.

Three expensive but nonpaintable caulks

Along with the paintable caulks, we also tested three nonpaintable silicone-rubber products. They turned out to be very good, but they were expensive (we paid more than $4 for a standard cartridge of each). And the fact that you can't paint over them is a serious shortcoming.

The three included two Dow Corning products, *Silicone Rubber Sealer (White)* and *Silicone Rubber Sealer (Clear)* (Dow Corning Corp., Midland, Mich.), as well as *G.E. Clear Silicone Caulk & Seal* (General Electric Co., Waterford, N.Y.). Our tests showed that all three were easy to apply and would be relatively long-lived. All showed little shrinkage and resisted mildew well. *The Dow Corning White* remained white after aging.

Since none of these products can be painted, however, you won't be able to cover them to make them match the area they adjoin. Indeed, paint won't even stick to adjacent areas onto which you may have spread the silicone sealer during application or leveling-off, even if you wipe off the sealer carefully. If you ever intend to paint such abutting areas, you should protect them with masking tape before you caulk. Furthermore, since you can't use paint to add weather protection to the caulk, you must depend on the caulk to protect itself. All three got slightly tacky in our weathering test; in outdoor use, they'd probably pick up dirt faster than the other high-rated caulks.

All in all, we don't think the silicones are worth their high cost for the kind of extensive, general caulking needed on the outside of your house. And for that reason, we have not included them in the Ratings. But they'd be the best choice for specialized jobs—caulking around a tub, say—where you want a durable, highly elastic joint.

Recommendations

Any of the caulking compounds that placed high in the Ratings should prove to be durable. The choice among them will depend on the particular job you have to do. (There is one caution to keep in mind: Our tests were conducted be-

20 Ways to "tighten" the house

tween 1976 and 1978, so some brands we tested may no longer be available.)

The *M-D Speed Load* combined low price with a top-rated performance. We found it easy to apply, reasonably dirt- and mildew-resistant. It also did well in our outdoor aging test. But it's not the best choice for caulking joints in a white house unless you're planning to paint over the caulk later—it discolored as it aged. And it will tend to stain adjacent areas more than most other caulks.

The *Sears Polyurethane* and the *M-D Perma-Calk* also did well in our outdoor aging test, but even though they were durable they would not be our first choice for a general-purpose caulk. Both of them can be difficult to apply and had other problems as well.

The *Weldwood Acrylic,* the *G.H. Eternaflex 1045,* and the *Macco Super Caulk LC130* were good all-around caulks. They withstood our tests well, and each offered a somewhat different combination of performance characteristics. The *Weldwood* showed high shrinkage, making it a good choice for caulking inside corners; the *GH* had good dirt- and mildew resistance; and the *Macco* had good whiteness after aging.

Ratings: Exterior caulking compounds

Listed in order of estimated overall quality, based mainly on judgments of durability. Closely ranked models differed little in overall quality. All can be painted and are nominally white (but most discolored to some degree after aging). Except as noted, all were judged unlikely to sag in vertical joints or to stain. Unless otherwise indicated, prices are averages of those paid in mid-1975 by CU's shoppers for standard-sized gun cartridges (10½ to 11½ fl. oz.). Some may no longer be available.

	Price	Type	Ease of application	Shrinkage	Resistance to mildew	Resistance to dirt pickup	Whiteness	Comments
M-D SPEED LOAD CAULKING COMPOUND WHITE (Macklanburg-Duncan Co., Oklahoma City) **A Best Buy**	77¢	Oil	Good	Moderate	Good	Good	Poor	Did well in outdoor aging test. Judged more likely to stain than most. Price as of Sept. 1978.
WELDWOOD ACRYLIC CAULK (Weldwood Packaged Prod., Roberts Consolidated Industries, City of Industry, Calif.)	$2.18	Acrylic latex	Good	High	Poor	Good	Fair	More suitable than most for use in inside corners, due to high shrinkage. Price as of Sept. 1978.
GH ETERNAFLEX 1045 ACRYLIC LATEX SEALANT (Gibson-Homans Co., Cleveland)	$1.74	Acrylic latex	Fair	Moderate	Good	Good	Variable	Judged slightly thin for easy application. Price as of Sept. 1978.
MACCO WHITE ACRYLIC SUPER CAULK LC130 (Macco Adhesives/SCM Corp., Wickliffe, Ohio)	$1.89	Acrylic latex	Good	Moderate	Fair	Good	Good	Price as of Sept. 1978.
DEXALL BUTYL RUBBER CAULK (Deshler Prod., Sherwin-Williams Co., Cleveland)	$1.57	Butyl rubber	Good	High	Good	Good	Poor	More suitable than most for use in inside corners, due to high shrinkage.
SEARS HIGH PERFORMANCE ACRYLIC LATEX CAULK 38101 (Sears, Roebuck)	$2.26	Acrylic latex	Good	Moderate	Good	Good	Variable	
DEXALL ACRYLIC LATEX CAULK (Deshler Prod.)	$1.63	Acrylic latex	Good	Moderate	Fair	Good	Poor	Useful life judged only average; uprated somewhat because of performance in other characteristics.
SEARS POLYURETHANE RUBBER BASE SEALER CAULK 38211 (Sears, Roebuck)	approx. $3	Polyurethane rubber	Fair	Low	Good	Good	Poor	Performed best of all caulks in outdoor aging test. Judged difficult to tool smoothly. Solidifies in a few weeks, in CU's experience; use up quickly. Contains toluene diisocyanate, a sensitizer; avoid breathing vapor or contact with skin or clothing. Price as of Sept. 1978.
UGL ACRYLIC LATEX CAULK (United Gilsonite Lab., Scranton, Pa.)	$1.68	Acrylic latex	Fair	Moderate	Fair	Good	Poor	Judged slightly thin for easy application.
M-D ACRYLIC LATEX CAULK (Macklanburg-Duncan Co.)	$1.57	Acrylic latex	Fair	Moderate	Good	Good	Poor	Judged slightly thin for easy application.
RUTLAND ARCHITECTURAL GRADE CAULK (Rutland Fire Clay Co., Rutland, Vt.)	96¢	Oil	Good	Moderate	Good	Good	Poor	
M-D PERMA-CALK WHITE (Macklanburg-Duncan Co.)	$4.79	Polysulfide rubber	Fair	Moderate	Good	Poor	Poor	Did well in outdoor aging test. Useful life judged longer than most, but downrated because caulk judged slightly thin for easy application and more likely to stain than most. Has odor many people may find objectionable. Avoid contact with skin. Price as of Sept. 1978.

(Ratings continued on next page.)

	Price	Type	Ease of application	Shrinkage	Resistance to mildew	Resistance to dirt pickup	Whiteness	Comments
WARDS ACRYLIC LATEX CAULK 5418 (Montgomery Ward)	$1.29	Acrylic latex	Good	Moderate	Fair	Fair	Poor	
STAY-TITE NO. 45 CAULKING COMPOUND (Stay-Tite Prod. Co., Cleveland)	69¢	Oil	Fair	Moderate	Fair	Good	Poor	Judged difficult to tool smoothly.
SEARS ACRYLIC LATEX CAULK 38001 (Sears, Roebuck)	$1.23	Acrylic latex	Good	Moderate	Fair	Poor	Fair	
POLYSEAMSEAL ADHESIVE CAULKING (Darworth Inc., Avon, Conn.)	$1.94	Latex	Fair	Moderate	Good	Good	Poor	Judged slightly thin for easy application.
DAP BUTYL-FLEX CAULKING (Dap Inc., Dayton, Ohio)	$2.02	Butyl rubber	Fair	High	Good	Poor	Poor	Judged difficult to tool smoothly.
UGL THERMAKING CAULK (United Gilsonite Lab.)	81¢	Oil	Poor	Moderate	Good	Good	Poor	Useful life judged longer than most, but downrated because caulk judged slightly thin for easy application, difficult to tool smoothly, and more likely to sag in a vertical joint and to stain than most.
GH BUTYLOID RUBBER CALK (Gibson-Homans Co.)	$1.64	Butyl rubber	Fair	High	Poor	Fair	Poor	Judged difficult to tool smoothly.
RELY-ON (Dap, Inc.)	67¢	Oil	Good	Moderate	Fair	Good	Poor	Judged much more likely to stain than most.
GH DRAFTITE CALKING COMPOUND (Gibson-Homans Co.)	48¢	Oil	Good	Moderate	Fair	Good	Poor	Judged more likely to stain than most.

■ *The following were judged of significantly lower quality than those above.*

WELDWOOD BUTYL RUBBER CAULK (Roberts Consolidated Industries)	$1.52	Butyl rubber	Fair	High	Good	Good	Poor	Judged difficult to tool smoothly.
G.E. WHITE MODIFIED SILICONE PAINTABLE CAULK (General Electric Co., Silicone Products Div., Waterford, N.Y.)	$5.99	Paintable silicone	Good	Moderate	Good	Poor	Good	Did poorly in outdoor aging test. Contains xylene, a flammable substance; avoid breathing vapor and avoid use near heat, sparks, or flame. Price as of Sept. 1978.
RED DEVIL LATEX CAULK (Red Devil Inc., Union, N.J.)	$1.16	Latex	Fair	High	Fair	Good	Poor	Judged slightly thin for easy application.
MACCO GUARDHOUSE BUTYL SEALANT BS120 (Macco Adhesives/SCM Corp.)	$1.59	Butyl rubber	Good	High	Good	Fair	Poor	
MACCO LATEX CAULK LC135 (Macco Adhesives/SCM Corp.)	$1.00	Latex	Fair	Moderate	Good	Good	Fair	Test samples varied greatly in viscosity; some were judged slightly thin, others slightly thick, for easy application.
M-D BUTYL RUBBER SEALANT (Macklanburg-Duncan Co.)	$1.51	Butyl rubber	Fair	High	Poor	Poor	Poor	Judged difficult to tool smoothly.
WELDWOOD LATEX CAULK (Roberts Consolidated Industries)	95¢	Latex	Good	Moderate	Poor	Good	Poor	

■ *The following were judged of significantly lower quality than those above.*

DAP ACRYLIC LATEX CAULK (Dap, Inc.)	$1.84	Acrylic latex	Fair	Moderate	Fair	Good	Good	Judged slightly thin for easy application.
RUTLAND WHITE BUTYL CAULK (Rutland Fire Clay Co.)	$1.40	Butyl rubber	Fair	Moderate	Good	Fair	Good	Judged difficult to tool smoothly. Judged more likely to stain than most.
STAY-TITE BUTYL RUBBER CAULK (Stay-Tite Prod. Co.)	$1.96	Butyl rubber	Fair	High	Fair	Good	Poor	Judged difficult to tool smoothly. Judged more likely to sag in a vertical joint than most.
GH 2045 LATEX CALK (Gibson-Homans Co.)	$1.09	Latex	Fair	Moderate	Poor	Good	Poor	Judged slightly thin for easy application. Judged more likely to stain than most.
RED DEVIL BUTYL CAULK (Red Devil, Inc.)	$1.47	Butyl rubber	Fair	High	Good	Fair	Poor	Judged difficult to tool smoothly. Judged more likely to sag in a vertical joint than most.
MACCO REAL SEAL CAULKING COMPOUND (Glidden-Durkee Div., SCM Corp.)	89¢	Oil	Fair	Moderate	Poor	Good	Poor	Judged slightly thin for easy application. Judged more likely to stain than most.

Ways to "tighten" the house

Weather stripping

If you feel a draft at doors or windows, it's a sign that weather stripping is needed. Not only does weather stripping reduce winter heat loss, it also reduces summer heat gain. It helps keep soot, dust, and other airborne contaminants out of the house, cushions the slam of a smartly closed window or door, and may even stop doors and windows from rattling in a sharp wind.

There's no lack of weather stripping material available. CU's shoppers purchased well over a hundred brands and varieties of weather stripping products in 1976. We tested them first by compressing them to various degrees and for various periods of time, then repeated the tests after we'd subjected them to an accelerated aging process. We also checked them for low-temperature flexibility and judged their resistance to abrasion.

Our conclusion: It doesn't pay to try to buy weather stripping by brand; quality differences among strips of the same type designed for the same use are minor. But it *does* pay to pick the right type of weather stripping for your particular installation—the types are not all interchangeable. Of course, *any* properly installed weather stripping is better than none at all.

Before you install weather stripping, you should first be sure that all your windows and doors fit snugly; if there are large gaps around them, a good do-it-yourself manual will tell you how to correct the problem. In addition, you'll need to caulk any gaps where the door or window frames meet the walls. Weather stripping seals only the contact points where windows or doors open and close within their frames. Note, too, that the use of weather stripping does not eliminate the need for storm windows and storm doors. Indeed, storm windows and doors themselves should be weather-stripped or caulked for best results. The work sheet on page 28 will help you calculate the amount of money weather stripping can save you during the heating season.

But what type of weather stripping to choose? The table on page 25, which lists types in order of estimated durability, gives some choices. You may, however, wish to make your choice based on installation considerations. So read the rest of this report before buying. Note that we've also described some strips that we did not test (notably, the various threshold seals). The durability of those types depends mainly on their soft components (foam, felt, vinyl, and the like); their longevity should approximate that of the weather stripping we did test.

Here's what we looked at.

Metal strip

Metal strips, sold in rolls as flat "tension" strips, can be highly efficient if correctly installed. One edge of the strip is nailed to a door or window frame; then the free edge is lifted

away from the frame. That way, a spring tension is developed that holds the strip against the door or window when it's closed.

The metal strips are not really difficult to install, though they are a bit trickier than some of the other types of weather stripping. For doors, the strips go inside the doorjamb at the top and on the sides. (The drawing below shows a bird's-eye view of a metal strip installed on a doorjamb.)

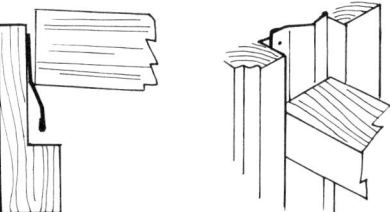

For double-hung windows, the metal strips go inside the side channels (see drawing) as well as at the top of the upper sash, the bottom of the lower sash, and where the two sashes meet. Awning (top-pivoting), hopper (bottom-pivoting), and casement windows are treated the same way doors are. Windows that slide horizontally can be considered double-hung windows on their sides. Properly installed, metal weather stripping is practically invisible. Look for strips with pre-drilled nail holes and brands that include an extra piece to fit over the striker plate (if for a door) and nails for installation.

Tubular gasket

Tubular gasket is basically rubber or vinyl plastic tubing with a ¼- to ½-inch lip or flange for nailing. Tubular

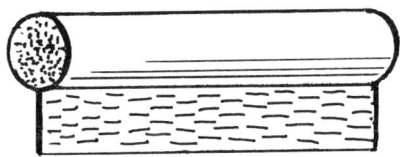

gasket is attached to door stops so that the slightly protruding tube is compressed when the door is closed (see drawing). On double-hung windows, it is nailed at the sides to the window frame, at the top and bottom to the rails of the sashes, and at the

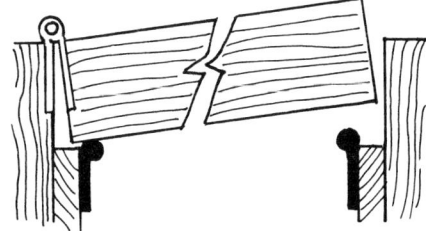

joint where the two sashes meet. CU prefers tubing filled with polyurethane or sponge rubber to tubing that is hollow. Tubing with flanges strengthened with wire or paper cord may last longer.

Weather stripping

Reinforced gasket

Reinforced gasket is a hollow vinyl tube that has a flange reinforced by an aluminum strip. It comes pre-

punched with holes for nailing, and you install it in much the same way as the tubular gasket described above, with the vinyl-tube side compressed against the door or window.

Reinforced felt

In this type, felt has been reinforced by aluminum. It is best used where little abrasion is expected—on a door

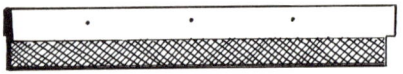

stop or the bottom of a window, for example (see drawing), but not at the side of a window, where it would be rubbed when the window is opened and closed. It's also best not to expose felt fully to the weather, since fungi, insects, and moisture can attack the felt. Wool felt should maintain a seal longer than felt made of other fibers, but it is not as durable as the gaskets.

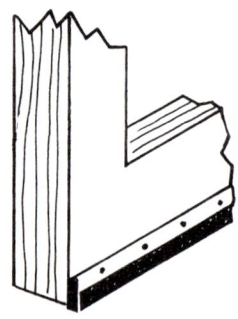

Nonreinforced felt

In our survey we found nonreinforced felt in strips up to ⅜ inch thick and some 5/16 to 1¼ inches

wide. You nail on most varieties, though at least one brand comes with an adhesive backing. Non-reinforced felt shares with reinforced felt the vulnerability to abrasion, weather, and the like, and is probably best used in protected locations, such as around a door opening (see drawing). Felt compresses

relatively little and is therefore best suited for sealing gaps that are narrow and uniform. All-wool felt is best but costs more than felt of other fibers.

Rigid strip

This type has resilient strips, such as plastic foam or tubular gasket, that come preattached to wood or alumi-

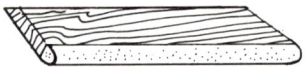

num molding. That, in turn, is nailed or screwed onto a doorjamb. The strips are primarily for use on door frames and usually come in a kit that contains two long pieces for the sides of the jamb and a shorter piece for the top. The strips are cut to size with a standard saw (if wood-backed) or a hack saw (if aluminum-based), fitted snugly against the closed door, and secured with nails or screws every eight to twelve inches. Properly installed, the strips blend in with the door frame and can be painted to match the molding. Metal strips that provide slots, rather than holes, allow you to loosen attaching screws and reset the strip to compensate for an aging or worn seal.

There's a potential problem with wood-reinforced strips—the foam or other glued-on sealing material may become detached from the wood in time, especially if the wood is exposed to alternating periods of dry and humid weather. Perhaps to counter that possibility, at least one brand secures its vinyl-gasket sealing material in a groove in the wood. That strip, however, is 1¾ inches wide, about an inch wider than most others; it might not fit some doors.

Foam strip

Our survey turned up foam strips of various widths and thicknesses. Some are glued on, usually by means of preapplied adhesive protected by a peelaway paper covering. Others come without adhesive. Foam can be used as a short-term weather stripping and can be removed without leaving marks. The most durable variety, we judge, is vinyl foam, followed by neoprene sponge, sponge rubber, and foam polyurethane, in that order. You can

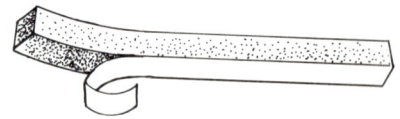

use foam strips wherever you would use felt, but, unlike felt, foam can seal cracks that are relatively wide, nonuniform, or both.

Weather stripping for door bottoms

Your leak-sealing isn't done until you've dealt with the spaces under the doors to the outside. You have a number of options.

Sweep. A sweep is perhaps the easiest to install. Typically, it's a metal-reinforced piece of plastic that you trim to door width and screw onto the face of the door at the bottom. It's meant to be installed on the outside face of doors that swing out, on the inside face of those that swing in. If the pre-drilled screw holes are slotted, you can lower the sweep later on to compensate for wear. The sweep is quite effective, even on doors without a threshold, but it's exposed to view. A sweep may also drag across carpeting. To solve that problem, consider buying an automatic sweep, which retracts when the door opens and lowers again when the door closes.

24   Ways to "tighten" the house

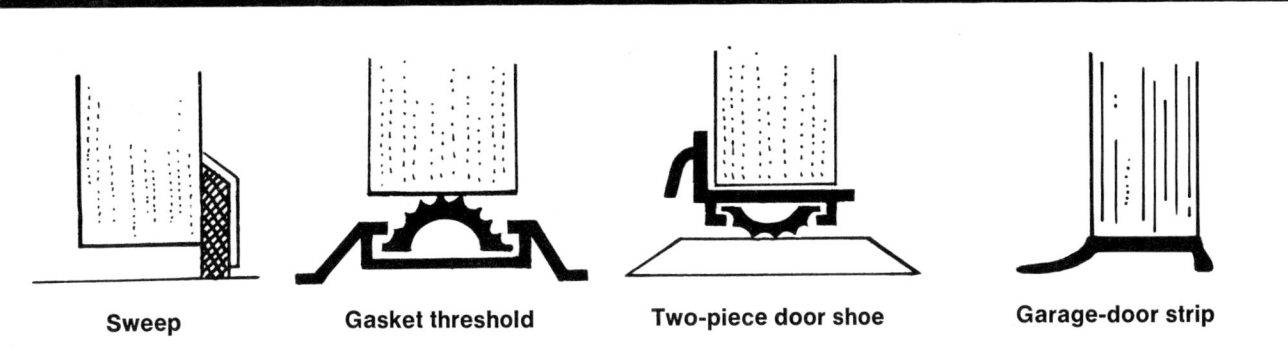

Sweep   Gasket threshold   Two-piece door shoe   Garage-door strip

Gasket threshold. A gasket threshold replaces an existing threshold or provides a threshold where there is none. It's essentially a metal molding with a broad vinyl hump running along its top face. The closed door compresses the hump and makes the seal. Gasket thresholds are available in a number of heights and they seal well, but they leave the gasket exposed to foot traffic that will eventually reduce the effectiveness of the seal. You'll then have to replace the gasket, but that's usually an easy job.

Two-piece door shoe. A more protective installation is the two-piece door shoe. The shoe, with its gasket, slips over the bottom of a door, where it's protected from the wear and tear of foot traffic. As a bonus, a "drip cap" that sheds rain is often included. The door shoe can be used with any threshold that isn't worn down in the middle. The gap under the door must be large enough to allow installation of the shoe (see drawing). If it isn't, you'll have to remove the door and trim it for the extra clearance. The slotted screw holes through which you attach the shoe allow for adjustment.

Garage-door strip. There are wider and longer strips designed primarily for use on the bottom of an overhead garage door. The gaps along the garage floor at this location are likely to be relatively large and nonuniform, calling for thicker material. CU tested several garage-door strips for resistance to petroleum products and found that all were satisfactory in this respect. The strips are easy to install—they are usually nailed to the bottom of the door. One precaution: you should be sure that the strip does not prevent easy latching of the door.

TYPES OF WEATHER STRIPPING FOR DOORS AND WINDOWS

Listed in order of estimated overall durability. Prices given are those found in New York City area late in 1976. In some cases, price ranges cover costs of same material in different widths, thicknesses, or both.

Type	Material	Approx. cost per ft.	Estimated overall durability*	Suitable under compression?	Suitable when subject to abrasion?	Suitable for non-uniform gaps?	How installed
METAL STRIP	Brass or bronze	18¢ to 21¢	E	Yes	Yes	No	Nail
	Aluminum	9¢ to 11¢	VG to E	Yes	Yes	No	Nail
TUBULAR GASKET	Vinyl or rubber, foam-filled	20¢ to 23¢	VG	Yes	Yes	Yes	Nail/Staple
	Vinyl or rubber, hollow	8¢ to 12¢	VG	Yes	Yes	Yes	Nail/Staple
REINFORCED GASKET	Aluminum and vinyl	13¢ to 14¢	VG	Yes	Yes	Yes	Nail
REINFORCED FELT	Wool felt and aluminum	Approx. 10¢	G	Yes	No	No	Nail/Staple
	Nonwool felt and aluminum	8¢ to 13¢	F to G	Yes	No	No	Nail/Staple
NONREINFORCED FELT	Wool	8¢ to 10¢	G	Yes	No	No	Nail/Glue/Staple
	Other	4¢ to 7¢	F to G	Yes	No	No	Nail/Glue/Staple
RIGID STRIP	Aluminum and vinyl	30¢ to 60¢	G	Yes	No	Yes	Screw
	Wood and foam	16¢ to 20¢	F	Yes	No	Yes	Nail/Screw
FOAM STRIP	Neoprene or rubber	10¢ to 21¢	F	Yes	No	Yes	Glue/Self-stick
	Vinyl	5¢ to 8¢	F	Yes	No	Yes	Glue/Self-stick
	Polyurethane	7¢ to 14¢	P to F	Yes	No	Yes	Glue/Self-stick

*E, Excellent; VG, Very Good; G, Good; F, Fair; P, Poor.

Weather stripping

Windows: Escape routes for heat

In simple terms, a window is a glassed-over hole in the wall. It admits light into the house and—to a greater extent than you may realize—allows heat to escape. The amount of heat lost can be considerable.

Windows contribute to heat loss in two ways: First, through conduction, or the flow of heat through the glass itself. (In this sense, glass is no different from other solid materials, which also conduct heat.) Second, through air leakage around the window frames. You can reduce both types of heat loss by installing storm windows.

Up to now we've used the term *storm window* when referring to any type of window that offers greater insulating ability than a single-pane window. Strictly speaking, however, a storm window is a separate sash that can be removed during the summer months or permanently installed outside the existing window frame; inexpensive storms that can be installed on the interior side of the window are also available. Removable storm sash has a single thickness of glass or plastic. A combination storm-screen, the permanently installed variety, has a screen (for summertime ventilation) plus two panes of glass that can be moved up and down in tracks in the storm's frame. Thermal windows, which replace existing windows, have two—sometimes three—thickness of glass in the same sash. Units with two thicknesses are known, logically enough, as *double-glazed* windows; units with three panes are called *triple-glazed*. (The sealed spaces between the panes of some thermal windows are filled with a dry gas; this does not improve the window's insulating ability, but does help prevent condensation between the panes.) Both storms and thermal windows offer the same insulating advantage: multiple layers of glass separated by an air space. Storms offer the added advantage of reducing air leakage around the frame.

The work sheet at the end of this report (page 28) will help you estimate how much you can save on fuel during the heating season by modifying the windows on your house. In order to make sense out of the work sheet, though, you need to know more about conduction and air leakage.

First, conduction. A window, like other parts of a house, has an R-value that characterizes its resistance to heat flow. A single pane of ordinary window glass has an R-value of about 0.9—not exactly large, considering that an uninsulated wood-frame wall with wood siding has an R-value of about 5. In other words, a square foot of window will conduct heat more than five times as fast as a square foot of uninsulated wood-frame wall. In terms of the house as a whole, if 15 percent of the total wall area is taken up with windows, then that house will lose just about as much heat through the windows, via conduction, as it does through the walls.

Adding storm sash or thermal windows raises a window's total R-value to between 1.6 and 2.5, depending on the amount of air space between the panes. As we noted earlier, doubling the R-value of a material cuts the amount of heat flow in half. So, while the windows will still allow a fair

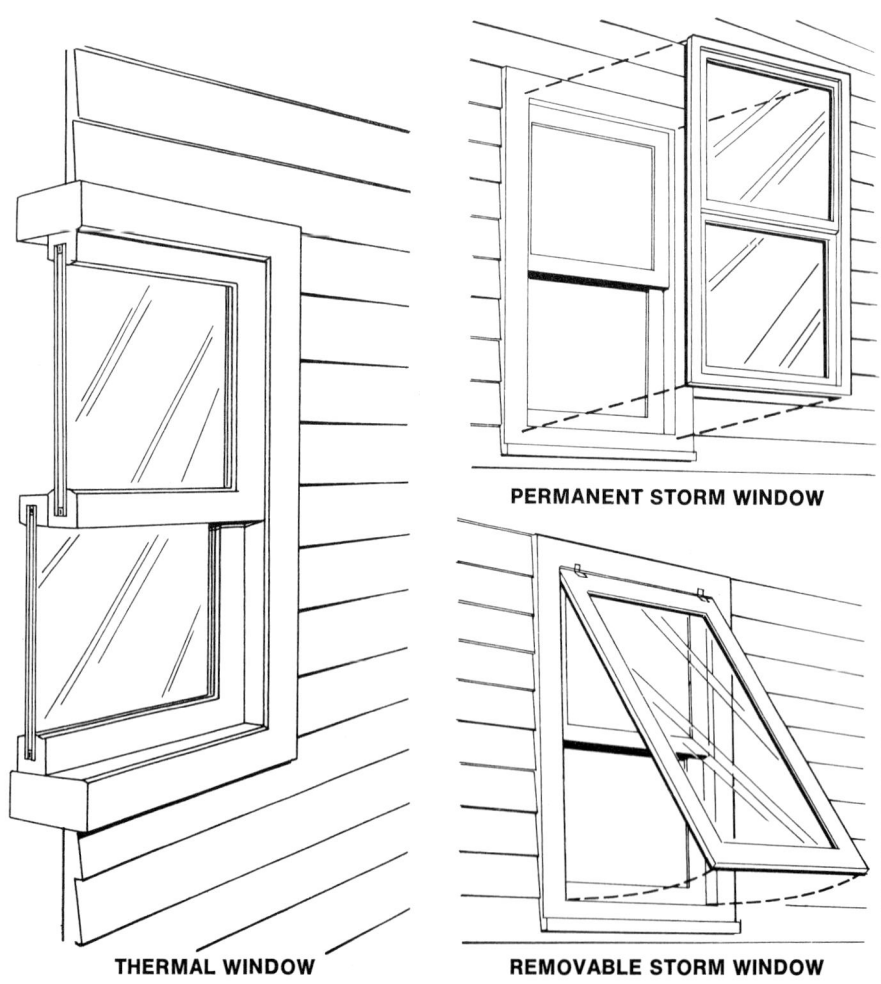

THERMAL WINDOW

PERMANENT STORM WINDOW

REMOVABLE STORM WINDOW

26   Ways to "tighten" the house

amount of heat to escape, with storms or thermal windows, the losses will be substantially less.

In calculating the conduction saving, you need to consider only the type of glazing (storm sash, double-glazed, or whatever) and the air space between the panes. The materials used for the window frame and the presence—or absence—of weather stripping have little effect on conduction; weather stripping can have a considerable effect on air leakage, which we will look at next.

Now for air leakage. Cracks around windows—at the sides of the sash and, on double-hung windows, in the space between the upper and lower sash—allow warm air to escape and cool outdoor air to take its place. The warm air moves because of differences in air pressure between the inside and outside of a house's walls. The air-pressure differences are largely the result of temperature differences and wind forces; walls that face the wind sustain high pressures, and leeward walls sustain relatively low pressures. Because air-leakage losses vary from window to window and from day to day, it's difficult to obtain an accurate estimate of those losses over the course of a year. So, when considering air leakage, you need to put your windows in one of three general categories: A *loose* window is one that rattles perceptibly in high winds, or one that rattles when you shake it in its frame. A *tight* window is one that is weather stripped and doesn't rattle. And a window that falls somewhere between the two extremes is *average*. In addition to reducing conductive losses, storm windows help reduce losses due to air leakage. The air-leakage saving is determined, first, by the type of windows your house now has; second, by the type of windows you want to add; and, third, the presence (or absence) of weather stripping. The type of glazing is not a factor in this instance. However, if you're replacing loose single-glazed windows with well-fitting thermal windows, there will be some air-leakage saving—the equivalent of weather stripping loose windows. There would be little air-leakage saving if you replaced average or tight windows with thermal windows.

Adding up the losses (and the saving)

As complicated as they may seem at first glance, the tables on pages 30 and 31 are rather simple to use. They show, for eight climatic zones, the amount of heat saved by reducing losses caused by conduction and air leakage. The air-leakage tables show the amount of heat that can be saved by adding storm windows alone, or by adding storm windows plus weather stripping.*

Once you know how much heat can be saved, it's then possible to calculate the amount of fuel you can save each heating season if you install storm sash or thermal windows. The work sheet explains how to do the calculations, but a few examples can illustrate the kind of saving possible.

Our hypothetical house in Columbus, Ohio, is in zone 4, a region with 5000 to 6000 degree-days per heating season. Let's say the house has 280 square feet of window, or about 15 percent of the total wall area. Let's also assume that all the windows in this house are double-hung, single-glazed, and have no weather stripping. The house, we'll say, is heated with natural gas. How much can the owner of this hypothetical house save by adding permanently mounted storm windows?

First, let's assume that the windows are loose. According to the table for conductive saving, changing from single glass to single glass plus storm windows saves 81 "heat units" per square foot of window, or 22,680 heat units per year for the entire house. (Each heat unit represents 1000 Btu.) Reducing air-leakage losses saves an additional 55,800 heat units per heating season (assuming a total "crack length" of 360 feet for the windows). By work-

The tables were adapted from methods set forth in the "Handbook of Fundamentals," 1977 edition, published by the American Society of Heating, Refrigerating, and Air Conditioning Engineers.

ing through the calculations, we see that the total saving equals about $210 per heating season.

Next, let's assume that the windows are average. According to our calculations, adding permanent storm windows alone would yield an annual saving of about $100.

Now let's assume that the homeowner chooses to install weather stripping as well as permanent storm windows. The weather stripping won't change conductive losses, but it will reduce air-leakage losses a bit, even though the storm windows block most of the leakage. By adding weather stripping, with *permanent* storm windows, the homeowner could save an additional $5 or so.

Weather stripping makes much more of a difference with *removable* storm sash, however. If our hypothetical house had loose windows, removable storms would save about $130 a year; weather stripping would add about $55 to that saving.

Finally, let's consider the saving that weather stripping alone could bring. According to the tables, 42,840 heat units per year could be saved on our hypothetical house if its loose windows had weather stripping added. That translates into a saving of about $117 per heating season. With average windows, the saving would be about $30 per heating season.

As our examples show, the tighter your present windows are, the lower the annual saving. The examples also show that weather stripping alone can yield a large saving—especially on loose windows. In any case, it's important to keep in mind that these estimates represent a saving *in addition to* other weatherization measures, such as insulation or caulking.

Some fine points to keep in mind

The air-leakage savings we've calculated are approximate and somewhat conservative. If your house is in an especially windy location, the numbers in the tables could be two or three times larger. Even so, our tables give you a reasonable basis for estimating the saving that storm windows can bring. If, using our conservative figures, you find the saving to be worthwhile, fine; if your actual saving proves to be larger than you had estimated, so much the better.

If you decide to install removable storm windows, note that they must fit well (tight, that is) and be weather stripped to achieve the saving we've calculated. Permanent storm windows should be caulked. As for inexpensive plastic storm windows (the type that fit inside your present windows), they should yield a saving comparable to that from removable storm windows, if they fit tightly and don't "flap."

The type of window you buy will depend on the amount of money you have available; taste (some people want storm windows to seem unobtrusive, others are less concerned about looks); and the ease with which they can be installed and removed. But no matter what type you choose, any storm window—properly fitted and installed—can help reduce your heating bills to a significant degree.

How much can you save by modifying your windows?

By using this work sheet, you can calculate the amount of money you can save on fuel by installing storm sash or thermal windows on your home. You can also use part of the work sheet to estimate the saving from weather stripping alone. We've included, as examples, calculations for adding permanent storm windows and for weather stripping on our hypothetical house in Columbus, Ohio. Here are the steps you should take.

1. Determine the total area of the windows in your house. The area should be entered in the Window Saving Calculator, below, as square feet, not square inches. To calculate square footage easily, measure the height (in inches) and the width (in inches) of each window. Multiply the two numbers, then divide by 144. Repeat for each window, then add together all the areas. (Our Columbus house has 280 square feet of window area.) Enter window area for your house in column 1.

2. Find the conductive heat saving. The map on the facing page divides the country into eight heating degree-day zones. Find the zone for your area, then turn to the table of Conductive Heat Saving (page 30) for that zone. The numbers show the heat units (thousands of Btu) saved per square foot by installing various types of windows—storm sash, double-glazed, or triple-glazed thermal. Move down the left-hand column to find the type that most closely matches the windows you now have. Then read across until you come to the column that most closely matches the type you want to install. What you will find is the approximate amount of heat saved per square foot. In our example, we've assumed single-glazed, double-hung windows that will be augmented with permanent storm windows. The table for the Columbus area (zone 4) shows a saving of 81 heat units per square foot. Enter heat units saved in column 2.

3. Multiply columns 1 and 2. Enter the result in column 3.

Note: If you are replacing average or tight windows with thermal windows, skip steps 4, 5, and 6.

4. Measure the cracks around the windows. This will allow you to calculate the heat to be saved by reducing the amount of air leakage. The crack length for each window will be twice the height plus twice the width; if you have double-hung windows, also add the width in the middle of the window, where the two sashes meet. Crack length must be entered in the Calculator in feet, not inches; so make all the measurements in inches, do the necessary addition, then divide by 12. Do the same for each window. (Our Columbus house has a total of 360 feet of crack.) Enter total crack length in column 4.

5. Determine the air-leakage saving. Find the air-leakage table for your zone. Move down the left-hand col-

---

WINDOW SAVING CALCULATOR

1	2	3	4	5	6	7	8	9	10	11
Total window area	Conductive heat saving per sq. ft.	Total conductive saving	Total crack length	Air-leakage saving per ft.	Total air-leakage saving	Overall heat saving (Col. 3 + Col. 6)	Fuel factor	Heat saved per fuel unit	Fuel cost	ANNUAL SAVING
280 × 81 = 22,680	360 × 155 = 55,800	78,480 × 0.013 = 1020.24 × $0.21 = $214.25
___ × ___ = ___	360 × 119 = 42,840	___ × 0.013 = 556.92 × $0.21 = $116.95
___ × ___ = ___	___ × ___ = ___	___ × ___ = ___ × ___ = $___
___ × ___ = ___	___ × ___ = ___	___ × ___ = ___ × ___ = $___

28   Ways to "tighten" the house

umn to find the type of window that most closely matches what you now have—loose, average, tight, with or without weather stripping, Read across the table to find the type of window that most closely matches what you want to install. What you will find is the amount of heat to be saved by reducing air-leakage. If you are replacing loose windows with thermal windows; use the saving given for weather stripping loose windows in your zone. (The saving is 155 heat units for our hypothetical house.) Enter the air-leakage saving in column 5.

6. *Multiply columns 4 and 5.* Enter the result in column 6.

7. *Total the heat units to be saved.* Add column 3 and column 6. Enter the total in column 7.

8. *Enter the fuel factor.* This is a number that takes into account the different amounts of heat produced by different fuels. The factor for oil is 0.01; for natural gas, it's 0.013; for electricity, it's 0.29; for propane, it's 0.059 if you buy it by the pound, 0.013 if you buy it by the gallon. Enter in column 8 the factor appropriate for your heating system. (It's natural gas in our example.)

9. *Multiply column 7 by column 8.* Enter the result in column 9.

10. *Factor in the cost of fuel.* Find out how much you pay for oil, natural gas, electricity, or propane—not the total monthly bill, but the rate for a basic unit of fuel (see Chapter 1, page 12). Your monthly statement should give the rate, but if it doesn't call your utility company or fuel dealer. Our hypothetical homeowner pays 21 cents per therm for natural gas, entered in the Calculator as $0.21, not 21.

11. *Multiply column 9 by column 10.* Enter the result on line 11. The result will be your total saving in dollars, per heating season, if you add storm windows.

To calculate the saving for weather stripping alone:

A. Disregard conductive saving, and begin your calculations with step 4. Measure the total crack length for your windows, then determine the heat saved by reducing air-leakage losses. Enter the data in columns 4 and 5.

B. Multiply columns 4 and 5, and enter the result in column 6.

C. Enter the fuel factor in column 8, then multiply column 6 by column 8. Enter the result in column 9.

D. Enter the fuel cost in column 10. Multiply columns 9 and 10. Enter the result in column 11. The result will be the total saving in dollars, per heating season, that weather stripping will provide. The calculations for our Columbus house are shown on the second line of the Calculator.

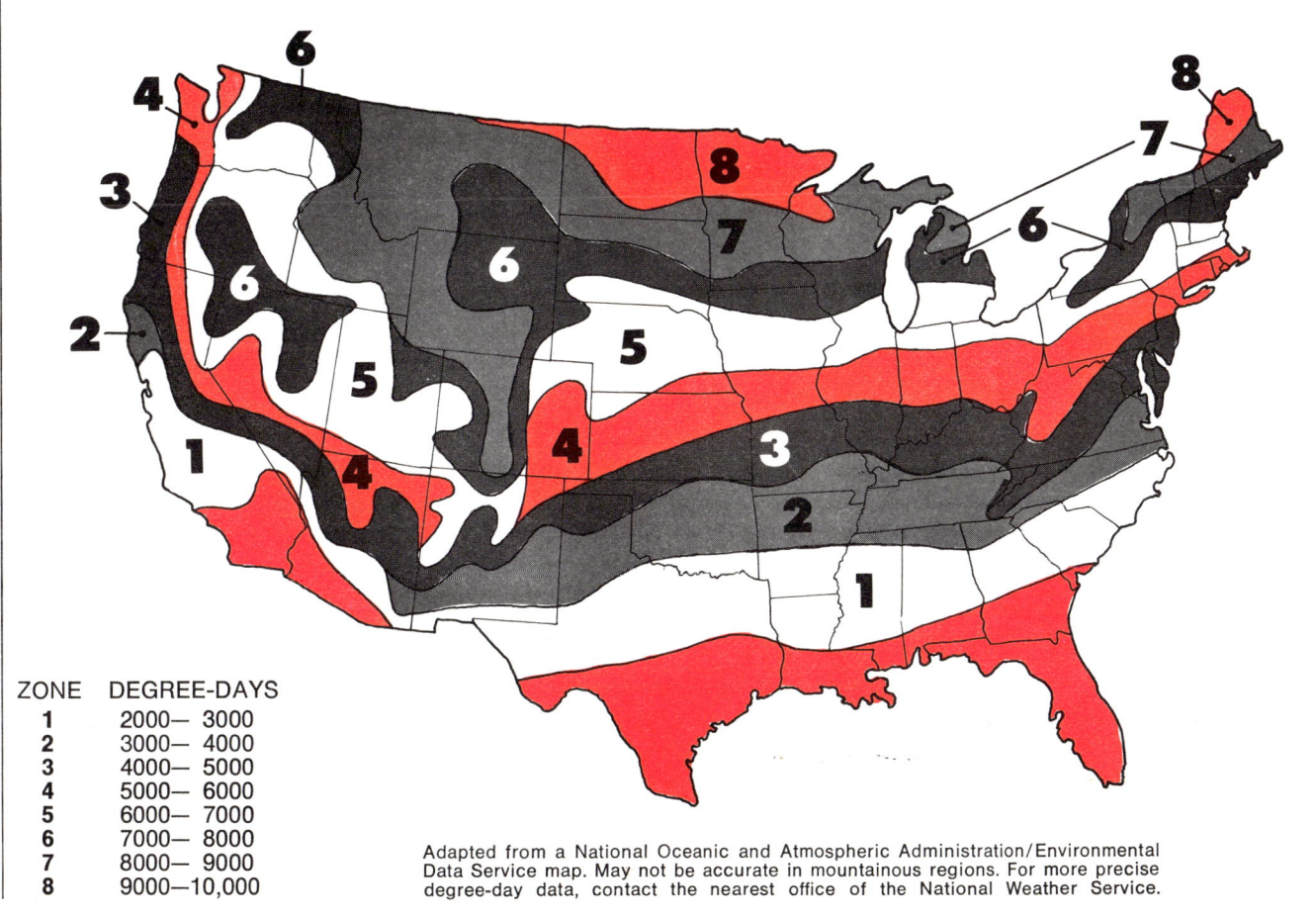

ZONE	DEGREE-DAYS
1	2000— 3000
2	3000— 4000
3	4000— 5000
4	5000— 6000
5	6000— 7000
6	7000— 8000
7	8000— 9000
8	9000—10,000

Adapted from a National Oceanic and Atmospheric Administration/Environmental Data Service map. May not be accurate in mountainous regions. For more precise degree-day data, contact the nearest office of the National Weather Service.

CONDUCTIVE HEAT SAVING

(Heat units per square foot per year, by degree-day zone. Numbers in parentheses indicate amount of air space, in inches, between panes of glass.)

ZONE 1

CURRENT WINDOWS	Double-glazed (3/16)	Double-glazed (1/4)	Storm windows (1 to 4)	Double-glazed (1/2)	Triple-glazed (1/4)	Triple-glazed (1/2)
Single glass	30	32	37	38	44	49
Double-glazed (3/16)		2	7	8	14	19
Double-glazed (1/4)			5	6	12	17
Storm windows (1 to 4)				1	7	12
Double-glazed (1/2)					6	11
Triple-glazed (1/4)						5

ZONE 2

CURRENT WINDOWS	Double-glazed (3/16)	Double-glazed (1/4)	Storm windows (1 to 4)	Double-glazed (1/2)	Triple-glazed (1/4)	Triple-glazed (1/2)
Single glass	41	45	52	53	61	68
Double-glazed (3/16)		3	10	11	20	27
Double-glazed (1/4)			7	8	16	23
Storm windows (1 to 4)				1	10	16
Double-glazed (1/2)					9	16
Triple-glazed (1/4)						7

ZONE 3

CURRENT WINDOWS	Double-glazed (3/16)	Double-glazed (1/4)	Storm windows (1 to 4)	Double-glazed (1/2)	Triple-glazed (1/4)	Triple-glazed (1/2)
Single glass	53	57	66	67	78	87
Double-glazed (3/16)		4	13	14	25	34
Double-glazed (1/4)			9	10	21	30
Storm windows (1 to 4)				1	12	21
Double-glazed (1/2)					11	20
Triple-glazed (1/4)						9

ZONE 4

CURRENT WINDOWS	Double-glazed (3/16)	Double-glazed (1/4)	Storm windows (1 to 4)	Double-glazed (1/2)	Triple-glazed (1/4)	Triple-glazed (1/2)
Single glass	65	70	81	82	95	106
Double-glazed (3/16)		5	16	17	31	42
Double-glazed (1/4)			11	12	26	36
Storm windows (1 to 4)				1	15	26
Double-glazed (1/2)					13	24
Triple-glazed (1/4)						11

ZONE 5

CURRENT WINDOWS	Double-glazed (3/16)	Double-glazed (1/4)	Storm windows (1 to 4)	Double-glazed (1/2)	Triple-glazed (1/4)	Triple-glazed (1/2)
Single glass	76	82	95	97	112	125
Double-glazed (3/16)		6	19	21	36	49
Double-glazed (1/4)			13	14	30	43
Storm windows (1 to 4)				2	17	30
Double-glazed (1/2)					16	29
Triple-glazed (1/4)						13

ZONE 6

CURRENT WINDOWS	Double-glazed (3/16)	Double-glazed (1/4)	Storm windows (1 to 4)	Double-glazed (1/2)	Triple-glazed (1/4)	Triple-glazed (1/2)
Single glass	88	95	109	111	130	144
Double-glazed (3/16)		7	22	24	42	57
Double-glazed (1/4)			15	16	35	49
Storm windows (1 to 4)				2	20	35
Double-glazed (1/2)					18	33
Triple-glazed (1/4)						15

ZONE 7

CURRENT WINDOWS	Double-glazed (3/16)	Double-glazed (1/4)	Storm windows (1 to 4)	Double-glazed (1/2)	Triple-glazed (1/4)	Triple-glazed (1/2)
Single glass	99	107	124	126	147	163
Double-glazed (3/16)		8	25	27	47	64
Double-glazed (1/4)			17	19	39	56
Storm windows (1 to 4)				2	23	39
Double-glazed (1/2)					21	37
Triple-glazed (1/4)						17

ZONE 8

CURRENT WINDOWS	Double-glazed (3/16)	Double-glazed (1/4)	Storm windows (1 to 4)	Double-glazed (1/2)	Triple-glazed (1/4)	Triple-glazed (1/2)
Single glass	111	120	138	141	164	182
Double-glazed (3/16)		9	28	30	53	71
Double-glazed (1/4)			18	21	44	62
Storm windows (1 to 4)				2	25	44
Double-glazed (1/2)					23	41
Triple-glazed (1/4)						18

Ways to "tighten" the house

AIR-LEAKAGE SAVING

(Heat units per linear foot per year, by degree-day zone)

ZONE 1

CONDITION OF CURRENT WINDOWS	Weather stripping	Permanent storm windows	Permanent storm windows and weather stripping	Removable storm windows	Removable storm windows and weather stripping
Loose fit (no weather stripping)	55	72	73	31	58
Loose fit (with weather stripping)			18		3
Average fit (no weather stripping)	15	18	20	3	16
Tight fit (with weather stripping)			6		1

ZONE 2

CONDITION OF CURRENT WINDOWS	Weather stripping	Permanent storm windows	Permanent storm windows and weather stripping	Removable storm windows	Removable storm windows and weather stripping
Loose fit (no weather stripping)	76	100	101	44	81
Loose fit (with weather stripping)			25		5
Average fit (no weather stripping)	20	25	28	5	22
Tight fit (with weather stripping)			8		2

ZONE 3

CONDITION OF CURRENT WINDOWS	Weather stripping	Permanent storm windows	Permanent storm windows and weather stripping	Removable storm windows	Removable storm windows and weather stripping
Loose fit (no weather stripping)	97	127	129	56	103
Loose fit (with weather stripping)			32		6
Average fit (no weather stripping)	26	32	36	6	28
Tight fit (with weather stripping)			10		2

ZONE 4

CONDITION OF CURRENT WINDOWS	Weather stripping	Permanent storm windows	Permanent storm windows and weather stripping	Removable storm windows	Removable storm windows and weather stripping
Loose fit (no weather stripping)	119	155	157	68	126
Loose fit (with weather stripping)			39		7
Average fit (no weather stripping)	31	39	44	7	34
Tight fit (with weather stripping)			12		2

ZONE 5

CONDITION OF CURRENT WINDOWS	Weather stripping	Permanent storm windows	Permanent storm windows and weather stripping	Removable storm windows	Removable storm windows and weather stripping
Loose fit (no weather stripping)	140	182	185	80	148
Loose fit (with weather stripping)			46		9
Average fit (no weather stripping)	37	46	51	9	40
Tight fit (with weather stripping)			14		3

ZONE 6

CONDITION OF CURRENT WINDOWS	Weather stripping	Permanent storm windows	Permanent storm windows and weather stripping	Removable storm windows	Removable storm windows and weather stripping
Loose fit (no weather stripping)	161	210	213	92	171
Loose fit (with weather stripping)			53		10
Average fit (no weather stripping)	43	53	59	10	46
Tight fit (with weather stripping)			16		3

ZONE 7

CONDITION OF CURRENT WINDOWS	Weather stripping	Permanent storm windows	Permanent storm windows and weather stripping	Removable storm windows	Removable storm windows and weather stripping
Loose fit (no weather stripping)	182	238	241	104	193
Loose fit (with weather stripping)			59		11
Average fit (no weather stripping)	48	59	67	11	52
Tight fit (with weather stripping)			19		4

ZONE 8

CONDITION OF CURRENT WINDOWS	Weather stripping	Permanent storm windows	Permanent storm windows and weather stripping	Removable storm windows	Removable storm windows and weather stripping
Loose fit (no weather stripping)	203	265	270	116	216
Loose fit (with weather stripping)			66		12
Average fit (no weather stripping)	54	66	75	12	58
Tight fit (with weather stripping)			21		4

Insulation:
When enough is enough in the wintertime

Of all the energy-saving products on the market today, insulation is getting the hardest, and most successful, sell. By all accounts, nearly 5 million homeowners bought insulation in 1977—double the number in years past. Some types of insulation have been in short supply, and the demand shows no sign of abating.

It's not hard to understand why insulation is so sought-after. Several state governments and local utility companies are offering homeowners tax credits, low-cost loans, and other inducements to add insulation. Federal tax credits for insulation and other energy-saving products (assuming Congress approves them) would be an extra scoop of ice cream on an already tall sundae of incentives.

But the big reason for the demand for insulation is the promise of lower fuel bills. The claimed savings vary, but one trade association maintains that proper Insulation could cut heating and cooling bills by half.

There's no question that every home should be adequately insulated—as one part of the national effort required to reduce the amount of oil, natural gas, and electricity used. In CU's view, however, insulation is being oversold as a conservation tool. If your house already has some insulation, adding more may not be the best course to follow because the money invested will often yield a surprisingly small saving of energy and money. As we noted at the beginning of this chapter, the NBS found that adding more insulation to the attic of its test home yielded the smallest saving—only 6 percent.

What's more, installing insulation does have its drawbacks. Blowing it inside walls or other finished areas can be chancy, since there's no way to be sure that the area has been filled properly. Faulty installation can also lead to moisture condensation within walls, ceilings, and floors. Urea-formaldehyde insulation tends to shrink once it's installed, and loose-fill types may settle in time. In addition, the safety of nearly every type of insulation has been questioned—sometimes with cause.

Why insulate?

Nearly any material will slow the flow of heat, but some materials do a better job than others. Six inches of fiberglass insulation, for instance, is as effective as a brick wall more than eight feet thick. As we noted in Chapter 1, the measure of a material's ability to retard heat flow is known as the R-value; the higher the R-value a given material has, the better it is as an insulator. In estimating your home's insulation needs, think only in terms of R-value, not in terms of a specific type of material or in terms of inches of insulation. It's the R-value that matters most. Four and a half inches of insulation rated at R-4 will be as effective as six inches of insulation rated at R-3.

R-values are additive, so that two fiberglass batts, each rated R-19, together yield R-38. The siding, roofing, and flooring in a house also have R-values of their own, albeit small ones. An uninsulated attic floor isn't R-0; it's normally anywhere from R-2 to R-4.

A little more than a generation ago, when oil and natural gas were cheap, most homes were built with little or no insulation. It was no great economic hardship to let the furnace run and keep the house comfortable. But in the mid-1950s, when electric heat started to gain acceptance from homeowners and the cost of home heating began to rise, insulation became important. Now that all forms of energy are expensive, *some* insulation is a must for every house.

But how much insulation is enough? According to government and industry officials, insulation levels considered adequate four or five years ago are now thought to be too low. Hence the call for higher R-values, on the theory that more insulation saves more energy and more money.

Federal insulation standards, used by the Federal Housing Administration and other mortgage agencies, are being raised. Manufacturers, trade associations and others are also promoting high levels of insulation. A heating-oil contractor in CU's area recommends at least six inches of attic insulation. And the CertainTeed Corp., a major manufacturer of fiberglass insulation, says homeowners should add "at least six inches" to what they now have in the attic. The Homefoamers, a supplier of urea-formaldehyde insulation, recommends "at least eight to ten inches of cellulose, rock wool, or fiberglass" in the attic—but adds that "if you don't insulate the walls, what you've done in the attic just isn't enough."

The most widely circulated set of recommended R-values comes from Owens-Corning, the largest fiberglass-insulation manufacturer in the country. The company conducted a "consumer education" campaign in the fall of 1977, running full-page advertisements in seventy-nine newspapers and several national magazines. The ad did present some worthwhile basic information, along with a map that gave *"economical amounts of insulation to have."* Homes in the warmest parts of the United States need six inches (R-19) of insulation in the attic, according to the map, while homes elsewhere need from 9½ inches to one foot (R-30 to R-38) of attic insulation. What kind of economies can homeowners realize by following Owens-

Corning's recommendations? Admittedly, they will vary, but the ads include a chart of impressive estimates of savings, ranging from $679 a year for an all-electric home in Albany, New York, down to $80 a year for a home in Los Angeles with gas heat and electric air conditioning.

Why not R-50?

Even though those savings might hold true—sometimes—they oversimplify the economics involved, because you *can* insulate a house to a point where the money spent on insulation far exceeds the money saved on fuel. As one official at the Department of Housing and Urban Development put it, "You could put in R-50 and you would save energy. But it wouldn't be cost-effective."

That crucial point was acknowledged by the engineers and other officials CU contacted. An engineer at Owens-Corning explained that the company's recommended R-values might not, in fact, be economical for everyone. They were devised for new homes that use electric heat, he said, and don't always apply to homes that use oil or gas. "If you live in Atlanta and heat your home with gas, it may not pay to add anything if you already have R-19 in the attic. There is a point of diminishing returns," he said.

Several factors determine when the returns begin to diminish: the cost of fuel, climate, the cost of new insulation, and the amount of time you're willing to wait to recover that cost. Still, there's some evidence that the optimum amount of insulation (from an economic standpoint) is usually somewhere below the widely recommended levels.

In the Detroit area, the Michigan Consolidated Gas Co. has helped 180,000 homeowners insulate their attics through a program that began in late 1973. By most standards—and according to the ads from Owens-Corning—Detroit homes should have attic insulation equivalent to at least R-33. Not so, a Michigan Consolidated representative told CU: "We estimated that R-19 insulation in the ceiling would reduce gas consumption by about 17 percent. Once you get past that level, you hit the point of diminishing returns. We've gone back and checked consumption data for specific houses and, on that basis, we're right on the numbers." Owens-Corning, for one, recommends wall insulation equal to R-19. But added wall insulation doesn't even figure in the Michigan Consolidated program, because the cost of getting the insulation into the walls outweighs any fuel saving, the representative said.

Further south, where winter weather is somewhat milder, the Tennessee Valley Authority has begun a five-year insulation program that is expected to affect some 800,000 homeowners. Here, too, the utility recommends R-19 attic insulation even though most other quoted optimum levels are higher for that area. In a small test program, the TVA installed insulation, caulking, and weather stripping in seventy electrically heated homes in Alabama, Mississippi, and Tennessee; on average, utility bills dropped 33 percent, or $120, for those homes in 1977. According to David Lamb, the engineer in charge of the program, the TVA could have pegged the new insulation levels at R-30 but chose not to. The added cost of the insulation, he said, would outweigh the additional saving in fuel.

What's best for your house?

Michigan Consolidated, the TVA, manufacturers, and others all use roughly the same kind of calculation to arrive at their recommended insulation levels. The arithmetic is fairly simple, but does allow for some variation, which is why different recommended R-values result.

It is possible for you to estimate how much money you can save if you put insulation in your house. The work sheet on page 36 tells you how. It may seem like a fair amount of work, but once you've done the estimating we recommend, you'll be able to judge where to spend your money wisely—whether it's for extra attic insulation, new insulation in walls or crawl spaces, or for some other kind of energy-saving product. As we explained in Chapter 1, you have to weigh the potential saving against the cost of the insulation. That way, you'll learn how quickly installing insulation will pay for itself and have a means of judging it against another energy-saving measure.

Suppose, for example, that our homeowner in Columbus, Ohio, wants to insulate the attic. Assume that the attic has 666 square feet of floor area, no insulation, and that the house is heated with natural gas costing 21 cents per therm. According to our calculations, installing R-19 insulation would save about $100 per heating season.

(By way of comparison, storm windows would save roughly $100 to $200 on our hypothetical house, depending on the condition of the house's old windows.)

The saving would be much less if this hypothetical Ohio home already had some attic insulation. With, say, R-11 in place, an additional R-19 (for a total R-value of 30) would save less than $15.

That kind of minuscule annual saving might lead the homeowner to consider leaving the attic at R-11 and insulating the walls instead. This time, suppose the house has 1600 square feet of uninsulated wood frame walls with wood siding. The walls now have an R-value of 4. By hiring a contractor to inject urea-formaldehyde foam, the homeowner can bring the walls to R-20. The annual saving: slightly more than $100.

Keep in mind that these examples are *only* for the heating season. For a discussion of insulation's effect on air-conditioning requirements, see page 57.

Just as recommended R-values differ, so do desirable payback periods. The Farmers Home Administration uses thirty-three years (the life of an FmHA mortgage); the National Association of Home Builders uses a seven-year period, since that's the average number of years a family spends before moving on to another house. There's no one number of months or years that's right for every house. But by calculating the saving for different amounts of insulation, or for different areas of the house, you will learn where added insulation may bring the greatest saving—and where the savings will mount up most quickly.

What about the effect of inflation? It's a safe bet that the cost of fuel will rise—and higher fuel costs will shorten the payback period for insulation. But there's no way to predict when the prices of fuel will increase, or how large the increase will be. In our view, it makes sense to put your energy-conservation dollars where they will do the most good *now*. The best investment today will also be the best investment in the future, regardless of higher fuel prices or higher material costs.

If your calculations do show that it will take a considerable time to save enough on fuel to recover the cost of insulation, you should consider investing in other energy-savers first. These include: storm windows (page 26); exterior caulking (page 17) and weather stripping (page 23) to eliminate drafts around doors and windows; an energy-saving thermostat (page 40); or one of several fuel-saving devices discussed in the next chapter.

What's available?

Your calculations may show that additional insulation will pay for itself in a fairly short time. The question you then have to answer is: What kind of insulation will work best? It's more important to understand the differences among types of insulation than to recognize brand names. There are several varieties, each with its own advantages and disadvantages. They include the following (all R-values given are *per inch*).

BATTS AND BLANKETS
Fiberglass or mineral wool (R-3.1).
Suitable for use in unfinished areas, batts and blankets can be a do-it-yourself item. They are made in standard thicknesses (generally yielding total R-values of 11, 13, 19, and 22), and in widths meant to fit between wall studs and floor joists.

They are available with or without a vapor barrier—necessary for most types of insulation (not just fiberglass) to minimize moisture condensation in walls, floors, and ceilings. Fiberglass and mineral wool present a very remote fire hazard.

LOOSE-FILL
Cellulose (R-3.7), mineral wool (R-3.1), perlite (R-2.6), fiberglass (R-2.3), and vermiculite (R-2.1).

These materials are suitable for use in both finished and unfinished areas. They can be poured into place between exposed floor joists or blown into finished wall or floor cavities. Pouring insulation is a job most homeowners should be able to handle themselves; blowing in insulation is a job for an experienced contractor. Any loose-fill material may settle in time, thus lowering its R-value. Except for improperly treated or badly installed cellulose, the risk of fire from loose-fill is remote.

FOAM
Urea-formaldehyde (R-4.8).

Suitable for use in finished walls, urea-formaldehyde does present some problems. High temperature and humidity can cause the foam to deteriorate and can cause a formaldehyde odor to linger after installation. The foam also deteriorates when exposed to light or open air. Some studies indicate that the foam shrinks for several months after installation, drastically reducing its effectiveness as an insulator. The material will burn, but presents very little risk of fire inside wall cavities. Proper installation is essential; components of the foam must be mixed correctly, injected at the proper pressure, and injection holes must be left open to allow water to evaporate and the foam to cure. Urea-formaldehyde foam must be installed by a contractor—and the contractor must be chosen with special care.

PLASTIC FOAM BOARDS
Urethane (R-5.9), polystyrene (R-4.5), and beadboard (R-3.6).

These products are suitable for use as exterior sheathing, or to cover finished walls. To insulate finished walls (something you can do yourself if you're a fairly accomplished do-it-yourselfer), panels of material are attached to an existing wall, then covered with a vapor barrier and, for fire protection, gypsum board at least ½-inch thick. Plastic boards don't shrink or settle, but they are combustible. They *must* be covered with a fire-retardant material, as specified by your local building code.

Installing insulation properly

No matter what type of insulation you use or who does the installing, there are five points to keep in mind.

1. It's important to include a vapor barrier (a sheet of foil, plastic, or treated paper) facing the inside of the house to minimize moisture condensation, which could soak insulation and lower its R-value. Moisture might also cause studs, joists, and sheathing to rot, and exterior paint to blister. If you're insulating finished walls, apply two coats of oil-based or aluminum paint to the inside walls for some protection against condensation.

2. Don't block vents in eaves or crawl spaces with insulation; they are important for temperature and moisture control.

3. Keep insulation away from the top and sides of recessed lighting fixtures and other heat sources. (If you're planning to use loose-fill, you'll need to install a shield of some sort to keep the material in place.)

4. If you're handling the insulation yourself, wear protective clothing—gloves, long-sleeved shirts and long trousers, a dust mask, and goggles—to keep dust or stray mineral wool fibers away from your skin, lungs, and eyes.

5. The R-values we have given are those generally accepted by both government and industry. Don't deal with contractors or suppliers who claim markedly higher R-values for these materials. If you're buying loose-fill insulation, check the label; it should give the number of square feet a bag will cover, the thickness of material for that area, and the resulting R-value. Follow that thickness

level carefully to be sure the insulation isn't spread too thin. If the label doesn't provide that information, don't buy the product.

Keep in mind that costs and installation problems will vary from one part of the house to another. Unfinished areas—attic floors, crawl spaces, basement walls or ceilings—are the easiest to get to and generally the least expensive to insulate. Finished attic floors and outside walls are the most difficult and costliest. In fact, it may not be wise to re-insulate walls that already have some insulation, according to the contractors and housing officials CU contacted. It's not necessary to re-insulate the entire house at once. If you find that your attic needs insulation, but your home-improvement budget will only allow you to cover half the area, fine; you will most likely save enough on fuel to recover that cost quickly. You can insulate the rest of the attic later.

Prices for insulation vary widely from one area of the country to the next, and some types—fiberglass and mineral wool in particular—may be hard to find at any price. If you're planning to install insulation yourself, shop for the best price. Otherwise, shop for the best *contractor*, even if that means paying a premium, to improve the chances of getting insulation installed safely and properly. (See Chapter 7, "If You Must Seek Professional Help.")

WHERE TO START ADDING INSULATION

In theory, every building surface that separates the living area from the outside should be insulated. However, you don't have to insulate the entire house at once. Start with the areas that are the easiest and least expensive, then do the more difficult and more expensive areas. Follow the general sequence indicated below.

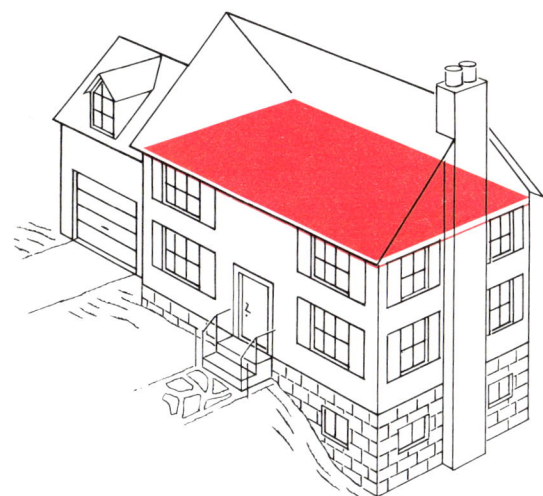

1. Unfinished attics; crawl spaces (not shown).

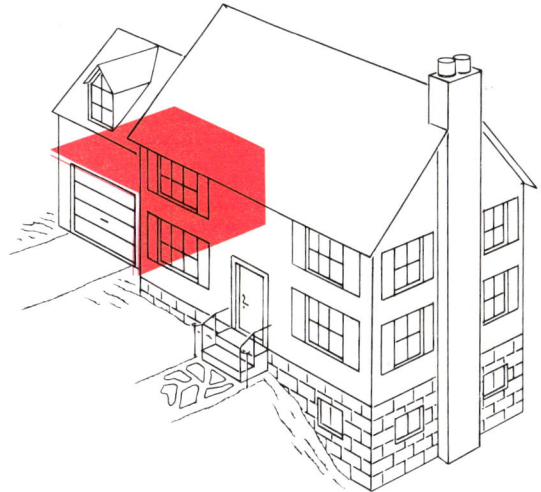

2. Walls and ceilings between unheated parts of the house (such as a garage) and living area.

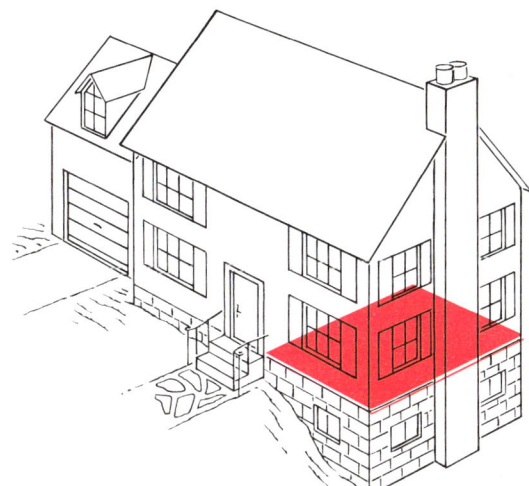

3. Ceilings in unfinished, unheated basements.

4. Exterior walls, including finished attics (left) and finished basements (not shown).

Insulation 35

How much insulation is enough?

This step-by-step work sheet will help you decide whether installing insulation will pay for itself within a reasonable period. Follow these ten steps for each surface (attic floor, basement walls, and so on) you are considering insulating.

1. Determine the current R-value of the area you wish to insulate. Begin with insulation already in place. In unfinished areas, you need only measure the thickness of any insulation you find. Finished walls and ceilings present more of a challenge. If an outside wall is noticeably colder to the touch than other walls in that room, there's probably no insulation inside. To be sure, use a screwdriver to probe carefully around the sides of an electrical junction box (*after* you've pulled the fuse or thrown the circuit breaker for that room). To check insulation under an attic floor, pry up a floorboard in an inconspicuous part of the attic and carefully probe. Measure the thickness of whatever insulation you find. If you can identify the type of insulation you have, turn to page 34 to determine its R-value per inch. Otherwise you'll have to estimate the R-value; a value of R-2.5 per inch is a reasonable estimate. Refer to the Building R-values table on the facing page to find the R-values for siding, shingles, and other parts of the house itself. (Our Columbus house, with an unfinished attic, no insulation, and a plasterboard ceiling, is R-2.) Add that value to the R-value for the existing insulation. Enter your current R-value in column 1 of the Insulation Saving Calculator below.

2. Select a new R-value. The kind of insulation you use will depend on what you can afford and what's readily available in your area. How much you add will depend on climate and the amount of insulation already in place. (With finished walls, the limit is the thickness of the wall cavity, typically 3½ inches.) For starters, use the insulation levels recommended for your area by insulation contractors, the local utility, or insulation manufacturers; if those levels don't prove to be economical, recalculate your saving, using a higher or lower R-value. Enter the R-value for added insulation in column 2.

3. Add columns 1 and 2. Enter the result in column 3.

4. Determine how much heat more insulation will save. The tables at the right show, for each degree-day zone, the "heat units" (thousands of Btu) saved per square foot by adding various amounts of insulation. Move down the left-hand column to find the number that's closest to your current R-value. Then read across the table until you come to the column that most closely matches the new R-value. What you find will be the approximate amount of heat per square foot you will save. In our example, moving from R-2 to R-20 (the closest value to R-21) in zone 4 saves 60 heat units per square foot per heating season. Enter heat saved in column 4.

5. Measure the area to be insulated—length and width of floors, height and length of walls. Be sure to subtract the areas of windows and doors. And, since there will be studs or floor joists in the way, allow for the area they occupy. If those structural members are approximately 16 inches apart, multiply the total area by 0.9; if they're nearly 24 inches apart, multiply the overall square footage by 0.94. The overall area of our sample house measures 666 square feet; joists are 16 inches apart, so the homeowner needs 600 square feet of insulation. Enter the area to be insulated in column 5.

6. Multiply columns 4 and 5. Enter the result in column 6.

7. Enter the fuel factor. The factor for oil is 0.01; for natural gas it's 0.013; for electricity it's 0.29; for propane, it's 0.059 if you buy it by the pound, 0.013 if you buy it by the gallon. Enter in column 7 the factor appropriate for your heating system.

8. Multiply column 6 by column 7. Enter the result in column 8.

9. Factor in the cost of fuel—the price you pay for a basic unit of fuel. Enter the fuel cost in column 9.

10. Multiply columns 8 and 9. Enter the result on line 10. The answer will be your total saving in dollars, per heating season, from insulation. The owners of our Columbus house would save an estimated $98 a year if they insulated the attic. (Note: If you have electric heat, but from a heat pump, divide the saving by 2.)

INSULATION SAVING CALCULATOR

Surface	1 Current R-value	2 R-value of added insulation	3 New R-value	4 Heat units saved per sq. ft.	5 Sq. ft. of surface	6 Total heat units saved	7 Fuel factor	8 Heat saved per fuel unit	9 Fuel cost	10 ANNUAL SAVING
Attic floor	2	+ 19	= 21	60	× 600	= 36,000	× 0.013	= 468	× $0.21	= $98.28
		+	=		×	=	×	=	×	= $
		+	=		×	=	×	=	×	= $

36 Ways to "tighten" the house

HEAT SAVING

(Heat units per square foot per year, by degree-day zone)

ZONE 1

CURRENT R-VALUES	NEW R-VALUES						
	10	15	20	25	30	35	40
2	25	27	28	29	29	29	30
3	15	17	18	18	19	19	19
4	9	11	12	13	14	14	14
5	6	8	9	10	10	11	11
10		2	3	4	4	4	5
15			1	2	2	2	3
20				1	1	1	2
25						1	1

ZONE 2

CURRENT R-VALUES	NEW R-VALUES						
	10	15	20	25	30	35	40
2	35	37	39	40	40	41	41
3	20	23	24	25	26	26	27
4	13	16	17	18	19	19	19
5	9	12	13	14	14	15	15
10		3	4	5	6	6	6
15			1	2	3	3	4
20				1	1	2	2
25					1	1	1

ZONE 3

CURRENT R-VALUES	NEW R-VALUES						
	10	15	20	25	30	35	40
2	44	48	50	51	52	52	52
3	26	29	31	32	33	34	34
4	17	20	22	23	24	24	25
5	11	15	17	18	18	19	19
10		4	6	7	7	8	8
15			2	3	4	4	5
20				1	2	2	3
25					1	1	2

ZONE 4

CURRENT R-VALUES	NEW R-VALUES						
	10	15	20	25	30	35	40
2	54	58	60	62	63	63	64
3	31	36	38	39	40	41	41
4	20	25	27	28	29	30	30
5	13	18	20	22	22	23	24
10		4	7	8	9	10	10
15			2	4	4	5	6
20				1	2	3	3
25					1	2	2

ZONE 5

CURRENT R-VALUES	NEW R-VALUES						
	10	15	20	25	30	35	40
2	63	69	71	73	74	75	75
3	37	42	45	46	48	48	49
4	24	29	32	33	34	35	36
5	16	21	24	25	26	27	28
10		5	8	10	11	11	12
15			3	4	5	6	7
20				2	3	3	4
25					1	2	2

ZONE 6

CURRENT R-VALUES	NEW R-VALUES						
	10	15	20	25	30	35	40
2	73	79	82	84	85	86	87
3	43	49	52	54	55	56	56
4	27	33	36	38	40	40	41
5	18	24	27	29	30	31	32
10		6	9	11	12	13	14
15			3	5	6	7	8
20				2	3	4	5
25					1	2	3

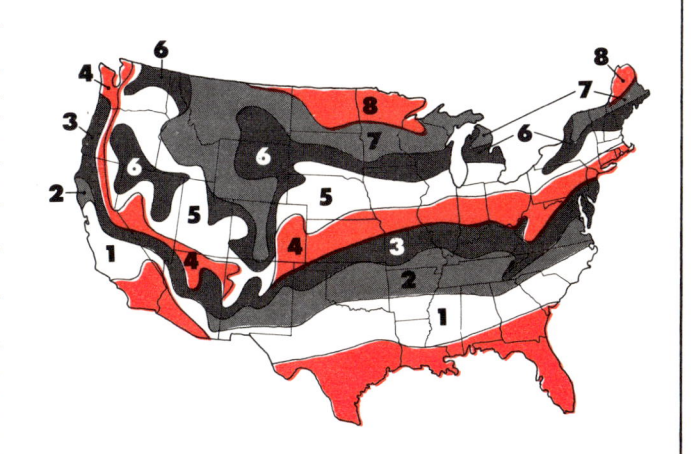

ZONE	DEGREE-DAYS
1	2000— 3000
2	3000— 4000
3	4000— 5000
4	5000— 6000
5	6000— 7000
6	7000— 8000
7	8000— 9000
8	9000—10,000

Adapted from a National Oceanic and Atmospheric Administration/Environmental Data Service map. May not be accurate in mountainous regions. For more precise degree-day data, contact the nearest office of the National Weather Service.

ZONE 7

CURRENT R-VALUES	NEW R-VALUES						
	10	15	20	25	30	35	40
2	83	89	93	95	96	97	98
3	48	55	58	61	62	63	64
4	31	38	41	43	45	46	46
5	21	28	31	33	34	35	36
10		7	10	12	14	15	15
15			3	6	7	8	9
20				2	3	4	5
25					1	2	3

ZONE 8

CURRENT R-VALUES	NEW R-VALUES						
	10	15	20	25	30	35	40
2	92	100	104	106	108	109	109
3	54	61	65	68	69	70	71
4	35	42	46	48	50	51	52
5	23	31	35	37	38	39	40
10		8	12	14	15	16	17
15			4	6	8	9	10
20				2	4	5	6
25					2	3	3

BUILDING R-VALUES
(For typical house construction)

WALLS
Uninsulated wood frame, with—
- Stucco — R-3
- Asbestos siding — R-3
- Wood siding — R-4
- Face-brick veneer — R-4
- Wood shingles — R-5

Brick — R-4
Concrete block — R-4

CEILINGS (under attics)
- Plaster or plasterboard — R-2
- Acoustical tile — R-3
  (Add 2 if attic has subfloor)

FLOORS (over basements, porches, and crawl spaces)
- Wood — R-3
  (Add 2 for finished ceiling in basement)

Insulation 37

Cellulose insulation: Handle with care

In December 1975, a fire damaged a home on the west side of Denver. City fire officials say it happened when cellulose insulation—installed only two days earlier—came into contact with faulty wiring. Cellulose insulation was also involved in two other fires in Denver that month.

Cellulose insulation was blamed for dozens of fires across the country in the mid-1970s. It may also have been responsible for corroded water pipes in other homes.

All types of insulation have their drawbacks. Insulation of any kind installed without proper moisture barriers and provision for venting can cause water condensation, which may in turn rot walls and roofs. Some varieties can produce an unpleasant odor when they're installed, and others will settle or shrink and lose some insulating value. And cellulose is not the only type of insulation that will burn. But cellulose, which is made from reprocessed paper, presents the greatest potential safety hazard, in our view. Cellulose is often used in attics, where exposure to lighting fixtures or electrical wiring can ignite it.

In addition, the rapid expansion of the cellulose insulation market in 1976 and 1977 only aggravated the safety problems. Fiberglass, the most frequently used type of insulation, was in short supply during those years. As a result, many homeowners turned to cellulose because it offers somewhat better insulating performance than figerglass for roughly the same price. The increase in cellulose production brought on a major problem in quality control, both in manufacturing and installing.

Cellulose must be treated with fire-retardant chemicals. But the chemical generally used, boric acid, was in short supply in 1977. (Sulfates, the second-line retardants, can cause corrosion problems.) Even if boric acid is used, it is essential that it be added to the cellulose properly; otherwise, the chemical can separate from the cellulose, leaving the material highly flammable.

Problems with cellulose have arisen even in carefully controlled insulation programs, such as the one run by the Tennessee Valley Authority (see page 33). The TVA did investigate suppliers and contractors before offering cellulose to its customers; even so, some of the material in four homes proved to be improperly treated and had to be replaced, according to a TV representative.

A number of standards have been prepared over the years to govern the flammability of cellulose. Those standards were not mandatory, however, and investigations have shown that the standards were not always followed. Homeowners, of course, had no way of differentiating between brands that met the standards and brands that merely claimed to meet them.

At last—a safety standard

Of all the fires involving cellulose, the ones in Denver were the most significant, since they led—slowly—to Federal action designed to make the material safer. Shortly after the fires occurred, the Denver District Attorney's office began investigating the safety of all types of insulation. In October 1976, the office petitioned the U.S. Consumer Product Safety Commission to issue mandatory standards for home insulation, but it took the CPSC more than a year to act on even a part of the petition.

Under pressure from Congress—where some legislators had severely criticized the CPSC for taking so long to deal with the cellulose insulation problem—the CPSC announced in November 1977 that its staff would "immediately begin drafting a Federal Register notice to announce the need for a mandatory rule for cellulose insulation." The notice appeared in March 1978—only to be followed less than two months later by a second notice, announcing that the agency was mothballing the rule-making machinery because Congress had, in effect, acted more quickly.

The Emergency Interim Consumer Product Safety Standard Act of 1978, which was passed in late June, was enacted in order to have some sort of standard in effect for the winter of 1978-79. The Act directed the CPSC to adopt parts of an existing Federal product specification as the basis for a mandatory safety rule. The CPSC can still prepare a permanent rule if the interim standard proves to be ineffective, according to the Act.

The Act includes the following requirements.

1. All of the cellulose insulation manufactured after September 8, 1978, must pass tests for flame resistance and corrosiveness as spelled out in Federal specification HH-I-515C. The specification allows for two classes of insulation: one with a "flame spread" of 0 to 25, a second with a flame spread of 25 to 50. (The lower the flame spread number, the slower the material will burn in a laboratory test.) The new safety standard is more rigid, however, allowing only flame spread ratings of 0 to 25.

2. Each bag of cellulose must carry the following statement: "ATTENTION: This material meets the applicable minimum Federal flammability standard. This standard is based upon laboratory tests only, which do not represent actual conditions which may occur in the home." As of August 1978, the CPSC had begun preparing requirements for a second label to spell out precautions to take when the insulation is installed.

3. The CPSC must keep pace with revisions to the Federal product specification, incorporating any changes it deems necessary into the safety standard. (In an awkward bit of timing, a new specification—with new flammability and corrosion tests—was published before the manda-

tory standard took effect. As this book went to press, the CPSC was considering whether to include the new tests in the standard.)

4. The CPSC must report to Congress every six months on the way it is enforcing the standard. Moreover, Congress required the CPSC to test insulation from 75 different manufacturers during the first year the standard is in force. According to a CPSC representative, the agency was planning to inspect every cellulose insulation plant and to test samples from at least 150 manufacturers. The testing would cover about one-third of the 450 to 500 manufacturers in business when the standard took effect.

Recommendations

The new standard can help alleviate some major problems, assuming that the CPSC can enforce the standard vigorously. But the standard, as it stood in August 1978, had one drawback, in our view: Manufacturers were not required to have independent laboratories conduct tests to certify that their products complied with the standard. The CPSC representative explained to CU that the agency might require such testing if the rate of compliance with the standard proved to be low.

Before the mandatory standard took effect, CU had recommended cellulose as the last choice for insulation, primarily because of the risk of fire. The new standard makes us somewhat less pessimistic. As the CPSC representative told CU: "We don't want people to be lulled into a false sense of security and think that they can just buy the stuff and dump it into their attics, assuming it's flameproof or fireproof. It's not. The standard provides some reasonable confidence that the product meets some minimum levels of safety. Proper installation is crucial."

If you choose to buy cellulose insulation, you should first take the time to find a reputable, experienced installer. You may be able to get help from your local utility company if it has a home-insulation program. Many utilities will supply names of contractors they consider reliable; others go further and inspect homes once the insulation has been installed.

Be sure the insulation you buy carries the required label statements. And—above all else—be sure the material is installed properly. It should be kept at least three inches away from recessed lighting fixtures, fan housings, and other heat sources (that can be done by building a simple shield around such heat sources). And be sure the insulation does not block attic vents.

If you already have cellulose insulation in the attic, it's a good idea to make sure it's fire-resistant. If the contractor who installed it will cooperate by sending samples to a testing laboratory, fine. Failing that, your local building inspector or fire department may be able to do the testing for you. If it doesn't pass muster, replace the cellulose with a safer material. Cellulose insulation in walls is less of a hazard, in our view, since the walls themselves offer a fair amount of fire protection.

3
Getting the most from the heating system

When Abraham Lincoln was a child, he studied by firelight, writing his lessons on a piece of wood. Or so the story goes. The fire gave off light, to be sure, but young Abe may have had another reason for huddling close to the hearth. It was warm there.

Back then, people stayed warm by tossing another log onto the fire, by bundling up, or, sometimes, both. Electric heating, furnaces, or boilers have since replaced the fireplace. And it's the thermostat that keeps the "fire" going by signaling the system to cycle on and off during the heating season to maintain the indoor temperature you want.

For Lincoln, firewood cost only the sweat needed to chop trees into logs. Fueling a modern heating system involves a much greater expense. How much depends, in part, on whether you get the most from your heating system.

We've seen how you can reduce your heating bills by installing caulking, weather stripping, storm windows, or insulation to enhance the house's ability to retain heat. The slower the heat escapes, the less heat the furnace needs to provide to maintain the temperature you want.

There are three ways you can save on fuel even if you have a "tight," adequately insulated house.

1. Lower the thermostat setting. By deliberately lowering the temperature setting slightly, you reduce the amount of heat required. Lowering the thermostat also helps reduce the loss of heat. As we noted in Chapter 1, the greater the difference between indoor and outdoor temperatures, the faster heat will escape, via conduction. Lowering the thermostat setting reduces the temperature difference, thus slowing the heat loss. (If you have electric heat, lowering the thermostat setting is really the only option open to you. Still, it's a step that can yield a worthwhile saving of energy and money.)

2. Get as much usable heat as possible from the fuel. Even the most efficient furnaces lose 15-25 percent of the energy contained in the fuel they burn—when they're operating. Those so-called "on-time" losses are, naturally, greater for less-efficient furnaces. Having the heating system cleaned and serviced can bring the furnace's heat output up to optimum levels. In addition, there are devices that can be added to the furnace to recover some of the heat that would otherwise be lost.

3. Reduce the loss of heat when the furnace is off. Heat will escape from the furnace even after the furnace shuts down. The "off-time" loss will continue, in fact, so long as the temperature inside the furnace is higher than the outside temperature at the top of the chimney. In the course of a heating season, off-time losses can about equal on-time losses. There are ways (discussed later in this chapter) to reduce off-time losses—but each approach has its drawbacks.

The reports that follow begin with the heating system's central control—the thermostat. We outline the range of saving you can expect by changing the temperature setting: Included in the report are descriptions of fourteen thermostats that can raise and lower the temperature without resetting, plus two thermostat "foolers." The second report explains some of the steps you can take to improve the performance of the heating system—ways to cut both on-time and off-time losses. The last two reports in the chapter discuss add-on hardware—flue heat recovery devices, which can reduce on-time losses somewhat, and flue dampers, which can cut off-time losses sharply.

Energy-saving thermostats

The simplest way to lower your heating bills is to turn down the thermostat. Begin by lowering your normal daytime thermostat setting to the coolest comfortable temperature. And if you set back the temperature further at night or when the house is empty, you can increase the saving even more.

No one can say precisely how much you will save by setting back your thermostat. But, in general, the greater the setback and the longer the setback period, the greater your saving will be. Both the kind of heating system you have and the weather conditions in your area will affect the actual amount of money you save.

A computer simulation prepared at the Oak Ridge National Laboratory shows the approximate saving that can be expected in a house that switched from a constant temperature of 68°F to two kinds of nighttime setbacks: from 68° during the day to 60° between 10 p.m. and 6 a.m., and from 68° to 55° in the same time period.

If, for example, there are about 4000 heating degree-days in your area, and you use a 68°-to-60° setback, you could save roughly $17 on every $100 you now spend for heating your home. And if you use a 68°-to-55° setback, you might expect to save $22 per $100 of your heating costs.

SAVING PER $100 OF PRESENT FUEL BILL (NIGHTTIME SETBACK)		
Degree-days	68° to 60°F	68° to 55°F
2000	$23	$30
3000	20	25
4000	17	22
5000	14	20
6000	12	18
7000	10	16
8000	9	14

As the table above shows, the greater the setback on your thermostat, the greater the saving. In addition, the warmer your area is, the higher the *percentage* of saving, though probably not the *total* saving. Don't be misled by the "saving per $100" figure. Homeowners who face cold winters run up very high fuel bills, and thus their overall dollar saving will probably be higher than those of people living in warmer climates.

How to achieve that saving

By lowering a conventional thermostat manually, you can save money without any additional expense. Admittedly, this can be a nuisance for some people. With a typical single-temperature thermostat, you may find that turning it down at night is a chore easily forgotten. And you may not like getting out of a warm bed in a cold house to turn the thermostat back up in the morning and then having to wait for the house to get warm.

If you forget to set back your thermostat at night, it means you're passing up a chance to save energy and money. You can do away with the nuisance and achieve a regular, consistent saving on fuel by installing a thermostat that controls to two temperatures so that the heat is automatically turned down at night and up again before you get up the next morning. Whether it is worthwhile for you to purchase such a thermostat depends on several factors: how long it takes for your home to get warm, where you live, whether you remember to lower the thermostat at night, and personal preference.

Multi-temperature, or setback, thermostats have been around for a long time, but their role in helping to save energy was not pointed up until fuel prices skyrocketed. These days, the market for these devices is flourishing. Consumers Union has looked at setback thermostats twice. Initially, we set out to find as many different brands and types as possible, a search that yielded eleven models which we checked in our laboratory. Not long after we finished those tests, several new automatic thermostats were introduced that promised to be easy to install and use. We bought samples of four brands and gave them to CU staffers to use in their homes—where some serious quality-contol problems quickly became evident.

We also tested two devices that perform the same function as a setback thermostat but for about half the cost. These devices will work with a conventional single-temperature thermostat and on existing household wiring.

This report explains how setback thermostats work and outlines some of the factors to consider if you decide to buy one of them. The table on page 45 gives key specifications for all the thermostats we tested, and the Listings on page 45 contain more information to help you choose among the types available.

How do setback thermostats work?

Most of the thermostats we checked can be preset to control at two temperatures—normal and setback. Adjustments made when you install the unit determine the amount of setback and its duration, though you can change these settings at any time.

Most of the thermostats have adjustable levers that set the two temperatures. The *Ammark Patriot* has a choice of two setbacks preset at the factory; the normal temperature can be adjusted, but the setback will always be either 5 or 10 degrees below the normal temperature, depending on the model chosen. The two *PSG Accustat* models use preset temperature sensors, which must be purchased separately. The *Accustat H3* controls at any of three specific temperatures selected, and the *Accustat LH2AS* controls at two. The temperature settings can be changed by installing new sensors. The manufacturer offers stock sensors that control seventeen different temperatures; sensors to control other temperatures can be ordered specially from the manufacturer.

As the table on page 45 shows, most of the thermostats are available in versions which can also control central air conditioning as well as heating.

The thermostats we checked control the duration of the setback period in one of four ways.

Clock. Nine units have a built-in 24-hour clock that regulates the duration of each setback period. Clock-timer thermostats are generally the most convenient to use because they work by themselves; once they're programmed, you don't have to do anything to get the setback desired. They're most useful for people who follow a regular schedule. Some models, noted in the Listings, also have a switch that you could use to override the clock. If the unit were set to reduce the temperature at 10 p.m., say, but you wanted to catch the late show on television, you could flip the override switch to leave the furnace on. Some of those with override switches return to clock operation at the end of the setback period; the *Ammark* clock unit has to be switched back manually to clock control. (The thermostats our staffers tested in their homes were clock-type units.)

Interval timer. The *Honeywell Semiautomatic Chronotherm* has a timer —much like a mechanical kitchen timer—as part of the thermostat. This allows you to vary the duration of the setback, within limits; the timer runs for a minimum of 2 hours and a maximum of 11½ hours. Setback begins when you wind up the timer; the thermostat automatically switches back to the higher temperature setting when the time has elapsed. While you have to set it every night, you can get up to a warm house. The *Semiautomatic* is well suited for people whose schedules vary, such as those who go to bed late one night and early the next. Light sleepers who might be bothered by the ticking of a mechanical timer should not choose this unit if it is to be in or near their bedroom.

Switch. Three models are even less automatic than the interval timer. You must flip a switch to change from one temperature to another. While you don't have to fiddle with temperature settings themselves, you must still remember to flip the switch each night (or other time you wish to change the temperature), and you still have to get up in a cold house in the morning. For that reason a switch-type thermostat is best suited to heating systems that have a quick warm-up time, such as a warm-air system.

One switch-type unit, the *Ammark Deluxe Series*, is intended for use with a "zoned" heating system, where the temperatures in different parts of the house can be regulated independently. It can be coupled with separate units to control various heating zones from a central location.

Photocell. The *Dynelco Therm-O-Guard* was the only unit checked that is controlled by a photocell. When light strikes the cell, the thermostat switches from one preset temperature to the other; when there is no light, the unit switches back. To be used during the heating season, the unit should be set so that it switches to the setback temperature when the lights are turned out at night. The *Dynelco* presents some drawbacks. It must be located in a place where light will strike it at the proper time, which means that you might have to move your thermostat from its current position. And if you get up before dawn in winter, you won't get up in a warm house—unless you rig up a timer light near the *Dynelco*.

What else is there to it?

There's more to an automatic thermostat than its switching mechanism. Other factors you should consider include the following.

Voltage. The thermostats we checked operate on a 24-volt circuit, but some conventional thermostats—most often those that control electric heating systems—run on 120 volts. The two aren't interchangeable. You'll have to use a voltmeter or call an electrician to find out whether your present thermostat is a high-voltage model. If it is, you may have to have extensive rewiring done to use one of these models or, more simply, you can rig up one of the "foolers" described below.

Conventional thermostats usually have two electrical connections, but some of the thermostats we checked required three or more. The specifications table (page 45) points out the number of connections needed to hook up each model. If your present thermostat has just two connections and you choose a model with three, you'll have to cope with snaking extra wires through your walls. The thermostats put through the home-use test were two-wire models, which are the easiest to install; none of our staffers had any trouble wiring the samples into place.

The *Knape & Vogt Thermotimer* is an add-on clock timer for conventional *Honeywell* round thermostats. It uses the existing thermostat and needs no additional wiring to run the clock (which is battery-powered).

A more elaborate add-on is the *Penn-Baso Timetrol*, which is wired into the circuit between the existing thermostat and the furnace. That's easy enough, but there's a catch: The *Penn-Baso* must be located in a "control area" where the temperature varies in direct relation to temperatures in the living area (the actual temperature readings in the two areas don't have to match). Finding a suitable control area for the *Penn-Baso* could be a nuisance, we think, but the unit was easy to install.

Anticipators. Most of the thermostats we tested have anticipators, which are controls that ensure that the thermostat signals the furnace to shut down as the house approaches the proper temperature. As noted in the table on page 45, some anticipators are adjustable; that is, they can be set to draw varying amounts of electricity and thus be compatible with a number of different furnace control circuits. The adjustable type can be more difficult to install, but we prefer them to fixed anticipators, whose electrical current requirements can't be adjusted. If a fixed anticipator doesn't prove to be compatible with the rest of the furnace control circuitry, a house could, in some cases, get too hot before the thermostat stopped calling for heat. In other cases, the thermostat could "short-cycle" and signal the furnace to shut down before the house had warmed up sufficiently.

Adjusting the setback periods. It can be a minor inconvenience to adjust any clock thermostat for variations in schedule (staying up late or getting up late). The *Honeywell CT200A* and the *Ammark Automatic Clock*, though, proved to be the most flexible. Both have an override switch, which allows you to change from one temperature setting to another without resetting the clock. The *Honeywell*'s override is "self-canceling," meaning that the thermostat automatically reverts to clock operation. So, by using the *Honeywell*'s override switch to lower the temperature and programming an automatic re-

42 **The heating system**

turn to the normal temperature, it's possible to change setback schedules with no further adjustments. On the *Ammark*, however, the override switch "locks" the unit into the temperature setting selected. The *Penn-Baso* also has a self-canceling override switch, but this thermostat's location outside the living area makes the switch inconvenient to use.

Those *Penn-Baso, Honeywell,* and *Ammark* models were the only ones we examined that can be set for more than one setback period per day; settings on those three are controlled with removable pins (one type of pin for normal temperature, another type for setback) that fit into the rim of a timer dial and trip an on-off switch as the dial rotates. The *PSG Accustat LH2AS* can also be easily adapted to some changes in schedule: It allows you to skip the setback period entirely up to four days during the week. To change the schedules of most other thermostats, you must adjust the temperature or clock settings.

Minimum and maximum setback periods. The models we checked have minimum setback periods ranging from 30 minutes up to 4½ hours; maximum setback periods range from 11½ to 23½ hours. If you want your house warm for most of the day and cool for only a few hours, you'll want a thermostat with a fairly short *minimum* setback. On the other hand, if you want to heat the house only in the evening, you'll want a unit with a fairly long *maximum* setback period.

Setback indicator. The Listings point out ways you can tell if a thermostat is at the setback setting or not. Some models have a thermometer that will give you a rough idea of what the house temperature is; others have visible switches or lights that indicate whether the normal or setback temperature setting is being used.

Number of temperature settings. Most of the models we tested will control only at two preset temperatures. The *PSG Accustat H3* will control at three.

Temperature range. A few of the thermostats can control at temperatures as low as 32°, others as high as 90°, but most models had a narrower operating range. Check the table to find the thermostat with the range of temperature settings that fit your needs.

Temperature and clock dials. Some of the staffers who tested the thermostats at home commented on the peculiar temperature and clock dials designed into these units. The *Honeywell CT200A*'s temperature dial, for instance, is marked in odd-numbered degrees—69°, 71°, and so on—while the others have temperature scales divided into even degrees. Clocks on the *Honeywell* and the *Ammark Clock* use conventional twelve-hour dials, but the *White-Rodgers,* the *Regutemp,* and the *Robertshaw* have twenty-four-hour dials. The unconventional dials took some getting used to, according to our panelists.

Problems at home

Our staffers had little trouble using the two-wire clock thermostats we gave them for home-use testing. But they had a lot of trouble getting the units to function in the first place. Several of the samples we purchased would not operate as received or soon failed. Samples of the *Honeywell CT200A* and the *White-Rodgers* arrived with defective parts, one *Regutemp* was delivered improperly wired, and a *Robertshaw* failed after a short period of use. There seemed to be no pattern to the defects. We were surprised at the number of faulty samples we encountered, and we consider the manufacturers' apparent lack of quality control to be deplorable.

Can you install one yourself?

Maybe. Some models, particularly the two-wire clock thermostats, are sold as do-it-yourself items, but they're really intended for people who understand basic electric wiring and are fairly handy around the house. If you're not entirely sure that you can handle the job, better hire a professional. Even then, there are some points you should know to be sure the thermostat is installed in the most suitable location. Keep the following in mind.

First, be sure the thermostat is located away from hot or cold spots—radiators, fireplaces, drafts, water pipes in the wall, and the like—and not on an outside wall. Be sure, too, that the unit is in an area that has good air circulation (but not a drafty area).

Second, keep in mind that a thermostat operates in response to the temperature of its immediate surroundings. So try to mount the thermostat in an area where the temperature is representative of the entire room or, if possible, of the entire house.

Third, set the two temperatures, normal and setback, according to comfort and *not* to the temperature markings on the thermostat dial. Those numbers can be inaccurate, so you should use them only for reference. Setting by comfort does take some time. Start by picking a point on the thermostat dial (68°, for the sake of argument), then wait at least two hours. If the room isn't comfortable, move the dial up or down a notch or two. Once you've found the right setting, stick to it; that will be the normal temperature. To decide on a setback temperature, start with a setting about 10 degrees lower than the normal temperature. Set the timing mechanism to switch to setback before you retire and return to normal before you get up. If the house cools down too much, try an 8-degree setback. And if the house is cold when you wake up, adjust the setback period so that it comes to an end earlier.

Fooling the thermostat

The *Fuel Sentry* (Fuel Sentry Corp., Mount Vernon, N.Y.) and the *Heat Watcher* (M. H. Rhodes, Inc., Avon, Conn.), both about $25 as of January 1977, are two "foolers" that can be used in place of a setback thermostat. They contain two-watt heaters that are to be fastened to the wall just below the thermostat. By heat-

Thermostats 43

ing the air around the thermostat, they trick it into acting as if the whole area is warmer than it really is.

The *Fuel Sentry* consists of two units connected by twelve feet of lamp cord—the heater unit to be positioned directly under the thermostat and a timer to be plugged directly into any nearby wall outlet. The timer that is supplied with the unit can be programmed for one setback period per day. In order to change the setback period or turn the heater on and off by hand, you need access to the timer in its outlet.

The *Heat Watcher* is a one-piece unit that contains an interval timer, much like a kitchen timer, with a ten-foot electrical cord. The unit has to be set manually to each setback period. Even though it's not completely automatic, the *Heat Watcher* can be useful for many who do not keep regular hours and who would therefore have to change the settings from day to day anyway. Access to the control is as easy as access to the thermostat itself. A possible drawback of the *Heat Watcher* is the annoyingly loud ticking.

With either device, establishing the desired degree of setback is somewhat more difficult than it would be with a setback thermostat. Heat emanating from the *Fuel Sentry* is controlled by a vane that can be opened and closed; from the *Heat Watcher*, by a sliding metal cover. Only by trial-and-error testing of various openings, checked by comfort (or by a room thermometer, not the one on the thermostat), can you arrive at a suitable setting.

Recommendations

If you follow a reasonably regular schedule, a clock thermostat will make night setback completely automatic. A two-wire clock thermostat combines convenience of use with ease of installation. Of the four thermostats that were tested by CU staffers in their homes, the *Honeywell CT200A* proved to be the clear favorite.

However, clock thermostats are generally more expensive than the other types, and you may not need or want such convenience. Both the interval-timer thermostat and the switch thermostats must be set back manually each evening; the switch type must also be reset in the morning. The photocell unit is a special case that may be useful in certain circumstances.

If you need only one setback period each day, you can choose from any of the models we checked. If you would like more, consider the *Honeywell CT200A* or the three-wire *Ammark Clock*, which provide from one to three setback periods per day. (As the Listings note, other clock-type thermostats are available in versions that control more than one setback period; CU has not tested them.) The switch type thermostats, which are controlled manually, can also be used for multiple setback periods.

Two other considerations may be important—the maximum and minimum setback periods you need and the compatibility of the unit with your present wiring. Both these factors may be checked in the table of specifications on the facing page.

Heating-equipment dealers, heating contractors, electrical supply stores, home centers, and hardware stores are the most likely sources of thermostats. If you can't find the one you want, the Listings include company addresses.

Note, however, that many of the samples purchased for our home-use test were defective when we received them or failed within a few hours. Be sure the retailer will exchange a defective sample before you buy any thermostat. And if the thermostat will not work with the furnace controller you have (an unlikely occurrence), be sure the supplier will exchange the thermostat for a different model. Save the sales receipt, because you might need it. Save the old thermostat; you might need that, too: If the new unit fails at night or on a weekend, you'll need something to keep the furnace going.

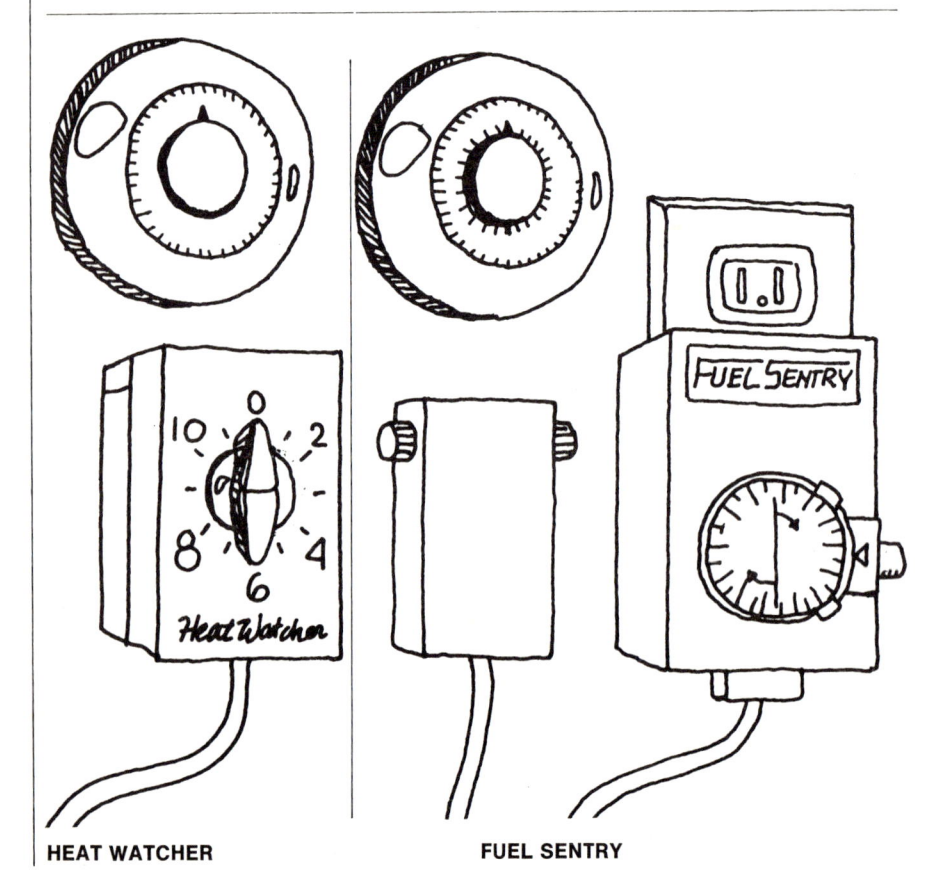

HEAT WATCHER   **FUEL SENTRY**

44   **The heating system**

SPECIFICATIONS FOR ENERGY-SAVING THERMOSTATS

Brand and model	Automatic setback periods per day	AUTOMATIC SETBACK PERIOD Minimum	AUTOMATIC SETBACK PERIOD Maximum	Temperature range	Electrical connections needed	Anticipator type
CLOCK TYPE						
AMMARK AUTOMATIC CLOCK 15015-0922	1 to 3	1 hr.	23 hr.	32°-86°F	3	Fixed
*HONEYWELL CHRONOTHERM T882A	1	4½ hr.	18½ hr.	54-86	4	Adjustable
*HONEYWELL CT200A-1	1 to 3	1 hr.	23 hr.	41-89	2	Adjustable
KNAPE & VOGT THERMOTIMER 202	1	1½ hr.	22½ hr.	[A]	[B]	[C]
PENN-BASO TIMETROL NIGHT SETBACK CONTROL A51AA-1	1 or 2	½ hr.	23½ hr.	40-90	[D]	None
*PSG ACCUSTAT LH2AS	1	1½ hr.	22½ hr.	[E]	3	None
*REGUTEMP I-99028	1	4 hr.	20 hr.	50-90	2	[F]
*ROBERTSHAW AUTOMATIC SETBACK THERMOSTAT T30-1141-411	1	1¼ hr.	22¾ hr.	50-90	2	Adjustable
*WHITE-RODGERS AUTOMATIC COMFORT-SET 1F70-1	1	4 hr.	20 hr.	55-90	2	[F]
INTERVAL-TIMER TYPE						
*HONEYWELL SEMIAUTOMATIC CHRONOTHERM T8084A	None [G]	2 hr.	11½ hr.	54-86	2	Adjustable
SWITCH TYPE [H]						
AMMARK DELUXE SERIES 15015-4187	None	None	None	32-86	3	Adjustable
AMMARK PATRIOT 15015-2531	None	None	None	32-86	3	Fixed
*PSG ACCUSTAT H3	None	None	None	[E]	2	None
PHOTOCELL TYPE						
*DYNELCO THERM-O-GUARD SST2	[I]	[J]	[J]	47-83	2	None

* Air-conditioning models available.

[A] Temperature range governed by Honeywell thermostat used with this unit.
[B] No additional wiring required beyond that used by present thermostat.
[C] Fits over existing thermostat; has no anticipator of its own.
[D] Requires up to 4 additional wires where unit is installed; no additional wiring is required at present thermostat, which remains in place (see report).
[E] Temperature settings controlled by sensors (see Listings).
[F] Non-adjustable by homeowner, but automatically compensates for varying amperage requirements in different control circuits.
[G] Has spring-type timer that must be wound manually to start a setback period.
[H] Switch-type setback thermostats are best used with heating systems with very fast warm-up time such as warm-air systems.
[I] Light-controlled photocell allows more than one setback period if artificial light is used.
[J] Setback period depends on light (see Listings).

Listings: Energy-saving thermostats

Listed by types; within types, listed in alphabetical order. Listings should be used in conjunction with the table of specifications above. Dimensions are given in order of height, length, and depth to next lower ⅛-in. All listed models operate on 24-volts a-c. Unless otherwise indicated, models were tested in CU's laboratory in 1977. Except as noted, prices are manufacturer's suggested retail, rounded to nearest dollar, as of October 1977. Prices do not include installation.

Except as noted, all: ◉ Control at 2 preset temperatures ◉ Control heating system only. ◉ Were judged suitable for installation in living area of house. ◉ Have external thermometers. ◉ Are also available in versions to control central air conditioning as well as heating (see table above).

CLOCK TYPE

Setback period started and stopped automatically by electric clock (included).

AMMARK AUTOMATIC CLOCK 15015-0922 (Ammark Corp., 12-22 River Road, Fair Lawn, N.J. 07410), $52. 2¾x5⅝x1⅝ in. Heater in unit controls setback to as much as 15° below normal temperature. Has switch that can be used to override clock control. During clock operation, warm thermostat cover is only indication unit is set for setback temperature. Has no external thermometer.

Thermostats 45

HONEYWELL CHRONOTHERM T882A (Honeywell Inc., Honeywell Plaza, Minneapolis, Minn. 55408), approx. $58. 3x6x2⅛ in. Setback range adjustable from 54°, to 3° below normal temperature. Optional power supply (model *R7305A*, approx. $29) can be used to power thermostat's clock; only 2 electrical connections required if power supply is used. No indication on thermostat whether unit is set for normal or setback temperature.

HONEYWELL CT200A (Honeywell Inc.), approx. $60, as of Sept. 1978. 3¾x6¾x2¼ in. Tested in 1978. Setback range adjustable from 41° to 3° below normal temperature. Has switch that can be used to override clock control; override self-cancels on next cycle. Has indicator to tell whether unit is set for normal or setback temperature. Two out of 5 samples received with inoperable clocks. Available through heating/air-conditioning dealers as Model *T8082A*.

KNAPE & VOGT THERMOTIMER 202 (Knape & Vogt, 2700 Oak Industrial Dr., N.E., Grand Rapids, Mich. 49505), $40. 4⅛x7⅝x 1¾ in. Battery-powered timer intended to be installed around conventional *Honeywell T85, T86,* or *T87* round thermostats. Uses single "C" cell. Setback adjustable between 14° and 2° below normal temperature. Setback and range depend on thermostat used. Clock control can be overridden; override self-cancels on next cycle if desired. Position of dial on thermostat indicates whether unit is set for normal or setback temperature. Optional dial ($5) can provide 2 setback periods per day, with 19½-hour maximum setback period.

PENN-BASO TIMETROL NIGHT SETBACK CONTROL A51AA-1 (Penn Div., Johnson Corp., 2221 Camden Ct., Oakbrook, Ill. 60521), $57. 6x5¾x2⅞ in. Has switch that can be used to override clock control; override self-cancels on next cycle if desired. Intended to be installed between present thermostat and heating plant, in "control area" (see report). Position of timer indicates whether unit is set for normal or setback temperature. Extra trippers available ($2 each) to provide up to 12 setback periods per day. Has no external thermometer. Judged not suitable for installation in living area of house.

PSG ACCUSTAT LH2AS (PSG Industries Inc., 1225 Tunnel Rd., Perkasie, Pa. 18944), $36; timer *TH-2*, $91; sensors, $7 each. Thermostat, 4⅝x4⅝x2¾ in.; timer,7⅞x4⅛x3 in. Temperatures controlled by preset sensors sold separately (see report). Standard sensors ($7 each) available for 40, 50, 60, 62, 64, 65, 66, 68, 70, 72, 74, 75, 76, 78, 80, 82, and 84 degrees. Sensors for other temperatures also available ($11.50 each). Separate timer intended to be mounted away from thermostat. Has switch on timer that can be used to override clock control; override self-cancels on next cycle. Timer can be set to skip setback periods up to 4 times per week. Switch position on remote timer only indication whether unit is set for normal or setback temperature. Has no external thermometer.

REGUTEMP I-99028 (Precision Products Co., Davidson, S.C. 28036), $52, as of Sept. 1978. 3¼x6x2½ in. Tested in 1978. Setback range adjustable from 50° up to whatever normal temperature is used. Position of timer indicates whether unit is set for normal or setback temperature. Also available with 2 automatic setback periods per day as model *Deluxe 1-90048*. One out of 3 samples did not function when received.

ROBERTSHAW AUTOMATIC SETBACK THERMOSTAT T-30-1141-411 (Robertshaw Controls Co., 100 W. Victoria St., Corona, Calif. 91720). $50, as of Sept. 1978. 3½x5⅜x2 in. Tested in 1978. Setback range adjustable from 0° to 10° below normal temperature. Position of timer indicates whether unit is set for normal or setback temperature. Available with 2 automatic setback periods per day as model *T30-1041-412*. Anticipator on 1 out of 3 samples failed during first week of use. Available through heating/air-conditioning dealers as model *TH-300-411A* (one setback period) and as model *TH-300-412A* (two setback periods).

WHITE-RODGERS AUTOMATIC COMFORT SET 1F70-1 (White-Rodgers Div., Emerson Electric Co., 9797 Reavis Rd., St. Louis, Mo. 63133), approx. $75, as of Sept. 1978. 3¼x6x2½ in. Tested in 1978. Setback range is adjustable from 55° up to whatever normal temperature is used. Position of timer indicates whether unit is set for normal or setback temperature. Also available with 2 automatic setback periods per day as model *1F70-201*. One out of 5 samples received with defective anticipator. Clock on second sample was defective as received.

INTERVAL-TIMER TYPE

Setback period started manually by setting mechanical timer for period desired; setback period stopped automatically at end of timer's cycle.

HONEYWELL SEMIAUTOMATIC CHRONOTHERM T8084A (Honeywell Inc.), approx. $44. 3x6x2⅜ in. Setback range adjustable from 54° to 3° below normal temperature.

SWITCH TYPE

Setback period started and stopped by manually operated switch. Switch position indicates whether unit is set for normal or setback temperature.

AMMARK DELUXE SERIES 15015-4187 (Ammark Corp.), $26. 2¾x4⅝x1¾ in. Heater in unit controls setback to as much as 15° below normal temperature. Thermostat cover is also warm to touch during setback. Has no external thermometer. Available with switch for remote unit as model *15015-4188* and with switches for 2 remote units as model *15015-4189*. Remote units designated *Ammark Slave 15015-4190* (see report).

AMMARK PATRIOT 15015-2531 (Ammark Corp.), $13. 2¾x-2¾x1⅜ in. 10° setback preset by manufacturer. Thermostat cover is also warm to touch during setback. Has no external thermometer. Also available with preset 5° setback as model *15015-2532*.

PSG ACCUSTAT H3 (PSG Industries Inc.), $22; sensors, $7 each. 4x4½x1½ in. This model accommodates 3 sensors; model *H2,* 2 sensors. See *PSG Accustat LH2AS*, above, for sensors available.

PHOTOCELL TYPE

Setback period started and stopped automatically when surrounding light level changes. Light-sensitivity of photocell is adjustable.

DYNELCO THERM-O-GUARD SST2 (Dynamic Electronic Controls Inc., 47 Mill Plain Rd., Danbury, Conn. 06810), $80. 3⅜x5x1½ in. Unit controlled by photocell (see report). For use in heating season, unit should be set to switch to higher temperature when light strikes it, lower temperature in the dark. Both high and low temperatures can be set independently from 47° to 83°. Indicator lights tell whether unit is set for normal or setback temperature.

Getting more from your fuel

In homes with electric heat the system's efficiency is so high that there's little or nothing that you can do to improve it. Furnaces fueled with oil or natural gas are a different story. On those systems, you can take some steps to improve the furnace's performance when it's running and other steps to reduce the loss of heat when the furnace shuts off.

Combustion efficiency (C.E.) is the term commonly used to describe how good a job a furnace does when it's running. In general terms, the combustion efficiency equals the percentage of the total energy contained in the fuel which becomes usable heat. Oil-fired or gas-fired furnaces have combustion efficiencies that range, at best, from 75 to 85 percent. That is, for every 100,000 Btu of fuel entering the system when the furnace is on, only 75,000 to 85,000 Btu stay within the house as usable heat. For the most part, the heat that's lost goes up the chimney, carrying with it the products of combustion.

Seasonal efficiency, on the other hand, measures the percentage of the total energy in the fuel which is available to heat the house over an entire heating season. Some studies, conducted by the Federal Government and private utility companies, have indicated that furnaces typically have seasonal efficiencies on the order of 50 to 60 percent. That is, for every 100,000 Btu of fuel the course of a year, only 50,000 to burned by the heating system over 60,000 Btu go ultimately to heat the house. As we noted in the introduction to this chapter, warm air will continue to escape up the flue even when the furnace is off. The annual loss of heat when a furnace is off roughly equals the annual loss of heat when the furnace is running.

There are ways to improve both combustion efficiency and seasonal efficiency. We'll deal with combustion efficiency first.

Getting more while the furnace is running

The first step toward trimming on-time losses is to have the furnace's C.E. checked. Chances are, the C.E. is somewhat below the maximum possible level. If the furnace hasn't been serviced recently, soot and dirt inside may block the flow of heat. The burner's nozzle and/or gas orifices may need to be cleaned and replaced, air inlets and controls adjusted and filters changed.

You could have the gas company or oil service company check the C.E. by measuring the temperature, smoke level, and carbon dioxide (CO_2) content of the gas entering the flue.

Actually, if you're really handy around the house, you can determine your furnace's C.E. on your own—provided that you're willing to spend about $120 for the required instruments. (You could share the cost with neighbors.) A *Tempoint* stack thermometer, to measure the temperature in the flue, cost us about $17, a *True-Spot Smoke Tester* cost us about $34, and a *Fyrite* CO_2 indicator was about $68 (prices as of July 1978). All the equipment was manufactured by Bacharach Instruments, Pittsburgh. To find this equipment locally, look in the Yellow Pages under "Heating Equipment" or "Heating Contractors." Before testing, though, you must drill a ¼-inch hole in the flue pipe (later to be plugged with a sheet-metal screw) to provide access for sampling the flue gases. The absence of such hole and plug is evidence that the furnace hasn't been tested for C.E.

If you have a relatively modern furnace (no more than ten years old), the C.E. should run close to 80 percent. Some older furnaces may not be able to reach more than 75 percent. But if the C.E. is less than 70 percent, a tune-up is imperative. A 5 percent improvement—from 70 to 75 percent, say—will save you $6.70 on every $100 of fuel you buy. As the table below shows, the more room there is for improvement, the more you stand to save.

Keep in mind that testing C.E. and improving C.E. are two very different propositions. If you decide that your furnace's C.E. needs upgrading, call in a qualified service technician to do the work. Tinkering with a furnace is not a job for do-it-yourselfers.

To get a better idea of the C.E. of typical home oil burners, we lent testing equipment to twenty CU staffers, technical and nontechnical. The average C.E. of their furnaces turned out to be 70 percent. On average, then, our staff panel could have saved a little more than $12 on every $100 worth of fuel by increasing their C.E. to 80 percent. The owner of the furnace with the worst C.E. in the panel group could have saved twice that much.

If you have an oil furnace, there are several ways to enhance its C.E. They include the following: *cleaning,*

SAVING PER $100 OF ANNUAL FUEL COST

Original combustion efficiency	55%	60%	65%	70%	75%	80%
50%	$9.10	$16.70	$23.10	$28.60	$33.00	$37.50
55		8.30	15.40	21.50	26.70	31.20
60			7.70	14.30	20.00	25.00
65				7.10	13.30	18.80
70					6.70	12.50
75						6.30

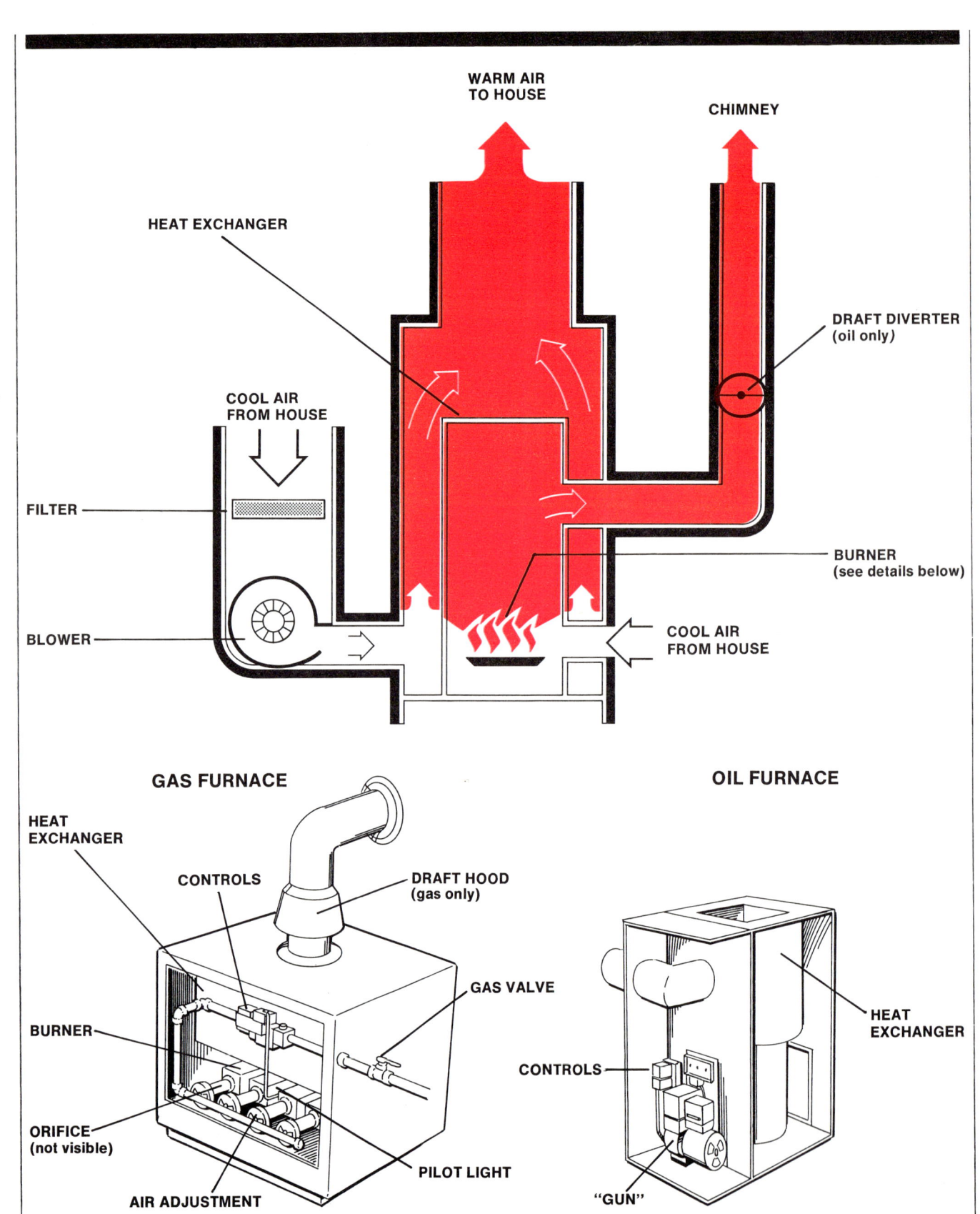

As the large drawing shows, a forced-air furnace draws in cool air from the house, passes the air over a heat exchanger to heat it, then circulates it back to the living areas. (Other heating systems work in the same general way, but circulate hot water or steam rather than air.) The smaller drawings point out the important parts of a gas-fired or an oil-fired furnace. The accompanying report outlines some of the steps that can be taken to improve a heating system's efficiency.

48   The heating system

to remove soot and dirt from the heat exchanger, the flue, and filters; *adjusting the air intake* to be sure the furnace gets the proper amount of air needed to burn oil completely, plus some excess air to ensure complete combustion (too little air will lead to excessive smoke, incomplete combustion, and an inadequate draft up the chimney, whereas too much air will draw excessive amounts of heat up the stack); *installing a nozzle of the proper size* to provide the optimum fuel delivery rate, and adjusting the pump pressure to meet the furnace manufacturer's specifications. Installing a new, more efficient "gun" (a job only an experienced service technician should handle) can also help.

If you have a gas furnace, there are fewer options available for improving its C.E. As things now stand, local building and fuel codes often prohibit modifications to a gas furnace or its flue, primarily for safety reasons. Short of periodic servicing and adjustment and making sure your burner's orifice is clean and properly sized, there isn't much you can do to change a gas furnace's combustion efficiency at this time.

Getting more while the furnace is off

It's an unavoidable fact that some on-time losses are necessary. A certain amount of heated air must escape up the chimney to carry the products of combustion away from the living areas of the house. Off-time losses, on the other hand, are almost always unnecessary.

Can anything be done to reduce off-time losses? The answer is a cautious yes—not because the techniques are exotic but because implementing them in existing home heating systems could be difficult, could violate local codes, and could be hazardous.

One way to eliminate off-time losses completely would be to have the furnace run continuously. But this is hardly practical, since it assumes a constant demand is imposed on the furnace throughout the winter. Other, more realistic approaches have been tested, sometimes with promising results.

One method is *derating*, or reducing the number of Btu per hour the furnace will deliver. This can be accomplished by installing a smaller gas orifice or oil nozzle. Derating causes the furnace to run longer in order to provide the same amount of heat. As the furnace's running time increases, its off-time (and off-time losses) decrease.

But before you call in a service technician to derate your furnace, consider these points. First, derating reduces the furnace's capability to deliver heat to your house. One limit to derating is the amount of heat you actually need on the coldest day of the year. If, on such a day, your furnace is firing virtually all the time, you shouldn't consider derating. Second, furnaces are designed for optimum combustion efficiency with a specific range of nozzles or orifices. If you derate the furnace, be sure the modifications don't significantly lower the furnace's C.E. Third, since derating causes the furnace to run more hours per year, it could

shorten the service life of the furnace.

Another way to reduce off-time losses—for gas furnaces only—is to replace the pilot light with *electronic ignition*. A pilot light wastes energy two ways: It consumes gas and it warms the air inside the furnace when the furnace is off; that warmed air helps create a draft in the flue which, in turn, draws warm air from the house and up the chimney. Many newer furnaces have electronic ignition built in. Some states, noted in Chapter 8, are mandating electronic ignition on new furnaces. Electronic ignition systems are also available for older furnaces. But before you turn off the pilot light, be sure the ignition device you buy meets local building codes. And have the device installed by a qualified heating contractor.

"*Direct venting*" is a way to reduce both on- and off-time losses. Gas and oil furnaces take in large quantities of air—usually warmed air from inside the house—to supply the oxygen required for combustion. And, when the furnace is off, some flow of warm air up the stack continues. If the furnace could draw its combustion air directly from outdoors it would reduce the loss of already heated air. Before you rig up a vent from the furnace to the outdoors, be sure your local building code permits this kind of venting. Here, too, have the work done by a qualified heating contractor. Homemade direct venting systems can lead to a host of problems, ranging from frozen water pipes to an insufficient amount of combustion air and excessive carbon monoxide levels.

Recovering heat at the flue

A properly operating furnace should extract all the heat possible from burning fuel—exchanging it for hot air, hot water, or steam—yet still provide a sufficient draft so that wastes will be sent up the chimney and a fresh supply of air drawn in.

It's generally agreed that, for an oil burner, the minimum permissible stack temperature (at the furnace outlet) is about 300°F; CU believes a similar limit should apply to gas burners. If the stack temperature drops much lower than that, the furnace may not have sufficient draft and may develop condensation problems in the flue. (Water vapor is a significant by-product of burning fossil fuels; if a gallon of oil were burned completely, a gallon of water would be produced.) But in many furnaces, especially older models, stack temperatures may soar as high as 800°. Clearly a lot of heat is getting away unnecessarily—heat that's going right up the flue.

There are devices that can recover some of the excessive exhaust heat and convert it into usable heat. CU tested six of these so-called "chimney robbers" in 1978. They perform, in effect, as secondary heat exchangers: A metal surface, heated by flue gases, transfers its heat to room air. Two of the devices are simply clamped over the flue pipe, drawing heat from the pipe itself. Four others, which all replace a section of flue pipe, use more elaborate heat-exchanger hardware plus a fan to circulate the heated air. As the drawings on page 52 show, details of construction and operation differ considerably among the six devices we tested.

A flue heat recovery device works best on a very inefficient furnace—one with very high stack temperatures; the amount of heat that can be reclaimed will diminish as stack temperatures fall. Most of the devices we tested were heavy, bulky, and could be difficult to clean. Most were also expensive, costing between $90 and $189 (in September 1978). We also looked at one $10.50 gadget, but it reclaimed almost no heat.

These devices won't necessarily lower your gas or oil bills. Unless you can move the reclaimed hot air to an area near the thermostat, the furnace will burn nearly as much fuel as it always does; you'll simply be getting slightly more usable heat from that fuel. In practice, the devices don't recover a large amount of heat (no more than 6 percent of the energy in the fuel burned, in CU's tests). And it's not practical to move that amount of heat more than about 20 feet away from the furnace. If there is an unheated room near the furnace (or a nearby room that's now warmed with a portable electric heater), then a flue heat recovery device can be useful.

But before you buy one of these devices, be sure it can be installed legally. A flue heat recovery device may not conform to the building code in your area.

Limits to heat recovery

We can't say exactly how much heat you'll be able to save with one of these devices, but we can provide some guidelines.

The absolute amount of heat any of these devices can recover depends on the stack temperature and the size of the furnace. A furnace rated at 140,000 Btu per hour will provide more reclaimable heat than a 100,000 Btu-per-hour furnace, if stack temperatures are the same. And on two furnaces of the same capacity, the one with the higher stack temperature will send the greater amount of heat up the flue. It is unlikely that any flue heat recovery device would provide a significant saving if the temperature of the flue gases entering the device were less than about 450°. This consideration more or less limits these devices to oil-fired furnaces or older gas-fired models, which have fairly high flue temperatures.

A U.S. Department of Commerce report suggests that a saving of 4 percent (for a 450° stack) to 8 percent (for an 800° stack) can be achieved with the *Air-O-Space,* which was the only model the Department of Commerce evaluated. Our tests tended to support those results.

The *Chimney Heat Reclaimer* was the most effective in our tests, recovering about 6 percent of the fuel burned in CU's specially equipped test furnace (a 140,000 Btu/hour model which was set to operate at stack temperatures between 575° and 600°). In that kind of situation, the *Chimney Heat Re-*

WHERE A FLUE HEAT RECOVERY DEVICE FITS INTO A HEATING SYSTEM

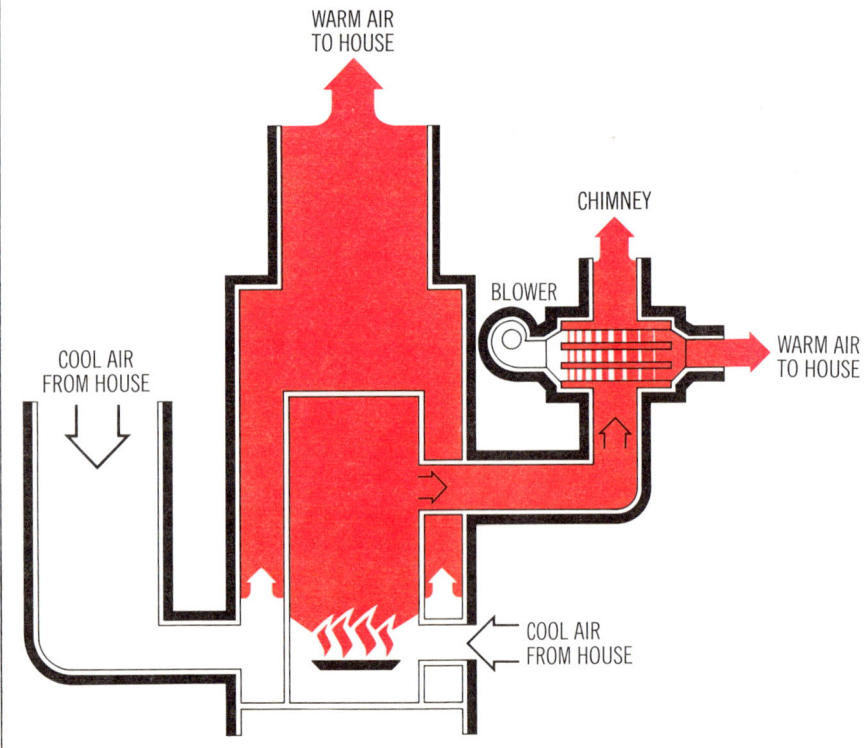

While a furnace delivers much of its heat to the house, some excess heat, in the form of hot air, escapes up the chimney. A flue heat recovery device (the top-rated *Chimney Heat Reclaimer* is shown in this schematic drawing) soaks up some of that heat; a blower on the device returns warm air to the house.

50 The heating system

claimer would recover some 8400 Btu of heat each hour the furnace was on. That's an essentially free supply of heat (excluding the original cost of the device) that matches the output of two 1250-watt electric space heaters (which also involve an original cost plus an operating cost of 9.5 cents an hour, based on a rate of 3.8 cents per kwh).

The *Fuelmiser* and the *Air-O-Space 5K* reclaimed somewhat less heat than the *Chimney Heat Reclaimer*, but they should provide useful amounts of heat in many situations. Least effective of all was the *Edmund 72,149*, which recovered well under 0.5 percent—about the same amount of heat given off by a bare flue pipe. (Specific amounts of heat saved can vary from furnace to furnace, although we judge that the top-rated devices will recover more heat than the others in any case.)

How usable is the heat?

An electric space heater will supply heat until the room reaches a preset temperature; a flue heat recovery device, on the other hand, will stop supplying heat when the furnace shuts down. That may leave the room too cool for your liking. Or—if the room happens to be very small—the recovery device might supply *too much* heat.

A flue heat recovery system can also create problems if you have a tankless coil in your boiler to provide hot water; production of hot water in the summer would then be accompanied by unwanted space heating. To avoid this problem on most of the fan-equipped models we tested, simply switch them off or unplug the fan. (Only the *Air-O-Space* heaters must be removed from the flue to be taken out of service.)

All of the fan-operated models have a stub of pipe to which stovepipe or ducting could be connected to move heated air away from the furnace. Most use a 6-inch-diameter pipe, but the *Fuelmiser* uses a 4-inch pipe and the *Recyclo-Heater* provides a 2⅛-inch-diameter stub. According to the manufacturer, heat from the *Air-O-Space* models can be ducted up to twenty feet away; the other manufacturers aren't as specific in their recommendations. We think you'll achieve the most satisfactory results with as little ducting as possible, since air velocities drop off sharply as the length of the duct increases.

Installation and maintenance

None of the devices was judged difficult to install, but some—especially the *Chimney Heat Reclaimer* and the *Fuelmiser*—may be too bulky to fit on your flue. To install one of these devices, you'll need between 10 and 24 inches of straight pipe between the furnace and the draft diverter (the component that controls the draft up the chimney). You'll also need ample space around the pipe to be able to install, service, and clean the device. (The *Edmund 72,149* requires very little clearance, but we see no reason to install it in the first place.)

The drawings that accompany the Ratings give key dimensions for each device, along with our estimates of the clearances required around the flue.

Before you install a flue heat recovery device, have a service technician adjust the burner and check the flue temperature. Have the temperature checked after installation, too. In some cases, a flue heat recovery device could drop stack temperatures below 300°, which could bring on excessive condensation in the flue.

Instructions supplied with these devices ranged from reasonably complete to hopelessly inadequate. The *Recyclo-Heater*'s instructions, for example, failed to state which flue pipe sizes the unit would fit. (If the flue is smaller than the device, you may need to purchase an adapter; installing any device in a flue that's larger than the device is hazardous and violates many building codes.) The *Chimney Heat Reclaimer* came with no installation instructions and appeared to be intended more for contractor installation than the do-it-yourself trade.

The *Air-O-Space* heaters included instructions for permanent wiring; their short power cords might not reach an available electrical outlet. (Cords supplied with the other models were from four feet to nearly eight feet long.) In any case, be sure to route the cord away from hot surfaces, which can easily destroy plastic or rubber insulation.

All of the devices we tested should be cleaned periodically; a monthly inspection couldn't hurt with most of them. (The *Edmund 72,149* requires the least frequent cleaning, since a layer of dust isn't apt to reduce its minuscule contribution to heat recovery.) Cleaning can be a messy chore, involving brushing and vacuuming hard-to-reach sooty surfaces. If possible, use an old vacuum cleaner exclusively for this work.

Recommendations

Recovering heat from the furnace flue may sound like a good way to save energy. In fact, not too much heat can be reclaimed, and it can't be moved too far away from the furnace. You should consider installing a flue heat recovery device if your situation meets four conditions: if your furnace is incurably inefficient; if you need to heat an area within about twenty feet of the furnace; if your annual heating costs are so high that your saving will justify an investment of $90 or more; and if your local building code permits it. In short, a flue heat recovery device won't be useful on every furnace, but an effective one can be useful in certain situations.

The *Chimney Heat Reclaimer* was clearly the most effective device tested, recovering 6 percent of the heat in the fuel. It is bulky, though, and might not fit on all flue pipes. At $189, it was also the most expensive model tested. If installation space is a problem, look to one of the *Air-O-Space* heaters. They are fairly small and, because they mount only on one side of the flue pipe, offer more flexibility in installation. Note, however, that they recovered only about 3 percent of the furnace's heat in our tests.

Recovering heat at the flue 51

ANATOMY OF THE DEVICES WE TESTED

Each of the flue heat recovery devices we tested has its own method for extracting heat from the flue. And, as the drawings below show, some of the devices require a good deal of space around the flue for installation, servicing, and cleaning.

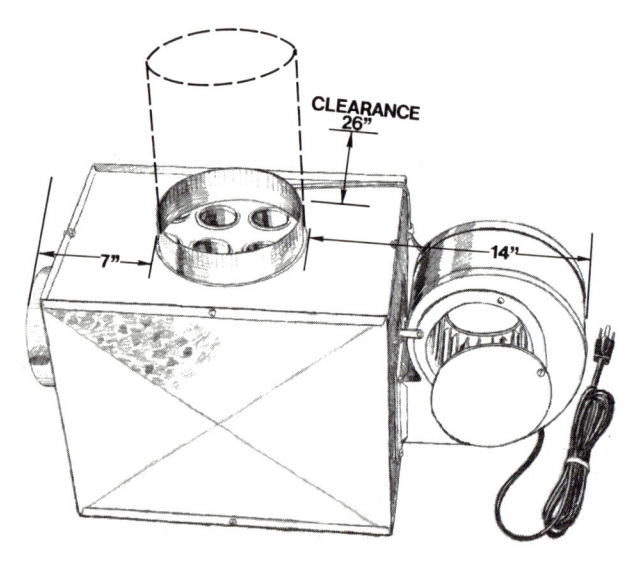

EDMUND FUEL MISER No. 19,255
Box contains twenty-four tubes through which flue gases are routed. Room air is heated as it's blown across the outside of the tubes, then discharged through duct at left.

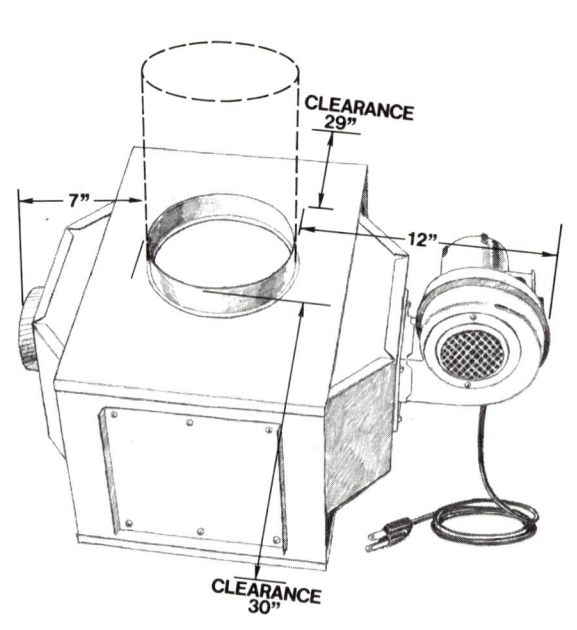

CHIMNEY HEAT RECLAIMER 2A
Room air is routed through eight tubes inside the device, while hot flue gases flow across the outside of the tubes. A blower, at right, forces the heated room air out through the duct at left.

AIR-O-SPACE HEATER 5K and 4K
Finned metal heat pipes (shown projecting into the flue pipe) extract heat from the flue. A fan blows room air over the pipes, then out through the exhaust duct at left. The *Air-O-Space 5K* has five heat pipes, the *4K*, four; otherwise, the two models are essentially similar.

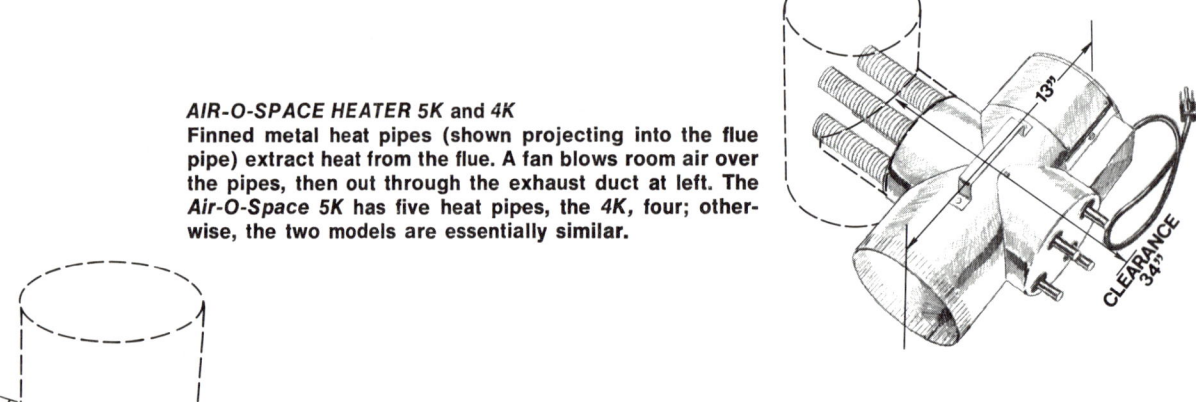

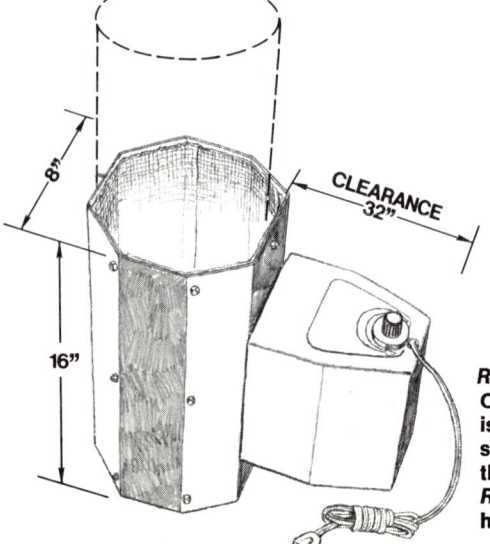

EDMUND No. 72,149
Rippled aluminum strips (sixteen in all) are wrapped around the flue to increase the radiation surface of the flue pipe.

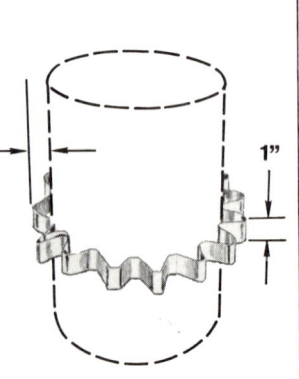

RECYCLO-HEATER
Octagonal tube, which clamps over the flue pipe, is lined with woven copper-colored pads that resemble large scouring pads. A blower mounted on the tube sucks air through the space between the *Recyclo-Heater* and the flue pipe, discharging heated air through an outlet (not shown).

52   The heating system

Ratings: Flue heat recovery devices

Listed in order of decreasing effectiveness in recovering heat from furnace flue. Heat-recovery percentages are the average, rounded to nearest ½ percent, of savings recorded on CU's oil-fired furnace. Specific savings will vary from one installation to another. Dimensions, including CU's estimates of clearance required for installation and servicing, are noted on the sketches on page 52. Flue-pipe sizes are for those models tested; other sizes (not tested) may be available. Except as noted, all require some modification to existing flue pipe, available a-c outlet, and ducting. Prices are list as of September 1978 and do not include installation.

CHIMNEY HEAT RECLAIMER 2A (Chimney Heat Reclaimer Corp., Plainville, Conn.), $189. Heat recovery: 6 percent. **Advantages:** Has adjustable thermostat and on-off switch to override thermostat, judged minor advantages. Can be cleaned in place by removing 2 access panels; cleaning brush supplied. **Comments:** For flue pipes up to 7-in. dia.; requires adapters for smaller pipes. Requires 11 in. of straight flue pipe for installation. Heated air outlet diameter: 4 in. Supplied with 90-in. power cord.

EDMUND FUEL MISER No. 19,255. (Edmund Scientific Co., Barrington, N.J.), $160. Heat recovery: 5 percent. **Advantages:** Has adjustable thermostat and damper to control velocity of outlet air, judged minor advantages. **Disadvantages:** Must be removed from flue pipe for cleaning; removable section weighs 27 lb. **Comments.** For flue pipes up to 7-in. dia.; requires adapters for smaller pipes. Requires 18 in. of straight flue pipe for installation. Heated air outlet diameter: 6 in. Supplied with 90-in. power cord.

AIR-O-SPACE HEATER 5K (Isothermics Inc., Augusta, N.J.), $170. Heat recovery: 3½ percent. **Advantages:** Requires less room for installation than most. **Disadvantages:** Must be removed from flue pipe for cleaning; removable section weighs 12 lb. **Comments:** For flue pipes of 6- to 8-in. dia.; requires adapters for smaller flue pipes. Requires 10 in. of straight flue pipe for installation. Heated air outlet diameter: 6 in. Supplied with 16-in. power cord.

AIR-O-SPACE HEATER 4K (Isothermics Inc.), $150. Heat recovery: 3 percent. Essentially similar to *Air-O-Space Heater 5K*, preceding, except has 4 heat pipes instead of 5. Removable section weighs 10½ lb. Supplied with 14-in. power cord.

RECYCLO-HEATER (General Products Corp., West Haven, Conn.), $90. Heat recovery: 1½ percent. **Advantages:** Has blower speed control and "off" switch, judged minor advantages. **Comments:** Only for flue pipes with 7-in. dia. Requires 16 in. of straight flue pipe for installation. Device clamps to outside of flue pipe; no modification to existing flue pipe required. Must be removed from flue pipe for cleaning; removable section weighs 11½ lb. According to the manufacturer, woven copper-colored pads must be changed annually; replacement pads available, $9.95. Heated air outlet diameter: 2⅛ in. Supplied with 47-in. power cord.

■ *The following model was judged significantly less effective in heat recovery than those preceding.*

EDMUND No. 72,149 (Edmund Scientific Co.), $10.50. Heat recovery: ½ percent. **Comments:** For flue pipes up to 9-in. dia. Requires total of 24 in. of straight flue pipe for installation. Device consists of sixteen rippled metal bands which are attached to outside surface of flue pipe; no modification to existing flue pipe required. No electrical connections required. No outlet for heated air.

The flue damper: Pros and cons of an energy-saver

A flue damper is a device that attacks the problem of off-time losses directly—it closes off the flue after the furnace shuts down to keep warm air within the house longer. The damper is nothing more than a circular metal plate fitted inside the flue pipe, typically operated by a motor linked to the furnace's controls. (If the device is installed in the flue itself it's called a *flue* damper; if it's put between the furnace and the draft diverter, it's called a *vent* damper. A damper by either name serves the same function, however, so we'll use the term *flue damper* to describe both types.)

When the thermostat calls for heat and the furnace goes on, the damper opens; when the furnace shuts off, the damper closes, keeping warm air from escaping. That way, the house cools off at a slower rate and the thermostat calls for heat less often. The damper doesn't snap shut the instant the furnace cycles off; some hot air, along with gases produced by the burning fuel, must escape as a safety measure.

The studies done so far—including CU's own tests—indicate that dampers can lower fuel bills from 10 percent to as much as 30 percent. Granted, that's a wide range, but the same variables that affect heat loss (temperature, climate, furnace size; and so on) also affect heat saving. In general, the more often your furnace cycles on and off, and the longer it stays off, the greater the saving possible with a flue damper.

Flue dampers have been used in Germany and other European countries since 1932, but in the United States they're a relatively new and controversial item.

A flue damper will save fuel; few people would dispute that. But engineers, fire-safety officials, and building inspectors in this country have been sharply divided over the possible hazards of the device. Some officials have maintained that the hazards outweigh whatever saving a damper may bring. In addition, the Federal Government has offered conflicting advice to homeowners. A few years ago, one agency advocated installing flue dampers as a worthwhile energy-saving measure. There weren't many dampers on the market then, however, and you probably would have violated your local building code if you'd tried to install one. Today, dampers are available that should meet local codes, but a second Government agency has recommended that homeowners put off buying one.

CU has been following the controversy over flue dampers for some time, and we have tested three early models of dampers. The tests we conducted measured some significant fuel saving, but they also uncovered some shortcomings in the design and operation of the dampers—shortcomings that underscore the controversy still associated with these devices.

Where have they been?

In 1965, a businessman named Charles Woolfolk helped finance the Save-Fuel Corporation, the first company in this country to manufacture flue dampers. The earliest models, which were much simpler than those now on the market, were priced at about $10. But Woolfolk and his associates soon learned that it was difficult to sell them. Contractor's couldn't install them: The devices couldn't pass the local building codes unless they'd been certified by a "nationally recognized testing agency"—in this case the American Gas Association (AGA) Laboratories (for gas furnaces) and Underwriters Laboratories (for oil furnaces). And they couldn't be certified because there was no set of standards for the laboratories to use in evaluating flue dampers. Woolfolk spent eight years trying, without success, to get such a standard written and adopted.

In Congressional hearings held in the spring of 1976 and later that year on the CBS-TV program "60 Minutes," Woolfolk charged that the AGA was opposed to flue dampers and that it had snuffed out attempts to produce a standard because the association was more interested in selling natural gas than in saving it.

Representatives from the AGA and the American National Standards Institute (ANSI) maintained that they were interested in conservation and did not oppose any fuel-saving device so long as it was safe. But flue dampers presented some serious safety questions, they said. If a damper failed in the closed position and the furnace cycled on, for instance, toxic products of combustion would be discharged directly into the house. And if the damper opened too slowly, some of those gases would spill into the house. According to AGA and ANSI, a standard could overcome those prob-

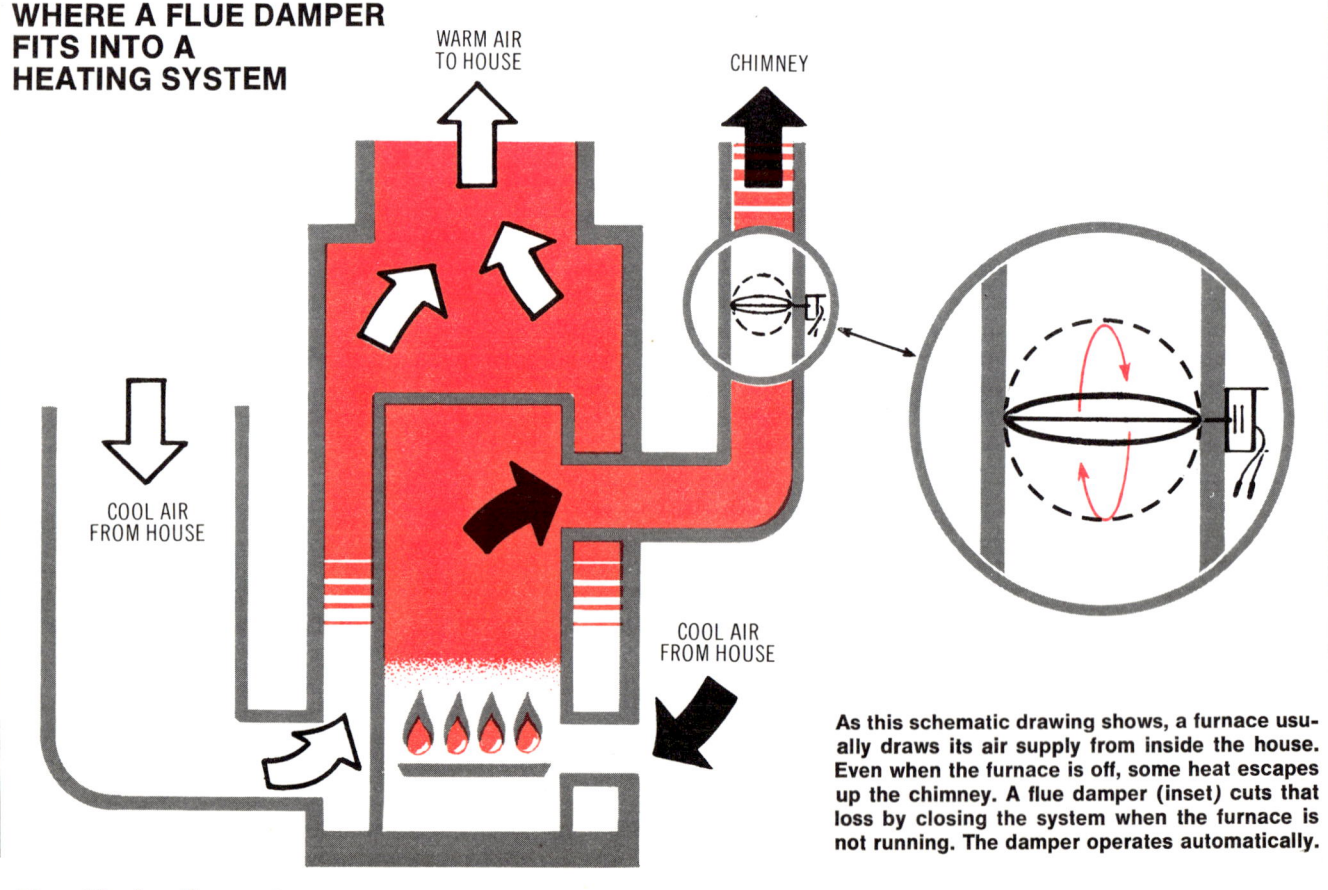

WHERE A FLUE DAMPER FITS INTO A HEATING SYSTEM

As this schematic drawing shows, a furnace usually draws its air supply from inside the house. Even when the furnace is off, some heat escapes up the chimney. A flue damper (inset) cuts that loss by closing the system when the furnace is not running. The damper operates automatically.

The heating system

lems, at least as far as the equipment itself was concerned; but they saw no way to keep dampers out of the hands of do-it-yourselfers. As a result, they believed it was impossible to ensure that proper installation procedures would always be followed. For that reason, in 1974 an ANSI committee voted down a proposed flue-damper standard.

The Congressional hearings had little immediate impact, but when "60 Minutes" aired Woolfolk's story before a nationwide television audience, the situation changed rapidly. The AGA set up a program to review various energy conservation products, including flue dampers. The Consumer Product Safety Commission hired a private testing laboratory to evaluate the safety of the devices. The Department of Energy hired a consulting firm to prepare a report on the fuel saving that dampers might produce.

The most significant response to the publicity came from ANSI, which set its committee to work with renewed vigor on a new standard for dampers on gas-fired furnaces. This time, a standard was approved; in November 1977, it was put in final form. Within six weeks, three manufacturers had obtained certification from the AGA Laboratories. UL, meanwhile, had developed its own criteria for evaluating dampers built for oil-fired furnaces and began testing the devices at about the same time AGA began its certification program. According to the manufacturers, both types of dampers can cost from $150 to $350, including installation.

Meanwhile, Woolfolk, who is still in the flue-damper business, has filed a $450 million antitrust suit against the AGA and others, charging once again that they conspired to keep flue dampers off the market.

Some serious problems remain

The ANSI standard for dampers deals extensively with safety questions. Among other things, it requires that dampers be installed only by "qualified" technicians, and it recommends procedures to be followed if both the heating system and the damper are to operate as they should. A number of people in the field, however, are still not convinced that the standard will always be followed. The worry is no longer solely that homeowners will botch an installation, but that heating contractors themselves don't know all the ins and outs of the dampers.

A recent Department of Energy report put it this way: "There is no way for the homeowner to be assured that the neighborhood contractor or fuel oil dealer has received adequate training in safe installation practices. There is no way of telling that the local code enforcement official inspecting the completed damper installation is competent to do so. No systematic program exists for training or certifying installers or inspectors. Nor does a program exist requiring annual follow-up inspections."

Things are different in Europe, where an estimated 2 million dampers are in use on gas furnaces. Most of the dampers are in Germany, where service technicians are specially trained and where chimney sweeps (who are actually technicians rather than soot-covered men carrying long-handled brooms) inspect home heating systems annually. As a result, the dampers installed since the late 1960s have reportedly had an accident-free usage record.

In the United States, both the AGA and a newly formed damper manufacturers' trade association have started to set up nationwide training programs for service technicians that were scheduled to be in operation by the fall of 1978.

CU's first look at flue dampers

CU conducted its first test of flue dampers in 1977, before a product standard had been written and when flue dampers were fairly hard to find. We purchased three models, all designed for oil-fired heating systems: The *Ad-Vant Stack Master* (Ad-Vant Industries Inc., Norristown, Pa. 19401), the *Flair Stack Pack* (Flair Mfg. Corp., Hauppauge, N.Y. 11787), and the *Trionic Heating System Sentinel* (Trionic Industries Inc., Harrisburg, Pa. 17112).

We tested them to gauge how much fuel a damper might save, and to judge for ourselves whether these dampers presented serious safety hazards, as some critics have claimed. We tested each damper on a specially instrumented boiler in CU's laboratory, and a staffer tested one model on the boiler in his home. CU is not suggesting that you buy one of these dampers, nor are we ranking them in order of estimated overall quality. The models listed by AGA and UL may be different from the ones we tested.

The dampers did work as fuel-savers; but, two dampers had drawbacks—some merely annoying, others serious.

An experienced service technician shouldn't find installation difficult. However, the *Sentinel* we bought lacked some important instructions, which were later supplied by the manufacturer. (According to the company, the *Sentinel* is now sold with a complete set of instructions.) In addition, one wire on the *Sentinel*'s controls was the wrong color. A green wire, which is customarily a ground wire, turned out to be a substitute for an orange one. The mistake could have led an installer to wire the damper incorrectly; that, in turn, could render the damper inoperative or trip a circuit breaker.

Two models, the *Sentinel* and the *Stack Master*, took fifteen seconds to open. That's rather slow and could be an annoyance on some furnaces, as the CU staffer learned. What happened was this: The slow-opening damper would prevent the burner from firing, and the furnace's controls would be "fooled" into sensing that the burner had malfunctioned. The furnace would then switch to a safety mode, requiring the controls to be reset manually. It should be noted that the slow start-up didn't always fool the heating system, but it did force our staffer to reset the furnace controls several times during the one-month home-use test. (The *Stack Pack* opens in about five seconds—fast enough, we judge, to keep most furnaces from being fooled.)

Each damper worked satisfactorily under normal conditions on the boiler in CU's laboratory. We then exposed them to a simulated "flue" temperature of more than 700°F—a temperature that could be reached in furnaces that need to be cleaned and serviced. The *Stack Pack* and the *Stack Master* worked fine at the higher temperature for hundreds of cycles. The *Sentinel* jammed, but the failure did not present a safety hazard. The damper's electrical safety controls continued to work as they should.

A more serious failure occurred on the *Stack Master*: An electrical relay welded itself shut. That in itself was not hazardous, but it did remove one safety feature from the system. If the damper had jammed or stuck in the closed position, the burner could still have fired. The *Stack Master* should have had an additional switch or interlock to prevent the damper from closing while the relay was shut.

As expected, the dampers reduced fuel consumption. On our test boiler, we produced the greatest saving—about 10 percent—when the heating system had short "on" cycles followed by long "off" cycles. As off-time decreased, so did the amount of fuel saved. We could not be quite as precise in measuring the fuel saving in our staffer's home. But by comparing fuel consumption with and without a damper, and allowing for variations in weather, our staffer estimates that the flue damper be used lowered his fuel bills by almost 15 percent.

Recommendations

There are still enough problems associated with flue dampers to keep CU from recommending them wholeheartedly. A damper isn't the only device that will save fuel. Other products, such as storm windows, caulking and weather stripping, and an energy-saving thermostat might make better investments—at least until the controversy surrounding flue dampers abates.

If you do buy a damper, be sure it carries a UL listing or has AGA certification. Investing in a damper makes sense—and saves money—if you can find a dealer who sells certified dampers, if the dealer has been trained to install them, and if the local building inspector is familiar with flue dampers and can thus ensure that yours is installed properly.

4
Keeping cool

Keeping a house comfortable during the winter is relatively simple: Turn on the furnace for heat and seal the house to keep heat indoors. During the summer, you can, of course, just close the doors and windows and rely totally on air conditioning for cooling and comfort—if you're willing to pay the price for the electricity the air conditioner demands. There are ways to reduce the cost—in energy and in dollars—of cooling a house, but to be most effective they require some ingenuity on your part.

To stay cool—and save some energy and money in the process—you need to work with the weather, not against it. In brief, working with the weather involves these strategies: First, minimize the amount of heat that's generated within the house. Second, shade the house to reduce the impact of the sun's heat. Third, close the house during the day to slow down the flow of heat in from the outdoors. Fourth, open the house at night to allow it to cool down rapidly. The report that follows, "Can Insulation Lower Your Air-Conditioning Costs?" explains those strategies in more detail.

Working with the weather doesn't mean you need to abandon air conditioning completely. But there may be circumstances where it makes more sense to use a whole-house attic fan, which can provide cooling for far less than the cost of air conditioning. We offer general advice on selecting and installing an attic fan; to help you further, we've evaluated eleven fans. Finally, we include two work sheets: one to help you choose a room air conditioner that's the proper size for the area it is to serve; a second to help you calculate the cost of operating the air conditioner.

Can insulation lower your air-conditioning costs?

Insulating the house can be an effective way to lower your fuel bills during the winter because insulation helps slow the flow of heat out of the house. And it's widely believed that insulation can substantially reduce air-conditioning costs as well. After all, if insulation helps keep heat in, shouldn't it also help keep heat *out* of the house during the summer? Unfortunately, it's not that simple.

Consumers Union engineers have taken a careful look at the effect of insulation on air-conditioning requirements, working out cooling needs for hypothetical houses and reviewing existing studies. The closer we looked, though, the more elusive any substantial saving became. Insulating the house may not cut air-conditioning costs, and even if it does, it may not be the most cost-effective way to do so.

Fortunately, there are other measures you can take to reduce the cost of cooling your house. We can't offer any precise estimate of the money those measures will save, but we can tell you why they are likely to be more effective than insulation. Before we outline the alternatives, we need to explain why insulation is more effective in the winter than in the summer.

How's the weather?

Winter weather affects heating requirements quite differently from the way summer weather affects cooling requirements. It's relatively simple to estimate how much heat will be required to keep a house comfortable. To a great extent, it depends on the difference between indoor and outdoor temperatures. The R-value of insulation in the house, the type of heating system, the construction of the house, and a family's living habits affect heating requirements. But, for any given house, the major factor is temperature, and the heating degree-day, as noted in Chapter 1, is a useful index for measuring heating needs.

Once you know the number of heating degree-days, you can calculate how much heat will be lost by conduction through the walls, floor, and ceiling of a house. By carrying

57

the calculations further, it's possible to estimate the amount of heat that can be *saved* by adding insulation.

It's not just the heat or the humidity

To understand the effect insulation might have on air-conditioning requirements, you have to look at humidity and temperature variations in detail.

First, humidity. Humidity is not directly affected by insulation. Insulation slows the flow of heat, and the rate of heat flow is determined only by temperature differences. If it's 85°F inside and 85° outside, there won't be any heat flow through the walls, regardless of the humidity. That's not to say you might not feel uncomfortable without air conditioning—only that insulation by itself wouldn't have an effect on the relative humidity inside the house.

Second, temperature. Let's assume for the moment that humidity is not a factor, and that you can use an air conditioner only to lower the temperature inside the house. (To keep the discussion fairly manageable, we're considering only central air-conditioning systems, not room air conditioners.) Can insulation reduce the amount of energy needed just to cool the house? Unfortunately, there's no simple answer.

If you have no insulation in the house, installing some might help lower your cooling bills. But if some insulation is already in place, adding more could yield only a fairly small saving. In that respect, insulating for air conditioning is no different from insulating for heating.

It's far more difficult to estimate how much energy it will take to air condition a house for summer comfort. There are factors other than temperature to consider, and there is no adequate single index (like the degree-day) that relates all those factors to energy use. The National Oceanic and Atmospheric Administration does compile cooling degree-day data but qualifies the data by saying, "The relationship between cooling degree-days and energy use is less precise than that between heating degree-days and fuel consumption."

There are four major factors that affect comfort and air-conditioning requirements.

1. Humidity. A room at 80° with 90 percent relative humidity may feel as uncomfortable as a room that's 85° or so but with only 50 percent relative humidity. The more uncomfortable you feel, the more likely you are to turn on the air conditioner.

2. The average difference between indoor and outdoor temperatures. Even in the warmest parts of the country, the average difference between indoor and outdoor temperature over the course of a cooling season isn't large. While there may be quite a difference during the hottest part of a hot day, there will be times when the difference is very small. Calculations for a saving in cooling costs must be based on the seasonal average difference, not hour-by-hour temperature shifts.

3. Outdoor temperature shifts. In many parts of the country, the temperature inside a house can often be higher than the outside temperature, especially where days are hot and nights are cool. During the winter, though, it's almost always colder outdoors than indoors.

4. Heat from the sun. The sun's heat is a minor factor in the winter, when the sun is low on the horizon. But during the summer, solar heat has an important effect on air-conditioning requirements. (Solar heat is one factor that can be controlled to some extent, as we'll explain below.)

Some limited estimates of summer energy requirements can be made. It is possible to take data on outside temperature and other factors (such as solar radiation), then calculate the amount of energy required to maintain a given indoor temperature. This approach is often used to determine how large a central air conditioner a house requires, and the calculations are generally made on a "worst case" basis to ensure that the cooling equipment will be adequate. The calculations are cumbersome, though—and they will tell you how large the air conditioner ought to be, not how much energy the unit will consume annually.

Furthermore, insulation will most likely have the greatest impact only in the warmest regions of the country —parts of Alabama, Arizona, Arkansas, California, Florida, Georgia, Hawaii, Louisiana, Mississippi, Nevada, Oklahoma, South Carolina, and Texas. And even in those areas, there are ways to save on cooling costs that may be more effective than insulation. To show what we mean, let's consider a hypothetical house in Houston, a city with about 3000 cooling degree-days a year.

We gave our hypothetical house the same dimensions as those for the Columbus, Ohio, house used as an example in Chapter 2—666 square feet of roof, 1600 square feet of walls (exclusive of glass), and no insulation. We also assumed the following: that the central air conditioner had an Energy Efficiency Ratio (EER) of 6; that it would be set to keep the house at a constant 78°; and that the windows would be kept closed at all times. By installing insulation with an R-value of 19 in the attic, we found the house's cooling requirements would be lowered by about $60 per cooling season.

In a second calculation, we assumed that the house already had R-11 insulation in the attic. Under those conditions, an *additional* R-19 (for a total R-value of 30) would save only an additional $6 per season.

There is a way to achieve a much more impressive reduction in cooling costs without adding that insulation. Simply by raising the indoor temperature from 78° to 80°, cooling requirements for that house would drop by one-fourth. Raising the thermostat setting reduces the air conditioner's running time. And, because of the relatively small average difference between indoor and outdoor temperatures, a change of a few degrees in the thermostat setting makes a large difference in cooling requirements. But lowering the house temperature from 78° to 75° would increase daily cooling requirements by more than one-third.

Further north, in Washington, D.C. (a region with 1000 cooling degree-days), the picture is drastically different. There, outdoor temperature shifts are greater than they are in Houston, and outdoor temperatures tend to drop below indoor temperatures at night. As a result, an uninsulated house in the Washington area would heat rapidly during the day and cool rapidly at night. Insulating the house would limit the daytime heat gain, but it would also limit how much the house would cool down at night. Consequently, insulation probably wouldn't lower cooling bills; it would probably change only the hours the air conditioner is used.

That's the theory, and it's been supported by the National Bureau of Standards study we discussed at the beginning of Chapter 2. The NBS outfitted a rather large ranch house near Washington, D.C., with storm windows and insulation in the ceiling, walls, and floor. The house was unoccupied and the windows and doors shut around the clock. NBS engineers maintained a constant indoor temperature and monitored the house's energy requirements. The engineers found that the insulation served, in effect, as a two-way roadblock, slowing the flow of heat into and out of the house. The result: no energy saving during the cooling season.

Work with the weather, not against it

Using nothing but central air conditioning is a simple—but expensive and wasteful—way to achieve comfort in the summer. There are reasonably simple, less expensive approaches you can take—if you're willing to work with the weather.

Controlling heat generated inside the house is a necessary first step. You should reduce the use of lights and appliances whenever possible and schedule dishwashing, clothes-drying, and other heat-producing chores for early in the morning or late at night, when it's cooler outside.

Next, find ways to reduce the effects of the sun. Sunlight strikes a house with greater intensity and for a longer period of time in the summer than in the winter, so heat builds up within the house far more than it would during the winter. The greatest heat gain occurs in the afternoon, when the temperature is high and the sun shines directly into west windows.

You can reduce the need for air conditioning considerably by blocking out as much sun as possible. Here are four ways to reduce the impact of solar heat through shading and ventilation.

1. Paved sidewalks and driveways reflect heat and glare into the house. They absorb heat during the day and radiate it at night. A green belt of lawns or shrubs planted next to the house will help reduce the effect of that heat on the house.

FOUR WAYS TO REDUCE THE SUN'S IMPACT

1. Greenery to block reflected heat

2. Light walls and roof

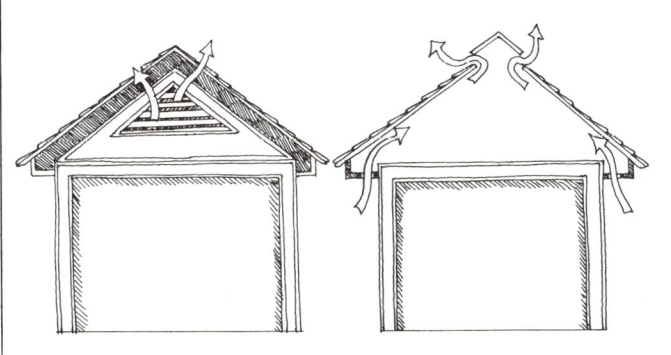

3. Adequate attic ventilation

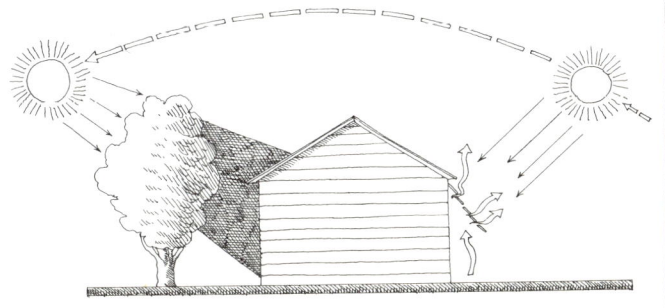

4. Trees and other shading devices

Insulation 59

2. Dark-colored roofs and walls can absorb twice as much heat as light-colored ones do. If your house needs a new roof or the siding painted, consider using light colors to improve the house's ability to reflect heat.

3. Unless there's some escape route, heat that builds up in the attic will radiate into the house. Be sure the attic is adequately ventilated—with vents in the gable ends, in the eaves, and/or along the ridge of the roof.

4. Because of the angle of the sun in summer, the windows on the east and west sides of a house become particularly vulnerable to the sun's heat. You can reduce heat gain by installing awnings, trellises, or other shading devices to protect those windows. Awnings should have ventilating slits or an air space separating them from the house; otherwise, they will become heat traps. A barrier of deciduous trees (not evergreens, which block out the sun in the winter), will also help solve this problem by shading the low early-morning and late-afternoon sun. The trees also help block heat reflected by neighboring houses. While exterior shading is far more effective, keeping interior shades or draperies drawn during the day will also be of some help in reducing the effects of solar radiation.

Blocking out the sun and controlling heat inside the house will help lower your cooling bills. But there are two additional steps you should take to achieve the greatest saving in an air-conditioned house.

First, raise the setting on your thermostat. If you move the setting up a few degrees, you will reduce the amount of time the air conditioner runs, thus lowering the cost of operation. Because of the relatively small average difference between indoor and outdoor temperatures, raising the thermostat setting can make a big difference, as our calculations for the house in Houston made clear.

Second, monitor the outdoor temperature. Whenever the outdoor temperature drops below the indoor temperature, it will pay you to turn off the air conditioner and ventilate the house in other ways. Opening the windows will help the house cool down; using a whole-house attic fan (discussed in the report that follows) or even using a window fan can hasten the rate of cooling. This approach will work best in areas where the difference between daytime and nighttime temperatures is the greatest.

Note that because insulation slows down the flow of heat during the day, the demands on the air conditioner are reduced. You'll see a substantial saving, however, only if you ventilate the house quickly on cool nights. In a study conducted in central New Jersey, residents who stopped running their air conditioners and opened the windows whenever the outside temperature dropped below 68° saw a 15 percent saving in their electric bills for those days. The saving you achieve will depend on several factors: the amount of insulation in the house, the temperature you maintain during the day, the amount of time you run the air conditioner, nighttime temperatures, and relative humidity.

To sum up, in most parts of the country, it's best to insulate for winter needs and consider any summertime saving to be a fringe benefit. If your house already has some insulation, adding more just for air-conditioning needs will probably yield only a small saving. In the warmest areas of the country, where houses may have no insulation, adding insulation can help reduce cooling costs, but we think it makes more sense to raise the thermostat setting and shade the house, rather than worry about the amount of insulation to install.

If you do add insulation, add it in the hottest walls and ceilings, not under the floor. The earth beneath the house is usually far cooler than the air, so insulating the floor closes off a useful escape route for unwanted heat. Even in an uninsulated house, you can save by using an attic fan of the proper size, or just by opening windows, rather than relying on an air conditioner.

Whole-house attic fans

A whole-house attic fan can be useful but it's clearly not a replacement for an air conditioner. An attic fan can pull air through the entire house, generating often-welcome breezes and cooling the house rapidly when the outdoor temperature drops. But an attic fan may not cool down a house as much as an air conditioner will, nor will it dehumidify the air.

Although attic fans don't cost much to operate, they're fairly expensive to buy and install. The models we tested ranged, in May 1978, from $84 plus shipping to $357. But those prices for the most part include only the fan assembly itself; blades, a motor, a drive belt, and a chassis to hold all the parts together. Shutters (to close off the intake and exhaust openings when the fan is idle), switches, and other hardware are generally extra. So is installation, which is a job beyond the range of the casual do-it-yourselfer. If you're adept at carpentry, you should be able to do most of the work yourself, but you should hire a licensed electrician to do the wiring. In CU's area, contractors typically charge from $500 to $600 for a fan plus installation.

We tested eight 36-inch fans (that's the blade diameter) and, to see what kind of performance we could achieve at lower cost, we purchased some 30-inch models from Sears, Montgomery Ward, and J.C. Penney. Six of the fans are single-speed models, four are two-speed, and one, the *Chelsea HVB36DA*, is a continuously variable-speed fan. We also took a look at wall shutters and other accessories.

The fans we tested are reasonably representative of what's available, although there are other brands and sizes on the market. The information that follows can also serve as general advice on how to choose and install a fan.

How much air do you need to move?

Before you settle on a specific brand or size, you need to calculate how powerful the fan should be. To determine the proper fan capacity for your house, calculate the volume of space (in cubic feet) to be ventilated. Multiply length × width × height of each room, hallway, and stairwell to be ventilated. You may not need or want to ventilate all the rooms in the house, or there may be out-of-the way rooms that would be impractical to ventilate. In any case, don't include closets, storage rooms, or the attic itself. In especially warm climates, the volume you wish to ventilate should closely match the fan's capacity, as measured in cubic feet of air per minute (cfm). Where summer temperatures are reasonably moderate, divide the volume by two to find the proper fan capacity.

The 36-inch fans we tested are rated by the manufacturers at 9700 to 11,300 cfm. There may be a catch to those ratings, though: Most appear to be based on "free air delivery," which represents a fan's performance when nothing blocks the air flow. But there's usually something that obstructs air movement, thus reducing the fan's performance. The size of the house, the layout of the rooms, and the location of the fan all have an effect on air delivery. Wall and ceiling shutters can also reduce air delivery, particularly on multi-speed fans at low speed.

To test the fans, we first monitored installations in several homes, then evaluated the performance of the fans in our laboratory over a range of conditions representative of actual use. The laboratory tests measured air delivery (cfm) and efficiency (cfm per watt).

Many of the 36-inch fans that were rated by their makers for about 10,000 cfm actually delivered between 6400 and 7700 cfm in our tests. The 30-inch models (two of which were rated for about 8000 cfm) actually delivered from 5000 to 6700 cfm. But a large fan didn't necessarily mean more cfm, we found. The 30-inch *Sears 6377*, for instance, turned in slightly higher air-delivery figures than the 36-inch *Chelsea HVB36DA*. Keep in mind, though, that the larger the fan, the quieter and more efficient it tends to be.

The Ratings on page 64 give the capacity of each fan, with shutters wide open, as measured by CU's engineers. If you're thinking of buying one of the tested fans, use our air-flow figures, not the manufacturer's.

If you can't find a fan with a capacity that's an appropriate match for your house, choose the next larger capacity available. A slightly oversized fan should have the reserve capacity needed for the hottest weather of the year but it won't cost much more to operate.

Cost, convenience, operation

While the installation of a fan involves a major outlay, keeping the fan running entails a relatively small expense. Let's assume that the fan runs 1000 hours a year on high speed, and that electricity costs 3.8 cents per kwh. At that rate, the *Lau Niteair RE36542S*, which uses a typical 480 watts, would cost only about $18 a year to run; cost of the other tested fans ranged from $13 to $25. Since the cost of operation is relatively low for all the fans we tested, we did not give it very much weight in our Ratings. It's more important to find a fan with the right capacity. We have noted those models that were more efficient and those that were less efficient than average in their use of electricity. Wattage figures are given for each fan primarily as an indication of the load imposed on the electrical circuit the fan is on.

A fan with a continuously variable speed control offers increased convenience, since it can be run at top speed for maximum ventilation, then throttled down to maintain whatever level of air movement you want. Two-speed models don't provide as much control over the fan's performance, but we think they're better than single-speed models. Sears, Montgomery Ward, and J.C. Penney offer a twelve-hour timer, which can be useful if you need to run the fan after you go to bed. It costs about $10.

In choosing a fan, you also need to select shutters—usually one set of ceiling shutters for the air-intake area in the ceiling between the living area and the attic, another set for the exhaust port in the outside wall of the attic. The ceiling shutters help prevent unwanted air circulation when the fan is off. (Don't rely on them to seal in heat during the winter; cover them in some way.) The shutters in the outside wall keep out rain and snow.

Most of the shutters we looked at had louvers made of aluminum reinforced with galvanized steel, and most had felt lips on the louvers to improve sealing. The *Ward* and *Penney* shutters, which lacked reinforcement, were flimsy. The *Ward* also has a lip that projects downward, a design that seemed to increase air drag. Some of the 36-inch shutters, as noted in the Ratings, are built in two sections separated by a narrow divider, a design that adds some reinforcement. We prefer them to single-section shutters. The shutters we've included in the Ratings are meant to be installed in attic walls, but ceiling shutters operate in similar fashion. The typical shutter is "automatic"; that is, the louvers open from the force of air moved by the fan and fall shut when the fan goes off.

An automatic shutter should be adequate with a single-speed fan. But if automatic operation doesn't work, you can add a motor drive or a simple pull-chain for controlled operation. A two-speed or variable-speed fan should probably be combined with controlled shutters because at low fan speeds there may not be enough air moving to keep the louvers fully open.

The drawings on page 63 show the three most typical fan installations: mounted horizontally over a ceiling opening, mounted vertically with a suction box or "plenum chamber" to direct air into the fan, and mounted on an attic wall so the entire attic becomes one big plenum. If you have a "loose" (meaning drafty) attic, a wall installation will generally require a high-capacity fan. (Note that the two *Penney* fans are intended only for ceiling installation.)

The location of the fan and the construction of the attic will also determine what type of shutters you need for maximum air flow. If the exhaust port has to be installed far from a ceiling-mounted fan, and if the attic is loose, then controlled shutters at the port might be best. Similarly, if the fan is mounted on an attic wall, you'd best use controlled shutters at the ceiling intake area for the most effective air flow. There's one other consideration: Automatic shutters may occasionally flap open in high winds, which may expose a wall-mounted fan to rain or snow; controlled shutters, which are held closed by spring action, offer somewhat better protection.

Chelsea offers both motor-drive kits or pull-chains for its shutters; other motor-drive kits are made by Dayton. Frigid offers a complete motorized assembly. The kits can be made to work with other brands of shutter or fan, but they were easiest to install on the shutters they were designed for. The shutter accessories are listed on page 65.

For some people, a small room fan may provide more comfort than a whole-house fan during hot, muggy daylight hours. But, as we noted in the previous report, a whole-house fan is most useful on summer evenings, when you'll want to ventilate the house quickly.

An attic fan can pull cooling air through the entire house, or only through a particular room or set of rooms. It all depends on which doors and windows you open. So, after a particularly hot day, you could air out the entire house by opening the bottom halves of the windows as far as they will go. Or, you could close off the bedrooms during the early evening hours to generate a stronger breeze in the dining room, living room, and kitchen. You'd ventilate the bedrooms later on. Where the night temperature drops markedly, continuous running of the attic fan all night may not be necessary; it might even make the bedrooms uncomfortably cool. Trial and error will establish the right schedule for your house under different temperature conditions.

Usually, the open windows and doors will far exceed the minimum intake area needed for optimum air flow, so you can safely cut down the opening to tailor the air circulation in the rooms. Limiting the number of windows open will increase the breeze but if carried too far the total exchange will be reduced. And be sure that at least one window or outside door is open before starting the fan at any time. If you don't, the fan could create enough suction to affect the operation of pilot lights—or even to pull soot out of the chimney.

Installing the fan

No matter how you install the fan, two openings will be required—one between the living space and the attic, a second between the attic and the outdoors. Normally, both those openings would be cut, framed, and shuttered. You can eliminate some of that carpentry, though at the expense of convenience. For example, you may be able to use an existing door to the attic as the intake area and install the fan in an attic wall. But then you'd have to open the door each time you use the fan. If your attic has windows, they could serve as the exhaust openings for a ceiling-mounted fan—if you were willing to make regular trips to the attic to open and close the windows.

There are other things to consider, and potential hazards to avoid, when installing an attic fan. These include the following.

Vent openings. The vent opening nearest the fan is generally the same size as the fan; a 3x3-foot shutter for a 36-inch fan, for example. The other required opening should be somewhat larger. To decide on its size, divide the fan's actual capacity (cfm) by 750. (Moving air should not exceed 750 feet per minute.) For example, if the fan delivers 8500 cfm, you'll need a little more than 11 square feet of unobstructed exhaust area (8500 ÷ 750 = 11.3). If the opening is to have insect screening, you'll have to double the size of the opening. Other grilles or louvers that obstruct the opening will also add to the required size of the exhaust area.

Noise. Compared with other motor-driven appliances, attic fans are not particularly noisy. The Ratings call out the quiet models and the noisemakers. The amount of sound you hear will depend on where the fan is installed (they're generally louder when mounted on the ceiling than when mounted on the wall) and how the unit is installed. If the fan chassis is attached directly to wall studs or ceiling joists, the hum, drone, and rumble of the fan will be transmitted into the living area. The *Fasco*, the *Lau Niteair*, and the *Ward* are supplied with resilient pads that could be used to make ceiling installation quieter. The *Chelsea* includes a mounting kit, suitable for wall or ceiling installations, that suspends the fan on springs. The *Chelsea* was not a noisy fan in the first place; the kit made it remarkably quiet.

Wiring. The fan's on-off switch (or speed control) should be mounted in a convenient location in the living area. It's easiest and least expensive to wire a fan into an existing circuit. But that may not always be practical, either because your local electrical code prohibits it or because existing circuits don't have the capacity to handle this kind of appliance. Most of the fans we tested put a brief but taxing load on an electric line when the motor was turned on; it was not unusual for the fans to draw 30 to 40 amps for a second or two on start-up. If you can use an existing circuit (and if your local code permits you to do so), consider the *Chelsea* or the *Fasco*, which had relatively low starting-power demands. In any case, be sure the fan and shutter motors are grounded, as a safety measure.

Safety. The whirling blades of these fans, as well as their exposed drive belts and pulleys, can be hazardous. The manufacturers stress that the fans are to be installed in areas that are not readily accessible to people or animals. The *Windmaker* offers a front blade guard for $43 and, for $83, a screened cage that fits over the back of the fan. Such a cage, or a homemade version, would be a useful safety addition, if there is family traffic near the fan.

None of the fans showed significant electrical leakage, and all but one have a built-in circuit breaker that interrupts the electric current if the motor overheats or draws excessive current. This thermal protection can prevent a minor malfunction from getting worse, and could conceivably prevent a fire. Only the *Frigid* lacks the safeguard; it landed at the bottom of the Ratings for that reason.

A motionless fan isn't necessarily off; a thermal overload protector or a thermostatic control (discussed below) could have idled the blades and left the electrical circuit live. If the fan starts up while you're servicing it, you could be seriously injured. To avoid that danger, have an on-off switch installed at the fan itself.

Protection in a fire. If a fire breaks out, the forced draft from a fan can be expected to increase the spread of flames and the intensity of the fire. That can be prevented by a fusible metal link that will melt in case of a fire, turning off the fan or causing motorized or manually operated shutters to close. The *Chelsea* has a switch with such a link. That switch is also sold separately as the *Chelsea S1A1* and should be usable with most other fans. A fusible link is also part of the *Chelsea* and *Frigid* shutter accessories we looked at, but the *Dayton* motor-drives lack the link.

Another fan accessory is a thermostatic control switch, which turns the fan on and off when tempera-

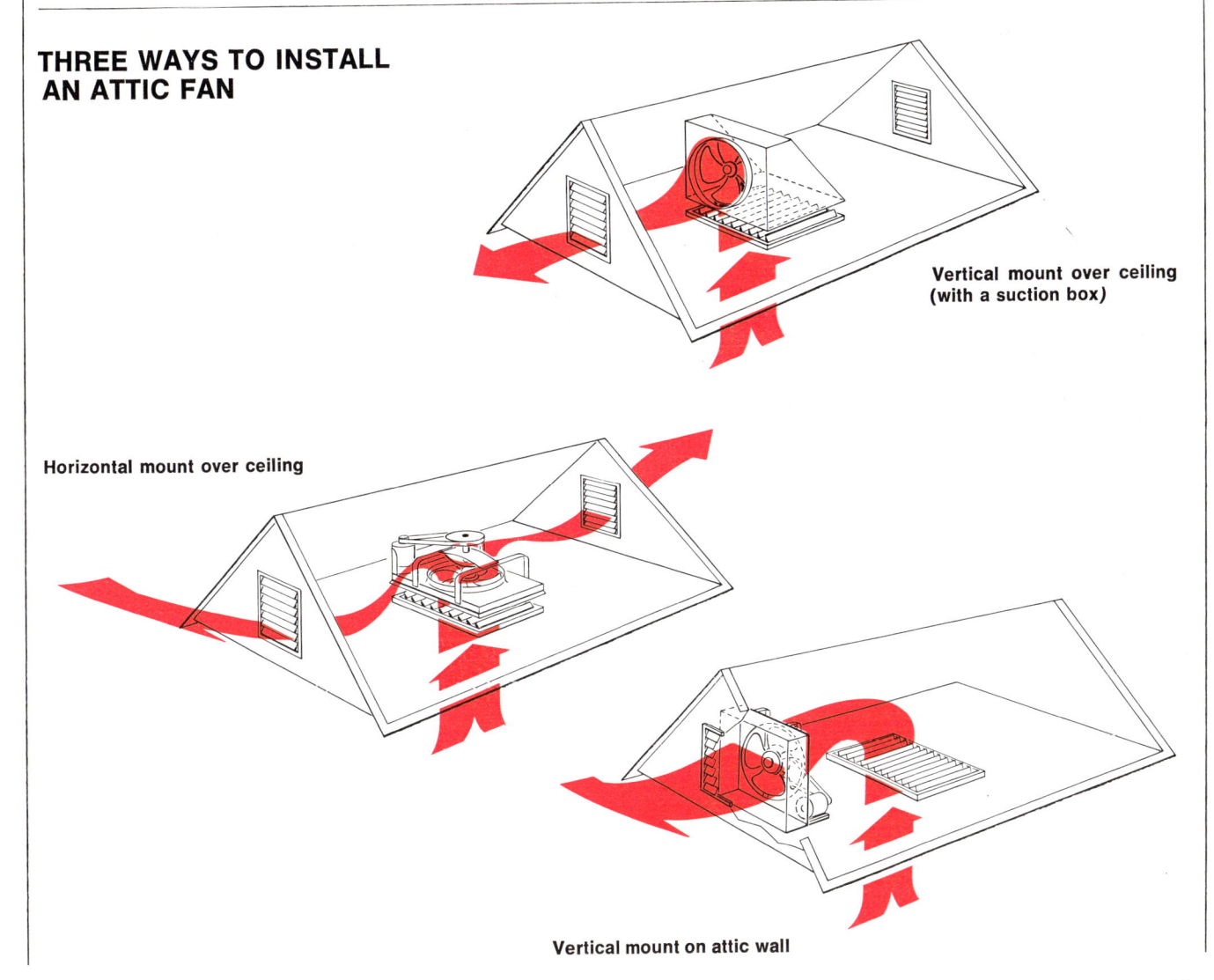

THREE WAYS TO INSTALL AN ATTIC FAN

Vertical mount over ceiling (with a suction box)

Horizontal mount over ceiling

Vertical mount on attic wall

Whole-house attic fans   63

tures reach certain levels. A thermostatically controlled fan can also be started by the heat of a fire, although overload protection built into a fan's motor should serve to shut down the fan in such an emergency.

Recommendations

The first step in choosing an attic fan is to measure the volume of the house, in order to determine how many cubic feet of air per minute the fan should deliver. Keep in mind that manufacturers' air-delivery figures should be discounted roughly 25 percent; the figures that we give in the Ratings are pretty close to the mark.

The air delivery you need won't automatically lock you into buying a fan of a given size. For example, *Windmaker* fans come in a 30-inch fan powered by a ½ horsepower motor might provide about the same performance as a 36-inch, ⅓ horsepower model. But the larger the fan, the quieter and more efficient it tends to be. A higher price doesn't necessarily mean a larger capacity. The top-rated *Chelsea HVB36DA*, for example, has many features that are extra-cost on other models, yet the fan delivers a modest 6600 cfm for a stiff $357.

You could get comparable capacity from the $84 *Sears 6377*, though its overall quality was not as high. Similarly, the *Fasco 3638LS* has almost the same capacity as the *Penney 2810*, but is priced about $90 higher. Those prices are for the basic attic fan; the cost of installation and accessories will usually increase the total cost by $200 to $400 or more.

Once you've determined your house's air-delivery requirements, you have to select wall and ceiling shutters and decide whether you want a single-speed or a multiple-speed fan. We favor multiple-speed models, combined with controlled shutters. That combination adds to the initial cost but offers slightly better fan efficiency and greater convenience.

You must also decide whether to mount the fan in the ceiling or in an attic wall. A wall installation tends to be quieter than a ceiling mount but might require a slightly more powerful fan if your attic is not tight.

Wherever the fan is installed, it may require a separate electrical circuit, either because local codes require one or because the existing wiring won't accommodate the added load.

Ratings: Whole-house attic fans

Listed in order of estimated overall quality. Air flow in cfm (cu. ft. per min.) and wattage listed are based on conditions CU judged to be representative of typical household installation. Actual air flow will differ from house to house. Ceiling shutters were inspected but not tested for performance. Prices are list as of May 1978. Except as noted, prices do not include mounting kits or switches; none of the prices include shutters, shipping (when required), or installation.

Except as noted: • All are single-speed models. • Fan bearings are sealed ball-type requiring no lubrication. • Motors have thermal overload protection. • Shutters listed are for use in attic walls. • Shutters are single-section type with felt seals and reinforced aluminum louvers that were adequately sturdy. • All have 1-yr. guarantee on parts and labor.

CHELSEA HVB36DA (Chelsea Fans and Blowers Div., Tuttle & Bailey Co., New Britain, Conn.). 36-in., variable speed. Air flow: 6600 cfm. 420 watts. $357, including mounting kit. Shutters, *Chelsea LWL36*, $86. **Advantages:** Motor has relatively low starting and running current demand, useful if fan is to be connected to an existing circuit. Overall construction somewhat sturdier than most. Mounting kit was highly effective in reducing noise. Has safety switch to interrupt fan circuit in case of house fire; switch also disconnects fan for convenience and safety when servicing. **Comments:** Model is essentially single-speed fan with solid-state variable speed control. Has 1-yr. guarantee on motor, 5-yr. guarantee on rest of fan. Also available as 1-speed *Chelsea HVB36*, $300, and as two-speed *HVB36T*, $330 (both not tested). *S36* ceiling shutter, $74.

FASCO 3638LS (Fasco Industries Inc., Fayetteville, N.C.). 36-in. Air flow: 7300 cfm. 400 watts. $253. Shutters, *Fasco 3136*, $89. **Advantages:** Fan efficiency somewhat better than average. Motor has relatively low starting and running demand, useful if fan is to be connected to an existing circuit. **Disadvantages:** Slightly noisier than most. Some motor wiring is external (judged safe), but fan requires some care in handling during installation to avoid damage to wiring. **Comments:** Shutters are two-section type; louvers lacked reinforcement but were adequately sturdy. Fan is convertible to variable-speed operation with *Fasco 630* control, $31.

J.C. PENNEY Cat. No. 2810 (J.C. Penney). 36-in., 2-speed. Air flow: High, 7200 cfm; low, 4800 cfm. 440/230 watts. $160. Shutters, *Cat. No. 1530*, $30. **Advantages:** Efficiency slightly above average at high speed, above average at low speed. Has wood-braced chassis for increased rigidity. **Comments:** Fan sold for ceiling mounting use; wall shutters not available. Louvers of ceiling shutters lacked reinforcement; construction relatively flimsy.

LAU NITEAIR RE36542S (Lau Industries Div., Phillips Industries Inc., Dayton, Ohio). 36-in., 2-speed. Air flow: High, 7700 cfm; low, 5400 cfm. 480/250 watts. $224, including 2-speed switch and mounting plate. Shutters, *Lau Niteair 556*, $85. **Advantages:** Fan efficiency above average at low speed. **Comments:** Has 1-yr. guarantee on motor, 5-yr. guarantee on rest of fan. Shutters are two-section type.

J.C. PENNEY Cat. No. 2786 (J.C. Penney). 30-in. Air flow: 5000 cfm. 330 watts. $105. Shutters, *Cat. No. 1522*, $25. **Advantages:** Somewhat quieter than most. Has wood-braced chassis for increased rigidity. **Comments:** Fan sold for ceiling mounting use;

wall shutters not available. Louvers of ceiling shutters lacked reinforcement; construction relatively flimsy.

WINDMAKER BE36-⅓ (Phil Rich Fan Mfg. Co., Houston, Tex.). 36-in. Air flow: 8400 cfm. 640 watts. $198. **Advantages:** Overall construction somewhat sturdier than most. **Disadvantages:** Fan efficiency somewhat below average. **Comments:** Has 2-yr. guarantee on motor and belt, 5-yr. guarantee on rest of fan. Manufacturer's shutters not tested; others available were not recommended for this model.

SEARS Cat. No. 6380 (Sears, Roebuck). 36-in. 2-speed. Air flow: High, 9200 cfm; low, 6300 cfm. 660/350 watts. $173, including 2-speed switch and mounting box. Shutters, *Cat. No. 6427*, $37. **Disadvantages:** Fan efficiency slightly below average at high speed, although somewhat above average at low speed. Motor has relatively high starting demand, a disadvantage if fan is to be connected to an existing circuit. Sleeve-type fan bearings require periodic lubrication. **Comments:** Shutters are two-section type.

WARDS Cat. No. 71028 (Montgomery Ward). 36-in. 2-speed. Air flow: High 7800 cfm; low, 5200 cfm. 510/290 watts. $155. Shutters, *Cat. No. 71056*, $40. **Disadvantages:** Noisiest model tested. **Comments:** 5-yr. guarantee on motor excludes labor after 1 yr. Shutter efficiency below average, particularly at high air-flow levels. Louvers lacked reinforcement and seals; construction judged relatively flimsy.

SEARS Cat. No. 6377 (Sears, Roebuck). 30-in. Air flow: 6700 cfm. 570 watts. $84. Shutters, *Cat. No. 6426*, $25. **Disadvantages:** Fan efficiency somewhat below average. Sleeve-type fan bearings require periodic lubrication.

WARDS Cat. No. 71029 (Montgomery Ward). 30-in. Air flow: 6400 cfm. 500 watts. $115. Shutters, *Cat. No. 71055*, $30. **Disadvantages:** Fan efficiency somewhat below average. Somewhat noisier than most. **Comments:** 5-yr. guarantee on motor excludes labor after 1 yr. Shutter efficiency somewhat below average. Louvers lacked reinforcement and seals; construction somewhat flimsy.

■ *The following model was downrated because its motor lacks overload protection (see report).*

FRIGID UT36 (Frigid Inc., Brooklyn, N.Y.). 36-in. Air flow: 6400 cfm. 490 watts. $210. Shutters, *Frigid SD36*, $70. **Advantages:** Overall construction somewhat sturdier than most. **Disadvantages:** Fan efficiency somewhat below average. Sleeve-type fan bearings require periodic lubrication.

Listings: Accessories for attic fans

Listed by types. Within types, listed alphabetically. Prices are list as of May 1978.

SHUTTER OPERATION KITS

Except as noted, all: ◉ **Were judged easy to install on shutters of the same brand.** ◉ **Are adaptable for use with single-section shutters of most other brands.** ◉ **Have a fusible link (see report).**

CHELSEA LXM (Chelsea Fans and Blowers Div., Tuttle & Bailey Co.), $17. Manual kit for wall shutters. Operates with chain pull, which works in either horizontal or vertical position.

CHELSEA SXMA (Chelsea Fans and Blowers Div., Tuttle & Bailey Co.), $18. Manual kit for ceiling shutters. Operates by vertical chain pull; action satisfactory but not smooth.

CHELSEA LXP (Chelsea Fans and Blowers Div., Tuttle & Bailey Co.), $55. Motorized kit for wall shutters. *Chelsea SXP*, $55, is motorized kit for ceiling shutters.

CHELSEA SXP (Chelsea Fans and Blowers Div., Tuttle & Bailey Co.), $55. Motorized kit for ceiling shutters.

DAYTON 2C832 (Dayton Electric Mfg. Co., Chicago), approx. $41. Motorized kit for two-section wall shutters. Fits 36-in. *Sears* and *Niteair* shutters without modification. Lacks fusible link for fire protection.

DAYTON 2C904 (Dayton Electric Mfg. Co.), $37. Motorized kit for ceiling shutters. Lacks fusible link for fire protection.

MOTORIZED SHUTTERS

FRIGID SD36M (Frigid Inc.), $120, motorized wall shutters. *Frigid C36M*, $125, motorized ceiling shutters. Each has a two-wire line cord that must be plugged into standard wall outlet. In CU's opinion, both models should be grounded when installed.

TIMERS

All have 12-hr. maximum timed interval, current rating of 7 amps, and were judged suitable for use with any of the fans tested.

J.C. PENNEY Cat. No. 2117 (J.C. Penney), $10. Timer dial lacked contrast, a possible disadvantage if mounted in area with low light level.

SEARS Cat. No. 4619 (Sears, Roebuck), $10. Has "constant-on" setting, an advantage if fan must run continuously for more than 12 hrs.

WARDS Cat. No. 71050 (Montgomery Ward), $10.

Room air conditioners: How to match the equipment to your needs

Some people need (or want) a room air conditioner to supply cooling and dehumidification to part of the house. For those people, the added comfort is worth the added cost. And there are ways to achieve that comfort without spending more than is necessary.

The first step is to match the air conditioner's capacity to the room it will serve. The Cooling-Load Estimate Form on the facing page will help you determine how large an air conditioner you need. Second, shop for a high-efficiency model. Look for the Energy Efficiency Ratio (EER) on the appliance label; the EER is the number of Btu the air conditioner delivers per watt of electricity. The higher the EER, the more efficient the air conditioner. Finally, use the Air-Conditioning Cost Calculator below to determine how much it will cost to run an air conditioner in your part of the country. By comparing operating costs for different brands, you'll be able to determine which ones will cost less in the long run even if they carry what may seem to be a high selling price.

1. Determine your cooling-season electric rate. In the example below, we've used the rate of 3.8 cents per kwh (entered as $0.038, not 3.8). Enter your electric rate in column 1.

2. Contact your local electric utility to learn the average number of hours of cooling for your area. (Our example shows 700 hours.) Enter cooling hours in column 2.

3. Multiply column 1 by column 2. Enter the result in column 3.

4. Refer to Step 11 on the Cooling-Load Estimate Form to find the total cooling load for the room you want to air condition. (Our example shows 5000 Btu.) Enter that number in column 4.

5. Multiply column 3 by column 4. Drop the last three digits from the result and enter that number in column 5.

6. Determine the Energy Efficiency Ratio (EER) of the brand and model you're considering. That number may be on the appliance label; if it's not, you can determine the EER by dividing the unit's wattage into its Btu output (Btu/watt=EER). (We've used, as an example, an EER of 8.8.) Enter the EER in column 6.

7. Divide column 5 by column 6. Enter the result in column 7. The result is the estimated cost, in dollars, to run the air conditioner.

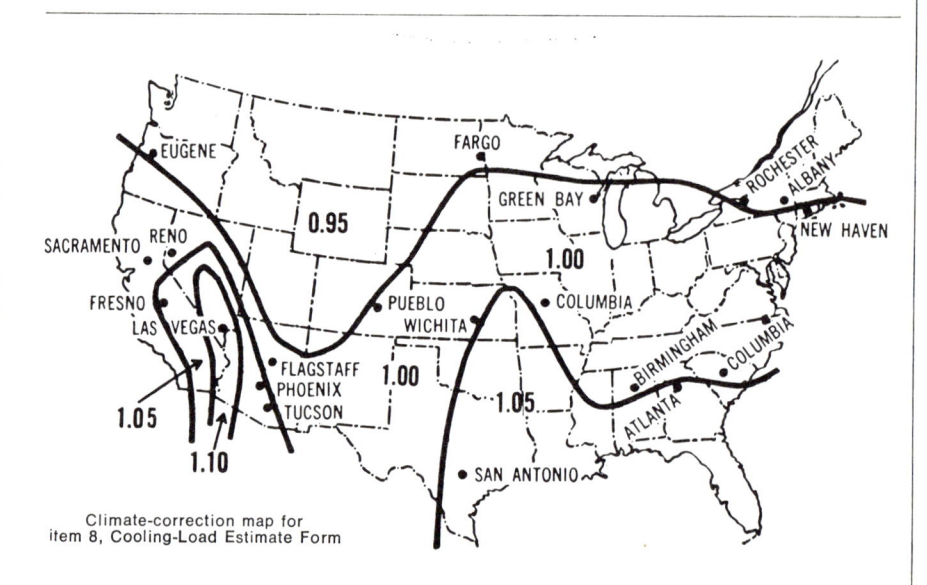

Climate-correction map for item 8, Cooling-Load Estimate Form

AIR-CONDITIONING COST CALCULATOR

1 Local electric rate	2 Average hours of cooling	3 Seasonal electric cost	4 Cooling load	5 Cost factor (drop last 3 digits)	6 Energy efficiency ratio (EER)	7 OPERATING COST FOR COOLING SEASON
$0.038	× 700	= 26.60	× 5000	= 133,000	÷ 8.8	= $ 15.11
$0.___	× ___	= ___	× ___	= ___	÷ ___	= $ ___
$0.___	× ___	= ___	× ___	= ___	÷ ___	= $ ___

66 Keeping cool

COOLING-LOAD ESTIMATE FORM FOR ROOM AIR CONDITIONERS

This form has been adapted from one published by The Association of Home Appliance Manufacturers (AHAM) in standard RAC-1.
NOTE—Where an air conditioner is to be used only for night cooling: The factor for item 1 is 200; disregard item 2; in item 4, the factor for heavy construction is 20, for all others, 30; in item 5, the factors are 5, 3, 7, 4, and 3.

HEAT GAIN FROM	QUANTITY	FACTOR	QUANTITY × FACTOR

1. DOORS AND ARCHES: Multiply the factor by the total width (linear feet) of any continually open doors or arches between room to be cooled and an uncooled space. Consider rooms connected by a door or arch more than five feet wide as a single large room for this and following calculations.

_____ ft. × 300 = _____

2. SUN THROUGH WINDOWS: Multiply window area for each exposure by applicable factor. For windows with inside shades or blinds, use factor for "inside shades." For windows with outside awnings (with or without shades or blinds), use factor for "outside awnings." Factors given are for single glass only. **For glass block, multiply factors by 0.5; for double glass or storm windows, multiply factors by 0.8.**

Enter at right only the largest figure from the column below

		No shades	Inside shades	Outside awnings	
Facing northeast	_____ sq. ft. ×	60 or	25 or	20 =	_____
Facing east	_____ sq. ft. ×	80 or	40 or	25 =	_____
Facing southeast	_____ sq. ft. ×	75 or	30 or	20 =	_____
Facing south	_____ sq. ft. ×	75 or	35 or	20 =	_____
Facing southwest	_____ sq. ft. ×	110 or	45 or	30 =	_____
Facing west	_____ sq. ft. ×	150 or	65 or	45 =	_____
Facing northwest	_____ sq. ft. ×	120 or	50 or	35 =	_____
Facing north	_____ sq. ft. ×	0	0	0 =	_____

3. CONDUCTION THROUGH WINDOWS: Multiply total square feet of all windows in room by the applicable factor.

Single glass .... _____ sq. ft. × 14 = _____
Double glass or glass block ..... _____ sq. ft. × 7 = _____

4. WALLS: Multiply total length (linear feet) of all walls exposed to the outside by the applicable factor. (Consider doors as part of the wall. Consider walls shaded by adjacent structures, but not by trees or shrubbery, as having "north exposure." "Light construction" means an uninsulated frame wall or a masonry wall 8 in. thick or less; "heavy construction" means insulated frame or masonry thicker than 8 in.) Also make computation for inside walls adjacent to uncooled spaces.

		Light construction	Heavy construction	
a. Outside walls				
North exposure	_____ ft. ×	30 or	20 =	_____
Other than north exposure	_____ ft. ×	60 or	30 =	_____
b. Inside walls (between conditioned and unconditioned spaces only)	_____ ft. ×	30 or	30 =	_____

5. CEILING: Multiply total ceiling area by factor for ceiling construction most nearly matching your ceiling.

Enter one figure only

a. Uninsulated with no space above ...... _____ sq. ft. × 19 = _____
b. Insulation 1 inch or more, no space above .... _____ sq. ft. × 8 = _____
c. Uninsulated with attic space above .... _____ sq. ft. × 12 = _____
d. Insulated with attic space above ...... _____ sq. ft. × 5 = _____
e. Occupied space above .... _____ sq. ft. × 3 = _____

6. FLOOR: Multiply the factor by the total floor area. Disregard this item if floor is directly on ground or over a basement.

_____ sq. ft. × 3 = _____

7. SUBTOTAL: Add the loads calculated in items 1 through 6.   SUBTOTAL = _____

8. CLIMATE CORRECTION: Multiply item 7 by correction factor, selected from map on page 66, for your locality.

_____ (item 7) × _____ (factor from map) = _____

9. PEOPLE: Multiply number of people who will normally occupy cooled space by 600. Use minimum of two people.

_____ × 600 = _____

10. ELECTRICAL EQUIPMENT: Determine total wattage for lights and electrical equipment in the cooled area (except the air conditioner itself) that will be in use when the conditioner is operating. Many appliances may give wattage on their nameplates; if not, multiply the nameplate amperage by the voltage for an estimate. Multiply the total wattage by the factor.

_____ watts × 3 = _____

11. TOTAL COOLING LOAD: Add items 8, 9, and 10. The result, in Btu per hour, should be matched fairly closely by an air conditioner's Btu/hr. rating.

TOTAL BTU/HR. = _____

Room air conditioners

5
Saving energy in the home's water system

No discussion of saving energy in the home would be complete without covering the subject of water.

As we noted in Chapter 1, heat for hot water typically accounts for about 20 percent of the energy used in the home. And there are several simple steps you can take to keep some of that energy from literally going down the drain.

The reports that follow focus on two major areas where you can save energy. We begin with the water heater, outlining ways to reduce the amount of energy and money needed to heat water and maintain its temperature. The second report covers ways to reduce by as much as half the amount of water (both hot and cold) you use in the shower. That report evaluates twenty-eight so-called "low-flow" shower heads and nineteen water flow restrictors.

The final report, "Conserving Water in the Toilet," may at first seem out of place because it doesn't deal with saving energy. We've included it because it's a useful supplement to our discussion of saving water in the shower. And, in this era of scarce resources, saving water of any temperature is becoming a very important consideration.

Early in 1978, the Water Resources Council, an independent Federal agency, said there could be "critical" water problems before the year 2000 in Arizona, California, Florida, Kansas, Nebraska, Nevada, New Mexico, Utah, Wyoming, and parts of the Pacific Northwest. But even in areas not associated with drought, the supply of water—along with purification and sewage-treatment facilities—may not be sufficient to keep pace with a growing population.

Many localities have begun to recognize the problem and are taking steps to reduce the amount of water that households use. Near Washington, D.C., for example, the Washington Suburban Sanitary Commission has been promoting voluntary water conservation for several years and now has rates designed to hold down consumption. Elsewhere, local plumbing codes are being tightened to require the use of water-conserving toilets, faucets, and showers in new and remodeled homes. In short, many people will have to learn how to use less water, just as they're now learning to use less energy.

By reducing the amount of water the toilet requires for each flush, you can significantly reduce your household's water consumption. The report that begins on page 74 explains how.

Reducing energy usage in the water heater

A word of caution at the outset: This report is full of numbers—in terms of Btu, kwh, gallons, therms, degrees, percent, dollars and cents. The numbers are necessary to explain how and where you can reduce the amount of energy you use—and, thus, the money you can save—for hot water. But if you can't face several pages of numbers, you'll do well to keep three principles in mind.

1. Lowering the thermostat setting on the water heater yields a double saving—it will reduce the amount of energy used to heat water in the first place, and also reduce the amount of energy used to maintain the temperature of the water inside the tank.

2. Increasing the amount of insulation on the tank can further reduce the amount of energy used for hot water. Some of the heat inside the tank inevitably escapes, via conduction, into the air around the water heater. Added insulation can reduce those losses.

3. Insulating the hot-water pipes will also yield a saving. The insulation reduces the amount of heat lost through the pipes into unheated areas of the house; it can also reduce the amount of time you wait for hot water to flow from the faucet, thus reducing the quantity of hot water you use. Insulated pipes give you hotter water at the tap, which allows you to reduce the temperature in the tank even further.

To explain those principles, and to show the kind of saving you can expect by following them, we need to unleash the numbers.

1. Lower the thermostat setting

For all practical purposes, electric water heaters do their job at 100 percent efficiency. Gas-fired models operate at about 75 percent efficiency; that is, about one-fourth of the energy contained in the gas goes up the flue, not into heating the water. There's not much that can be done to improve operating efficiency for either type of heater, but there is a way to lower the cost of operation.

Water typically flows into the heater tank at 50°F. If you have an electric heater, heating 100 gallons of that water to 150° requires slightly more than 24 kwh, which costs 92 cents (based on a rate of 3.8 cents per kwh). But if you lower the heater's thermostat setting to 120°, you reduce the cost of heating the water by about 30 percent, or 28 cents. The percentage saving will be the same for gas-fired water heaters, although the amount of money saved will be smaller. The table below shows what it costs (in both energy and money) to heat 100 gallons of water to various temperatures.

Even though lowering the thermostat on the water heater will save money, note that this approach does have one drawback: It effectively reduces the amount of hot water available. Since hot water for washing and bathing is usually a mix of hot and cold water, lowering the hot-water temperature can simply mean you will use more hot water and less cold. (To achieve the water temperature you're accustomed to, you'll most likely open the hot-water faucet a bit more and cut back on the amount of cold water.) But reducing hot-water temperatures *does* make a difference with a dishwasher, since that appliance consumes the same amount of water every time it's used. Lowering water temperature at the heater can also make a difference with a washing machine if you use it with a "hot" setting. (But you can also reduce hot-water consumption in a washing machine if you adjust the valves feeding water into the machine to achieve a desired temperature using a "warm" setting.)

To find the proper thermostat setting for your heater, begin by lowering the setting by about 10 degrees; if you still have enough hot water for your needs, lower the setting further. Check the performance of the dishwasher each time you lower the thermostat to be sure the water is hot enough to wash dishes satisfactorily. When you reach a point where the hot-water supply is inadequate, raise the setting a few degrees.

Lowering the thermostat setting also lowers the amount of money spent to maintain the temperature of the hot water (a cost we'll call *storage costs*, for brevity's sake). Storage costs, in terms of energy or dollars, account for about one-fourth of a heater's total operating costs.

To determine how great a saving in storage costs could be achieved by lowering the thermostat, we measured the cost of maintaining water at 155° in two relatively poorly insulated heaters—a 52-gallon electric model and a 40-gallon gas-fired heater. We then estimated the storage costs at 125°. (In each case, we assumed the heaters were in a room kept at about 70°.) The gas-fired model required 59,200 Btu per day to maintain water at 155°, which amounts to a cost of $45 per year, based on a rate of 21 cents per therm. The electric heater used 5.2 kwh per day, for an annual cost of $72. Lowering the thermostat setting on each heater, we found, would reduce the storage costs by about one-third to around $29 per year for the gas-fired heater, and to about $46 for the electric model.

But lowering the thermostat setting is not the only way to reduce the cost of storing hot water.

2. Add insulation to the tank

Hot-water tanks are insulated, of course, to reduce heat loss. Can that built-in insulation be improved upon significantly? It can. We formed that judgment after testing two identical products claiming the ability to improve a water heater's efficiency: the *Johns-Manville Water Heater Insulation Kit* ($20, Johns-Manville, Denver) and the *Sears Water Heater Jacket Insulation Kit 9412* ($20 plus shipping, Sears, Roebuck). (Both prices are as of January 1977.)

The insulation kits contain two sections of 1½-inch thick plastic-faced insulation batt—one section large enough to envelop the outer walls of the heater tank and another to cover the top (although you shouldn't cover the top of a gas heater). Also included are a collection of fastening tapes, some paper patterns to help in cutting the fiberglass sections to size, and a comprehensive set of instructions. Installation was judged easy; it took a CU technician about an hour and a half, working slowly and methodically, and taking notes throughout. One reason for taking special care is that fiberglass is nasty stuff to work with. Anyone who handles it is well advised to wear a dust mask, gloves, and a long-sleeved shirt—and not to leave pieces lying about, especially where children play.

To establish a before-and-after basis for comparison, we selected two water heaters that had shown comparatively high heat loss in previous tests (*Consumer Reports*, March 1976). They were the same two heaters referred to above. We set the controls on both heaters to "high" (corresponding to water temperatures of from 150° to 160°), placed them in a room maintained at a temperature of 70° to 75°, turned them on, and monitored their energy input. Then, with the insulation in place we redid the test.

COST OF HEATING 100 GALLONS OF WATER

Temperature raised from 50°F to —	GAS WATER HEATER Therms	Dollars	ELECTRIC WATER HEATER Kwh	Dollars
160°	1.2	0.25	26.9	1.02
150°	1.1	.23	24.5	.92
140°	1.0	.21	22.0	.83
130°	0.9	.19	19.6	.74
120°	0.8	.17	17.1	.65

Without the extra insulation, our electric heater used about 5.2 kwh per day to maintain the high water temperature; when the heater was insulated, the power demand averaged only 3.8 kwh per day, a reduction of 26 percent. Similarly, added insulation lowered the daily energy input to the gas heater from about 59,200 Btu to 45,000 Btu, or 24 percent. There are heaters better insulated and more efficient than the two we used in our tests; we would expect such heaters to benefit less from the extra insulation.

Still, you can achieve a noticeable saving with added insulation, especially if you combine the insulation with lower water temperature. The table to the right shows the approximate costs—in Btu or kwh per day and in dollars per year—for our 40-gallon gas heater and our 52-gallon electric model.

One footnote: If your water heater is in a finished space—kitchen, basement playroom, or the like—the heat being given off from the heater's walls is not actually being lost, since it supplements the furnace's output.

STORAGE COSTS

GAS WATER HEATER

Water temperature	No added insulation Btu/day	No added insulation Dollars/year	Added insulation Btu/day	Added insulation Dollars/year
155°	59,200	$45	45,000	$34
125°	38,000	29	28,600	22

ELECTRIC WATER HEATER

Water temperature	No added insulation Kwh/day	No added insulation Dollars/year	Added insulation Kwh/day	Added insulation Dollars/year
155°	5.2	$72	3.8	$53
125°	3.3	46	2.4	34

In such a situation the insulation jacket would provide little or no saving during the heating season, though it would help in reducing the heat load if that space were air conditioned in summer.

3. Insulate the pipes

When water pipes are full of hot water, they lose heat rapidly, via conduction, to the surrounding air. If the pipes pass through an unheated area, such as a crawl space, the heat is irretrievably lost. Pipes that pass through living areas also lose heat, but the loss is not irretrievable; you can't put the heat back into the water at that point, but the heat does help warm the area.

By insulating the pipes, you can help keep the heat in the water, where it belongs. The insulation also yields two fringe benefits: It can help you reduce the amount of water you use since you may not need to wait so long to get hot water out of a faucet. And, in the summer, reducing heat loss from the pipes may reduce your cooling needs.

Restricting the flow in the shower

Bathing accounts for a significant amount—about 30 percent—of a typical household's water usage. A good part of that water must be heated, making the bath a likely place to try to save energy and money. Simply lowering the thermostat setting on the water heater won't result in a saving, however, unless you also reduce the *amount* of water used. If you favor tub baths, you can, of course, simply use less water. In the shower, you may be able to cut the rate of water flow in half—thus reducing the amount of water used—without sacrificing the kind of shower you like.

A standard shower head delivers 5 to 6 gallons per minute (gpm) at full flow. We tested twenty-eight "low-flow" shower heads that deliver substantially less than 5 gpm; we found one, in fact, that gave an acceptable shower on less than 2 gpm. We also evaluated nineteen flow restrictors, simple devices that reduce the water that flows through the existing shower head. The stingiest restrictor reduced the flow rate to around 2 gpm.

The Ratings beginning on page 72 note which devices reduced flow the most, but it's impossible to say precisely how many gallons of water you will actually save, since individual showering habits vary. Some people turn the shower faucet on full blast, but others make do with a gentler stream of water. There are people who linger in the shower, and those who dip in and out quickly. The more time you spend in the shower, of course, the more water you use—and the more water you stand to save with one of these devices installed in your shower.

A new head or a restrictor?

The cheapest way to save is to install a flow restrictor. The ones we tested ranged in price from a mere 13 cents to about $7, as of May 1978. The more expensive types are cylinders that fit between the shower arm and the shower head. The less expensive types are inserts designed to be slipped into the threaded fitting of the shower head itself. A restrictor cuts water usage but it can also affect the shower's quality. A restrictor may well yield a less vigorous spray than you get from your existing shower head, or from the majority of low-flow heads we tested.

Low-flow shower heads are more expensive—from $3.50 to $27 for the ones we tested. One type of low-flow head, which we'll call "*regular*" for want of a better term, looks like an ordinary shower head. The regular models we tested all have an adjustable spray, but not all could produce both a soft shower and a tingly needle spray. "Aerating heads," the other type we looked at, mix the water with air. They're smaller than ordinary heads and have nonadjustable sprays.

With one exception, none of the devices we tested could be attached to a shower arm that ends in a ball joint. If that's the kind of arm your shower has, you'll need to have it replaced before you can install a low-flow head or a restrictor. (The *Water Guard* restrictor we tested included one device for threaded-pipe shower arms and a second device that the company claims will fit ball-joint arms.)

Metering the flow

Water consumption was a major factor in our Ratings. To represent a range of pressures available in municipal water systems, we measured flow rates at two static water-pressure settings—a moderate 50 pounds per square inch and a more forceful 80 psi.

On average, the aerating heads were the more economical type, using around 2 gpm at moderate pressure and about 2.5 gpm at the higher pressure. Water consumption for most regular heads was about 2.6 gpm at moderate pressure and 3 gpm at the higher pressure. The Ratings give water consumption for restrictors and low-flow heads at both static pressure settings.

How good a shower?

No matter what the flow rate, a shower is only as good as it feels. The head should be versatile enough to satisfy those who prefer brisk showers and those who don't. The spray pattern should provide good body coverage, so you don't have to twist and turn to get wet or rinse off soap. The spray should provide about the same amount of water wherever it hits your body, and the spray should also be free of streams that shoot off to the side. The head itself should swivel to direct the spray where you want it.

To evaluate the low-flow heads, we used a shower stall in our laboratory and asked staffers to shower with each of the heads, judging spray characteristics at all different spray settings. We also asked the panelists to tell us which shower heads they liked. They generally preferred the higher-rated models in each group over those further down in the Ratings. (A pleasant shower is a matter of personal preference, so our panelists' tastes may not apply to everyone.)

All the regular heads produced a gentle rain spray, but only eight delivered a second spray sufficiently sharp or needlelike for us to consider them truly versatile. The finest sprays from the other heads had no tingle; they seemed hardly different from the rain sprays. The Ratings note the range of sprays each head provided. Most of the aerating heads produced a sharp, forceful spray that we think should be pleasing to those who like needle showers. The one exception was the *Economizer CSF318*, which did not develop an active aerated spray, perhaps because it used a very small amount of water.

We also ran some of our showering tests at about 20 psi, to see how well the low-flow heads could handle low-pressure conditions. Most could still deliver an acceptably strong stream of water, we found; the Ratings note those that did a good job at low pressure and those that were noticeably weak. The Ratings also identify those restrictors whose measured flow rate was hardly affected by low pressure.

To test the performance of the flow restrictors, we tried them out on several types of standard shower heads whose needle spray tended to use less water than their rain spray. As expected, the sprays became less forceful. A restrictor rated at about 3 gpm provided a fairly decent needle spray with these heads, but we found we needed a 3.5 gpm restrictor in order to get a good rain spray.

Shut-off controls: Another way to save

You can achieve the greatest saving, of course, if you turn off the water while lathering up, using the shower only to wet yourself beforehand and to rinse afterward. Granted, that's a regimen that won't appeal to everyone, but if conservation matters more than pleasure, you should consider adding a shut-off control to your shower. Four of the aerating heads—the *Nova B6402*, the *Wrightway Aerating 6002*, the *Water Saving Deluxe Fuel Saver*, and the *Deluxe Savershower*—have that control as standard equipment. A similar control is a $3.95 option on the *Lovo*. Since shut-off controls make for additional water-saving, we consider them an advantage. We found that the water temperature tended to change—sometimes hotter, sometimes colder—when the controls were used. However, if you don't shut off the water completely, but let it trickle, you shouldn't experience temperature shifts.

We also tested two shut-off controls that can be installed between the shower arm and the existing shower head: The *Chatham E8* (Chatham Brass Co., 1500 W. Blancke St., Linden, N.J. 07036), $3.70, and the *Zin-Plas 180002* (Zin-Plas Corp., P.O. Box Q, Grand Rapids, Mich. 49501), $4.17 (prices as of May 1978). We found the *Zin-Plas* somewhat more convenient to use. It has a push-button control, so there would be no mistaking "on" from "off." The *Chatham* has a rotating on-off lever; if you turn the lever past the "off" position, the water will start to flow again.

Recommendations

A flow restrictor will allow you to conserve water and costs less to buy than a completely new shower head. Since several restrictors are priced at less than $2, you might want to try a few models, with different flow rates, to find the one that works best with your existing shower head.

However, if you find that a flow restrictor restricts enjoyment of your shower too much, then consider installing a low-flow shower head. The higher-rated regular heads are for those who want a spray that's adjustable from needle-sharp to rainlike. The top eight models offered the widest range of spray settings; of those, we judged the *Zin-Plas 241615* a Best Buy at $7.69. Aerating heads, the other type we tested, have non-adjustable sprays, but they were more economical with water, on average, than the regular heads. The *Nova* models and the *Economizer CSF318* had the lowest flow rates.

We had difficulty locating certain brands of flow restrictors and shower heads. While plumbing-supply houses should stock major brands such as *American Standard* and *Kohler*, others are available primarily by mail order. The Ratings include full addresses for all the distributors.

Ratings: Water-saving devices for showers

Listed by types. Within types, listed as noted. Flow rates given for static pressure settings of 50 psi and 80 psi, respectively. Prices are list as of March 1978 and do not include shipping.

FLOW RESTRICTORS

Listed in order of increasing water consumption. Judged likely to reduce intensity of shower spray. All will fit ½-in. threaded-pipe shower arm but, except as noted, cannot be used with ball-joint shower arm. Except as noted, devices did not maintain flow rate at low pressure. Unless otherwise indicated, all are chrome-plated brass cylinders.

NY-DEL ND76 (Ny-Del Corp., 740 E. Alosta Ave., Glendora, Calif. 91740), 98¢. Flow rates: 2.5 and 2 gpm. Rubber bushing inserted into shower mounting collar. Maintained flow rate at low pressure.

DOLE GS2GPM (Eaton Corp., Controls Div., 191 E. North Ave., Carol Stream, Ill. 60187), $4.25. Flow rates: 2.3 and 2.3 gpm. Maintained flow rate at low pressure.

DOLE GO2.50 GPM (Eaton Corp., Controls Div.), $4.25. Flow rates: 2.5 and 2.7 gpm. Maintained flow rate at low pressure.

AMERICAN STANDARD AQUAMIZER 1620.012 (American Standard Inc., P.O. Box 2063, New Brunswick, N.J. 08903), $4. Flow rates: 2.7 and 2.7 gpm. Maintained flow rate at low pressure.

OMNI A710 (Omni Products Inc., 55666B Yucca Trail, Yucca Valley, Calif. 92284), $3.80. Flow rates: 2.5 and 3 gpm.

WATERGATE SHOWER FLOW CONTROL (JKW 5000 Ltd., 10610 Culver Blvd., Culver City, Calif. 90230). $2.29. Flow rates: 2.6 and 3.1 gpm. Chrome-plated plastic cylinder.

STEDI-FLO 1007 (Chicago Faucet Co., 2100 S. Nuclear Drive, Des Plaines, Ill. 60018), $7.50. Flow rates: 2.9 and 2.9 gpm. Maintained flow rate at low pressure.

WRIGHTWAY 6205 (Wrightway Mfg. Co., 1050 Central Ave., Park Forest South, Ill. 60466), $3.39. Flow rates: 2.8 and 3.4 gpm.

ECONOMIZER CF535 (Moody Consumer Products, P.O. Box 15486/2201 S. Standard, Santa Ana, Calif. 92705), $3.75. Flow rates: 2.9 and 3.3 gpm.

CREST/GOOD 555 (Crest/Good, 325 Underhill Blvd., Syosset, N.Y. 11791), 80¢. Flow rates: 2.8 and 3.4 gpm. Dished stainless-steel washer inserts into shower mounting collar.

DOLE GM3.0GPM (Eaton Corp., Controls Div.), $4.25. Flow rates: 3.1 and 3.2 gpm.

WATER GUARD (Water Guard Div., Eden Enterprises, P.O. Box 370, Arroyo Grande, Calif. 93420), 25¢. Flow rates: 2.9 and 3.5 gpm. Epoxy fiberglass washer inserts into shower mounting collar. Supplied with second insert (not tested), which company claims will fit ball-joint shower arms.

WHAT-A-MIZER (What-A-Mizer Co., Div. D&J Associates, 730 Boston Post Rd., Sudbury, Mass. 01776), approx. $4.95. Flow rates: 2.8 and 3.8 gpm.

ZIN-PLAS WATER PINCHER COUPLING 180005 (Zin-Plas Corp., P.O. Box Q, Grand Rapids, Mich. 49501), $1.98. Flow rates: 3.1 and 3.5 gpm. Chrome-plated plastic cylinder. Maintained flow rate at low pressure.

NOLAND SFC3 (Noland Co., 2700 Warwick Blvd., Newport News, Va. 23607), 65¢. Flow rates: 3 and 3.6 gpm. Flanged plastic cylinder inserts into shower mounting collar.

MAT RESTRICTOR 2031 (Mat Mfg. Corp., 2112 Edison Ave., San Leandro, Calif. 94577), 60¢. Flow rates: 3.1 and 3.7 gpm. Rubber and brass disc inserts into shower mounting collar.

WATER SAVING COUPLING (Water Saving Co., 1641 Third Ave., NYC 10028), $2.50. Flow rates: 3.5 and 3.9 gpm. Chrome-plated plastic cylinder.

CONSERV-A-UNION 378CD (Waterbury Pressed Metals Div., WPM Inc., 407 Brookside Rd., Waterbury, Conn. 06720), $2.98. Flow rates: 3.6 and 4 gpm.

ECONOMIZER CF500R (Moody Consumer Products), 13¢. Flow rates: 3.4 and 4.3 gpm. Nylon washer inserts into shower mounting collar. May have to be filed down to fit some shower heads.

LOW-FLOW SHOWER HEADS

Listed by types, regular and aerating; within types, listed in order of estimated overall quality. Closely ranked models differed little in overall quality. All will fit ½-in. threaded-pipe shower arm but cannot be used with ball-joint shower arm. Regular heads have adjustable spray control; aerating heads are not adjustable.

Except as noted: ◉ Body coverage and spray uniformity were judged adequate. ◉ Spray was somewhat weak, but still acceptable, at low flow pressure.

REGULAR HEADS

AMERICAN STANDARD STEREO 1414.051 (American Standard Inc., P.O. Box 2063, New Brunswick, N.J. 08903), $27. Flow rates: Fine spray, 2 and 2.5 gpm; coarse spray, 2.6 and 3.1

72 The home's water system

gpm. Spray adjustable from very sharp needle to rainlike. Spray stronger than most at low pressure.

CHATHAM 443S (Chatham Brass Co., 1500 W. Blancke St., Linden, N.J. 07036), approx. $20. Flow rates: 3 and 3 gpm. Spray adjustable from sharp needle to rainlike. Spray stronger than most at low pressure.

ZIN-PLAS WATER PINCHER 241615 (Zin-Plas Corp., P.O. Box Q, Grand Rapids, Mich. 49501), $7.69. Flow rates: 2.7 and 3.1 gpm. Spray adjustable from fairly sharp needle to rainlike. Body coverage relatively wide. Spray stronger than most at low pressure. Swiveling range of head narrower than most. **A BEST BUY.**

BARON S850SD (Baron Mfg. Co., 14439 N. 73rd St., Scottsdale, Ariz. 85260), $12. Essentially similar to *Zin-Plas Water Pincher 241615*, preceding. According to the company, the designation of this model was *S950P* in May 1978.

AMERICAN STANDARD ASTRO-JET 1413.038 (American Standard Inc.), $15. Flow rates: Fine spray, 2 and 2.5 gpm; coarse spray, 2.7 and 2.7 gpm. Spray adjustable from moderately forceful and sharp to rainlike.

■ *The following 2 models were judged approximately equal in overall quality. Listed in order of increasing price.*

CHATHAM C2 with No. 104 FLOW CONTROL (Chatham Brass Co.), approx. $6. Flow rates: 2.2 and 2.9 gpm. Spray adjustable from moderately forceful and sharp to rainlike.

AMERICAN STANDARD ASTRO-JET 1413.079 (American Standard Inc.), $12. Flow rates: Fine spray, 1.9 and 2.4 gpm; coarse spray, 2.6 and 3.3 gpm. Spray adjustable from moderately forceful and sharp to rainlike.

■ *The following 9 models were judged slightly lower in overall quality than those preceding.*

CONSERVATIONIST MARK III (Eaton Corp., Controls Div., 191 E. North Ave., Carol Stream, Ill. 60187), $11. Flow rates: 3.1 and 3.2 gpm. Spray adjustable from moderately forceful and sharp to rainlike. Spray somewhat stronger than most at low pressure.

TIPTURN 3130 (American Consumer, Dept. SSH, Caroline Rd., Philadelphia 19176), $7.98. Flow rates: 2.8 and 2.7 gpm. Spray adjustable from mild rainlike spray to coarse, somewhat narrow spray lacking in uniformity. Swiveling range of head narrower than most.

KOHLER AUTEL K7371-3 (Kohler Co., Kohler, Wis. 53044), approx. $14. Flow rates: 3 and 3.1 gpm. Spray adjustment, judged inconvenient, hardly varied mild rain spray. Swiveling range of head wider than most.

NY-DEL 550-II (NY-Del Corp.), $3.50. Flow rates: 3.2 and 4 gpm. Adjusting the head caused moderately forceful rainliwe spray to break up. Spray adjustment judged inconvenient. Body coverage relatively wide.

ZIN-PLAS WATER PINCHER 141653 (Zin-Plas Corp.), $4.45. Flow rates: 2.8 and 3.3 gpm. Rainlike spray adjustable from moderately forceful to mild. Spray adjustment judged inconvenient and somewhat difficult to use. Swiveling range of head narrower than most.

WATER SAVING WATER SAVER (Water Saving Co.), $5.75. Essentially similar to *Zin-Plas Water Pincher 141653*, preceding, except has brass instead of plastic ball joint and mounting collar.

BARON S550W (Baron Mfg. Co.), $5.95. Essentially similar to *Zin-Plas Water Pincher 141653*, above.

CONSERV-A-SHOWER 379CD (Waterbury Pressed Metals Div., WPM Inc.), $5.98. Essentially similar to *Zin-Plas Water Pincher 141653*, above, except has brass instead of plastic ball joint and mounting collar.

WATERGATE WG75 (JKW 5000 Ltd.), $4.95. Essentially similar to *Zin-Plas Water Pincher 141653*, above, except swiveling range of head much narrower than most.

■ *The following 2 models were judged approximately equal in overall quality. Listed in order of increasing price.*

SPEAKMAN AUTO FLO S220AF (Speakman Co., P.O. Box 191, Wilmington, Del. 19899), $8.94. Flow rates: 1.9 and 2.1 gpm. Mild rain spray lacked uniformity. Adjusting the head caused spray to break up. Spray very weak at low pressure.

SPEAKMAN AUTO FLO S2252AF (Speakman Co.), $19. Flow rates: 2.4 and 2.8 gpm. Spray adjustment hardly varied from mild rainlike spray. Spray lacked uniformity.

AERATING HEADS

WATER SAVING DELUXE FUEL SAVER (Water Saving Co., 1641 Third Ave., NYC 10028), $10. Flow rates: 2 and 2.6 gpm. Produced forceful and fairly sharp spray. Has shut-off control, a potential water-saver. Swiveling range of head wider than most.

DELUXE SAVERSHOWER (Reis Enterprises, 15-37 Bell Blvd., Bayside, N.Y. 11360), approx. $10. Essentially similar to *Water Saving Deluxe Fuel Saver*, preceding.

ECONOMIZER CSF318 (Moody Consumer Products, P.O. Box 15486/2201 S. Standard, Santa Ana, Calif. 92705), $7.95. Flow rates: 1.3 and 1.5 gpm. Produced nonaerated, rainlike spray; very weak at low pressure. Body coverage relatively wide. Swiveling range of head wider than most.

WRIGHTWAY AERATING 6002 (Wrightway Mfg. Co., 1050 Central Ave., Park Forest So., Ill. 60466), $7.50. Flow rates: 2.3 and 3.1 gpm. Produced forceful and sharp spray. Spray somewhat stronger than most at low pressure. Has shut-off control, a potential water-saver. Swiveling range of head wider than most.

LOVO (Lovo Products Div., Vanderburgh Enterprises Inc., P.O. Box 138, Southport, Conn. 06490), $7.95. Flow rates: 2 and 2.6 gpm. Produced forceful and fairly sharp spray. Swiveling range of head wider than most. Shut-off control available as an option, $3.95.

ECO-FLO (Eco Products, 44 Post Road West, Westport, Conn. 06880), $13. Essentially similar to *Lovo*, preceding.

NOVA B6402 (Con-Serv Inc., 7879 Reading Rd., Cincinnati), $17. Flow rates: 1.7 and 2.1 gpm. Produced forceful and fairly sharp spray. Body coverage somewhat narrow. Has shut-off control, a potential water-saver. Swiveling range of head wider than most.

ECONOMIZER CS300 (Moody Consumer Products), $3.50. Flow rates: 2.7 and 3.4 gpm. Produced forceful and sharp spray. Spray stronger than most at low pressure. Swiveling range of head wider than most.

CONSERV-A-FLOW (Premium Equipment Ltd., 18 Shurre Pkwy., St. Charles, Mo. 63301), $20. Flow rates: 2 and 2.4 gpm. Produced forceful and fairly sharp spray. Spray somewhat stronger than most at low pressure. Body coverage a bit narrow. Swiveling range of head wider than most.

NOVA B6401 (Con-Serv Inc.), $13. Flow rates: 1.9 and 2.5 gpm. Produced forceful and fairly sharp spray. Body coverage somewhat narrow. Swiveling range of head wider than most.

Conserving water in the toilet

Each time a tank-type toilet is flushed, six to eight gallons of water go down the drain. Flushing the toilet, in fact, consumes almost half the water used each day by a typical household—about twenty-nine gallons of water per person, according to one estimate. That's a lot of water. There are ways—some effective, some not so effective—to save water with each flush.

You can, for example, reduce the amount of water in the tank, either by using a smaller tank or by displacing some of the volume in the existing tank. You can also tinker with the flush valve so that it closes more quickly, releasing less water into the bowl. The amount of water saved will depend on the design and size of the tank and the bowl. We can't predict exactly how much water could be saved by modifying the toilet, but you'd certainly save some.

Keep in mind, however, that any decrease, if carried too far, can interfere with a toilet's ability to flush away waste—particularly solid waste. It's the water falling from the tank into the bowl that pushes waste from the bowl down into the drainpipe. Lowering the water level in the tank or reducing the amount of water released hinders the toilet's ability to push waste from the bowl. There should be no problem with liquid waste, but if water usage is reduced too much, it might take two flushes to remove solid waste. And any saving would probably be canceled out.

Reducing the water in the tank also reduces the amount of water available to fill the trap (the water remaining in the bowl after you flush). That standing water is necessary to isolate the sewer pipe from the bathroom.

Consumers Union tested a variety of gadgets (twenty-seven in all) designed to reduce the amount of water a toilet uses. None of them worked any better than the do-it-yourself methods described below. But if for some reason you find it more convenient to install a manufactured device, we describe below the ones we tested. The Ratings begin on page 76. Performance aside, there's another problem with these commercial devices: availability. CU purchased most of its samples by mail, but the products we received carried different names and model numbers, or were made of different materials than the products we ordered. Company names and addresses also changed. We suggest you order by mail only if you can't find the device you want locally. The Ratings give complete addresses for manufacturers and suppliers.

The do-it-yourself approach

A few minutes spent tinkering with the toilet can yield a significant reduction in the amount of water it uses. Here's what to do.

1. Check for a leaky valve. Before you go to bed, pour some blue toilet cleaner into the tank but do not flush. Next morning, first thing—before anyone uses the toilet—check the color of the water in the bowl. If the water is blue, that's a sign that the flush valve or flapper valve is leaking and should be replaced. A leaky valve can waste more water than you can save with any device, homemade or otherwise.

2. Make your own bottle-dam. Take a one-gallon plastic bottle (such as a bleach or antifreeze container), cut off the neck, and weight the bottle with a few stones. Then sink the bottle in the tank so that it doesn't interfere with the flushing mechanism (see drawing below). The bottle will retain some water, thus reducing the amount of water that is used for each flush.

If the toilet works adequately with one bottle—that is, if solid waste flushes satisfactorily and if the trap refills properly—then sink another bottle in the tank to reduce water usage further. If the second bottle

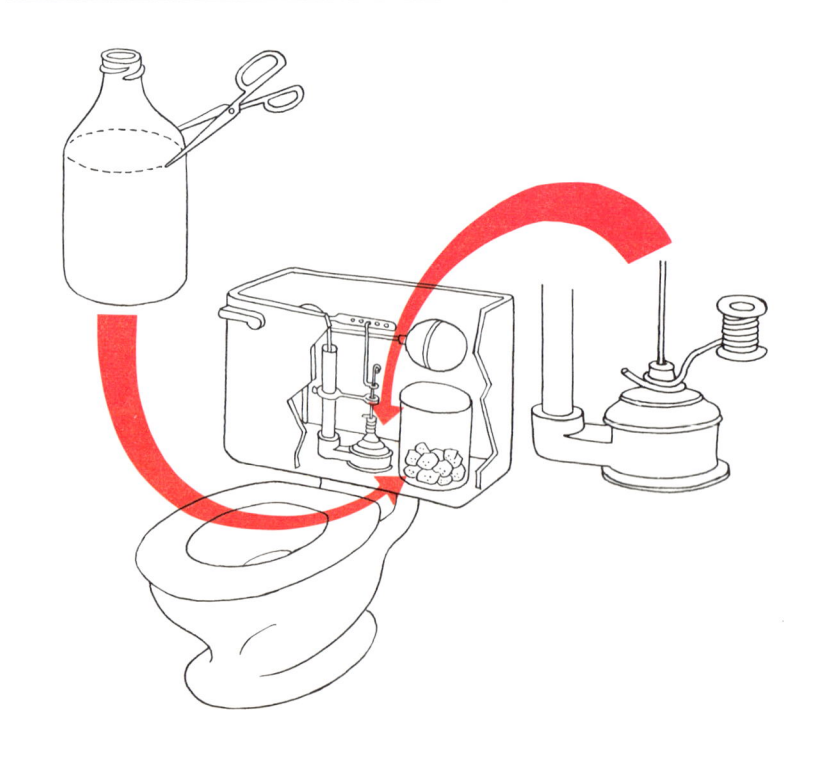

74 **The home's water system**

leads to less-than-adequate flushes, cut another half-inch off the top of the bottle. Keep reducing the size of the second bottle until the toilet flushes satisfactorily.

If you run out of room in the tank for more bottles and the toilet continues to work properly, then you might invest in a commercial dam, which should reduce water usage even more.

You may have seen suggestions that a brick be placed in a toilet tank to reduce the volume of water used. CU does not recommend this procedure because a brick will disintegrate over time, and bits of it could clog the plumbing or interfere with the flushing mechanism. Some people try to save water by bending the float arm down to reduce the water volume. While you can save a little bit of water this way, you probably won't save enough to offset the poor flushing performance that may result.

3. Create a dual-flush toilet. Take a piece of solid-wire solder (you can get some at a hardware store or home center) and wrap it around the valve, as shown in the drawing, to increase the valve's weight. Start with just a small amount of solder and add more later. This is a job that's easiest to do when the tank is empty: Turn off the water supply to the toilet, then flush to drain the tank.

The aim is to weight the valve so that just enough water leaves the tank to flush liquid waste before the valve closes. Once you've reached that point, you can flush as usual to dispose of liquid waste, but you'll have to hold the lever down to flush solid waste.

4. Measure the water in the trap. Once you've installed the bottles and the solder (or any other device), you must be sure the trap is full. Use a grease pencil or crayon to mark the water level in the bowl. Then pour about a quart of water into the bowl —slowly. If the water level doesn't rise above the mark you've made, the trap has filled. If the water level does rise above the mark, the trap has not filled, and you should remove some of the solder from the valve or shorten one of the bottles. Repeat the test to be sure the bowl refills properly.

5. Check the water exchange. Cutting down the amount of water used also reduces a toilet's ability to remove contaminated water. To check, use an ounce or so of toilet cleaner to dye the water in the bowl a deep blue. Then flush. If the water in the bowl is clear or just slightly blue after the flush, fine. But if it's still a pronounced blue, you'll have to increase the amount of water used to flush the toilet.

Note: You should replace leaky valves, measure the water in the trap, and check the water exchange (steps 1, 4, and 5) even if you install one of the water-saving devices we tested.

The gadgets

To evaluate our battery of commercial water-saving devices, we set up five conventional toilets in our laboratory so that we could measure water usage with and without each device. The amount of water consumed and ease of use were the major factors in our tests, but we also monitored the effect each water-saving device had on the ability of our toilets to flush solid waste (simulated in our tests with ping-pong balls, coarse sawdust, and pieces of sponge).

The types of devices we tested were the following.

Dams. Dams, a sophisticated version of our do-it-yourself bottle-in-the-tank, are flexible panels pressed into place in the tank. They block off a portion of the lower part of a tank, thus reducing the amount of water released into the bowl. But dams allow the tank to refill completely, maximizing water velocity when flushing. They can save somewhat more water than other devices tested since they can block off quite a bit of the tank without interfering with the flushing mechanism. Two we examined have features that will allow you to vary the water level once the dams are in position. A metal dam is preferable to a plastic one, we judged.

Weights. These devices cause the flush valve to close sooner than it normally would. With some, either the amount of weight added or the weight's position on the valve can be varied. An adjustable weight allows the toilet to be flushed normally to remove liquid waste, but the flush lever must be held down to clear solid waste. Other types weight the valve so much that the flush lever must be held down each time the toilet is used. The commercial weights we tested really have no advantage over the homemade variety. One weight, the *Econo-Flush #3*, is supplied with a small "metering" tank, which ensures that the trap refills after a flush. It worked, but sloppily and slowly.

Dual-flush units. In theory, a dual-flush mechanism should be good. The flush lever is moved in one direction to flush liquid waste (using very little water) and in the other direction to clear solid waste. The *Eco Flush* two-way flush mechanism was convenient to use, but we judged it difficult to install. And, since it's not adjustable, it may not give an adequate flush in all toilets. The other dual-flush unit we tested, the *Dual-Flo*, was judged to be poorly constructed and not durable.

Air bleeds. We looked at five devices that have the same effect as weights: Air bleeds release air from inside the ballcock or flapper valve, so that the valve closes more quickly. As with weights, air bleeds require the flush lever to be held down to clear solid waste. The bleeds we tested did work, but they could become clogged with water deposits or dirt. We prefer weights to air-bleed devices.

Replacement tanks. We bought two European-made toilet tanks that are smaller than conventional American-made tanks. As received, the *Geberit 35.000* and *30.000* tanks used as much water as a conventional tank. Once we'd figured out how to adjust the float arm and the valve (no instructions were supplied with the samples we purchased), we found that the *Geberit*s did use less water. In CU's judgment, though, the *Geberit* replacement tanks have no advantage over a dam.

We also tested the *Flushmate 2000 with AFC*, a complex replacement tank that uses air pressure to increase water velocity. The water that refills the tank compresses air above the water in a pressure tank; when you punch the *Flushmate*'s flush button, the compressed air pushes the water into the bowl with a fair amount of force. As a result, the unit consistently used between 2.5 and 3 gallons of water per flush—about half the amount normally used by a conventional toilet.

However, the *Flushmate* could not exchange the water in the bowl completely. Some dirty water remained in the trap after the flush and flowed into the bowl. Poor water exchange can be an unwanted side effect of any water-saving scheme, but it's impossible to correct on the *Flushmate* because the device is not adjustable. The *Flushmate* requires a minimum of 25 to 30 pounds of water pressure to function, while most conventional toilets will work at pressures as low as 20 pounds. In addition, the *Flushmate* is noisy at high water pressures.

Flush-valve stop. The *Water Saver* (the only valve stop we tested) works somewhat like a valve weight, causing the valve to shut as soon as the flush lever is released. The flush lever must be held down to clear both solid and liquid waste. The *Water Saver* prevents the valve from opening fully and tends to slow down the water leaving the tank.

How about a new toilet?

Buying an entirely new, water-efficient toilet is an extravagant way to save water. However, such a purchase may make sense if you're remodeling a bathroom or adding a bath to the house. A few areas, in fact, require water-saving fixtures in all new construction. The plumbing codes we've seen specify, among other things, that newly installed toilets must use no more than 3.5 gallons per flush.

For those in the market for a new toilet, we tested eight water-saving toilets built by major manufacturers, evaluating water usage and flushing performance. Most used slightly more than 3.5 gallons per flush, although a few used even more. Most of the toilets we tested performed less effectively than a standard toilet. Many provided less-than-complete water exchange during the flush. Only the *American Standard* and the *Kohler* could handle solid and liquid waste on a par with a conventional toilet.

Recommendations

Although we tested twenty-seven water-saving devices for toilets, we can't really recommend your buying any of them. A bottle in the toilet tank or a homemade weight for the flush valve should be just as effective as nearly all the products we tested.

If you'd rather buy a gadget, however, consider the *Toilet Tank Water Saver* or the *Mini-Flusher* dams; they may save a bit more water than other tank-displacement devices.

Of the new water-saving toilets we tested, the *American Standard* and the *Kohler* are the clear choices.

Ratings: Water-saving devices for toilets

Listed by types in order of estimated convenience and water-saving capability. Within types listed, except as noted, in order of estimated overall quality. Product designations are as given by companies as of May 1978. Prices are list and do not include shipping.

Except as noted: ◉ Amount of water saved will depend on toilet tank in which device is installed. ◉ Devices should work with most types of flush valve. ◉ All devices may not fit in all tanks due to variations in tank size and construction. ◉ All require adjustments after installation for optimum performance.

DAMS

Judged the most effective commercial devices for reducing water consumption. Except as noted, dams are supplied in two identical parts; dimensions given are length and height of each part.

MINI-FLUSHER MF544 (Con-Serv Inc., 7879 Reading Rd., Cincinnati), 8¾x5⅜ in., $6.95. Stainless steel covered with rubber; potentially more durable than plastic dams.

TOILET TANK WATER SAVER (G&E Products Inc., 2082 S. Grand Ave., Santa Ana, Calif. 92705), 7¼x5½ in., $4.95. Brass dam has foam rubber strips at edge for sealing. Potentially more durable than plastic dams.

■ *The following 7 plastic dams were judged approximately equal in overall quality. Listed in order of increasing price.*

WATER GUARD MARK II (Water Guard Div., Eden Enterprises, P.O. Box 370, Arroyo Grande, Calif. 93420), 7⅝x5½ in., $3.33. Kit contains flow restrictors for shower heads (see Ratings, page 72), and leak-detection tablets for toilet tank (not tested).

MOBY DIKE (Watersavers Inc., P.O. Box 22326, Cleveland 44122), 7⅞x5¼ in., $3.95.

WATER GATE WATER SAVERS WG76 (JKW 5000 Ltd., 10610 Culver Blvd., Culver City, Calif. 90230), 8x5¼ in., $3.95. Has pop-out plugs to increase adjustability of water level.

CREST/GOOD WATER SKIMP-R (Crest/Good Mfg. Co., 325 Underhill Blvd., Syosset, N.Y. 11791), 8⅝x5⅜ in., $5. Essentially similar to *Moby Dike*, above.

SAVEIT WATERSAVER SA720 (Ny-Del Corp., 740 E. Alosta Ave., Glendora, Calif. 91740), 16x5¼ in., $5.95. One-piece dam held in place by springs judged susceptible to corrosion. Has cutouts to adjust water level.

The home's water system

WATER SAVER 105 (Baron Mfg. Co., 14439 N. 73rd St., Scottsdale, Ariz. 85260), 8⅝x5½ in., $5.95.

JOHNNY WATER SAVER (Johnny Water Saver, P.O. Box 43190, Birmingham, Ala. 35203), 8⅝x5⅞ in., $6.95.

WEIGHTS

Judged nearly as effective as dams in reducing water consumption; can be used in conjunction with dams to maximize convenience and water saving. All require flush lever to be held down to clear solid waste; nonadjustable models require flush lever to be held down to clear liquid waste and solid waste. Except as noted, all can be adjusted to vary amount of weight or its position on valve assembly.

■ *The following 4 models were judged approximately equal in overall quality. Listed in order of increasing price.*

RD DESIGN WATER-THRIFT (RD Design, 5200 Bald Eagle Ave., White Bear Lake, Minn. 55110), $2.95. Kit with same name available with flapper valve to replace ballcock-type valve ($4.50).

MINI-FLUSH (Mini-Flush, P.O. Box 6373, Colorado Springs 80934), $3.49.

PLUMB SHOP WATER SAVER (Plumb Shop Div., Brass Craft Mfg. Co., 700 Fisher Bldg., Detroit 48202), $3.99. *Type A, Model PSWS11*, fits flapper-type valve; *Type B, Model PSWS12*, fits ballcock-type valve.

ECONO-FLUSH #3 (Water Save Inc., 3137 Capri Rd., Lake Park, Fla. 33410), $5.95. Has "metering" tank to ensure that trap refills, but tank refills slowly after flushing. Position of metering tank and water inlet tend to cause water to spill outside main tank when refilling.

■ *The following 2 models were judged approximately equal in overall quality. Listed in order of increasing price.*

ECONO-FLUSH (Schuyler Products Inc., P.O. Box 31, Kingston, N.Y. 12401), $1.95. Not adjustable.

ECOLOGY HELPER (Jenkins S.M., 106 W. Jefferson St., Falls Church, Va. 22046), $5. Not adjustable.

■ *The following model was judged lower in overall quality than those preceding.*

PLUMB SHOP WATER SAVER TYPE C, PSWS13 (Plumb Shop Div., Brass Craft Mfg. Co.), $3.99. Not adjustable. Claims to fit *American Standard* tilt valve No. 5. Did not fit tilt valve in our *American Standard* tanks.

DUAL-FLUSH UNITS

Judged slightly less useful than dams or weights in reducing water consumption. Both have flushing lever that moves in one direction for liquid wastes, in the opposite direction for solid wastes, a convenient arrangement. Devices are not adjustable; water usage is fixed.

3-B ECO FLUSH 6000 (3-B Mfg. & Supply Co., 6969 Worthington-Galena Rd., Worthington, Ohio 43085), $12.99. Replaces existing flush-valve assembly. Tank must be removed from bowl for installation, judged more difficult than other installation procedures.

GLOBALMAN DUAL-FLO 801 (Global America Corp., P.O. Box 246, El Toro, Calif. 92630), $14.95. Judged significantly lower in quality than model above. Flushing mechanism on one sample broke, and another sample failed to operate reliably. Includes replacement ballcock.

AIR BLEEDS

Similar to weights in operation, but judged susceptible to clogging or malfunctioning. All require flush lever to be held down to discharge solid waste; nonadjustable models require flush lever to be held down to clear liquid waste and solid waste. Except as noted, amount of air released can be varied.

■ *The following 2 models were judged approximately equal in overall quality. Listed in order of increasing price.*

FLUSHMASTER (Flushmaster Sales, 1333 Upton Place, Los Angeles 90041), $5.95. *Kit No. 1* fits ballcock-type flush valve; *Kit No. 2* fits flapper-type flush valve; *Kit No. 3* fits tilt-type flush valve.

CARLTON DIAL-A-FLUSH WATER SAVER (Carlton Industries Inc., 2630 Walnut Drive, Tustin, Calif. 92680), $7.95.

■ *The following model was judged slightly lower in overall quality than those preceding.*

DUO-FLUSH (Duo Flush Corp., P.O. Box 2406, Colorado Springs 80934), $3.50. Not adjustable.

■ *The following 2 models were judged approximately equal but significantly lower in overall quality than those preceding. Listed in order of increasing price.*

SAVWAY DUAL FLUSH SYSTEM (Savway Co., 930 Clarkson Ave., Brooklyn, N.Y. 11203), $4.98. Although air release is nominally variable, device did not perform dependably during CU's tests. Replacement flush valve required for use with tilt-type valve.

WATER PINCHER DUAL FLUSH 210002 (Zin-Plas Corp., P.O. Box Q, Grand Rapids, Mich. 49501), $5.95. Essentially similar to *Savway Dual Flush System*, preceding.

REPLACEMENT TANKS

Amount of water saved not dependent on present tank, which must be removed. Installation judged far more difficult than with other devices. All have plastic exterior.

FLUSHMATE 2000 with AFC (Water Control Products Inc., 1100 Owndale, Troy, Mich. 48084), $74. Uses air compressed by water pressure to force water into bowl at fairly high velocity. Uses between 2.5 and 3 gal. per flush, but reduced water usage led to inadequate water exchange. May not work on system with water pressure of less than 25 to 30 psi; somewhat noisy at high pressure. May not fit all toilet bowls.

GEBERIT Model 35.000 (Geberit Mfg. Inc., P.O. Box 2008, Michigan City, Ind. 46360), $37. Although tank can be adjusted to use less water than conventional tanks, as received it did not. Adjustments for float and flush valve are different than those on usual domestic toilets; no instructions provided with model received. Tank is insulated to reduce sweating during warm, humid weather.

GEBERIT Model 30.000 (Geberit Mfg. Inc.), $37. Essentially a reduced-volume version of *Gerberit Model 35.000*, preceding.

FLUSH-VALVE STOP

Flushing effectiveness judged lower than for other devices tested.

WATER SAVER (National Water Saver Co., P.O. Box 14408, Orlando, Fla. 32807), $2.50. Requires flush lever to be held down to discharge both solid and liquid waste. Not adjustable. Prevents flush valve from opening fully. Not for use on tilt-type valve.

Ratings: Water-saving toilets

Listed in order of decreasing flushing effectiveness, as judged in CU's tests. All are standard round-front bowls, with 12-in. rough-in. Other rough-in sizes should perform similar to models tested. Model numbers given are for white porcelain; other colors available. Prices are list as of May 1978 and do not include seat or installation.

AMERICAN STANDARD CADET 2122.448 (American Standard Inc., New Brunswick, N.J.), $77. Water usage: 3.7 gal. Water exchange judged good.

KOHLER WELLWORTH WATER-GUARD K3500-PB (Kohler Co., Kohler, Wis.), $80. Water usage: 4.2 gal. Water exchange judged good.

■ *Flushing effectiveness of the following 6 models was judged significantly lower than effectiveness of those preceding and not equal to that of a standard toilet.*

ELJER EMBLEM 901-0500 (Plumbingware Div., Wallace Murray Corp., Pittsburgh), $81. Water usage: 3.8 gal. Water exchange judged fair.

SEARS Cat. No. 49288 (Sears, Roebuck), $43 plus shipping. Water usage: 4.3 gal. Water exchange judged good.

CRANE RADCLIFFE 3143 (Crane Co., NYC), $73. Water usage: 3.6 gal. Did not wash inside of bowl properly. Water exchange judged fair.

ARTESIAN C4321 (Artesian Industries, Mansfield, Ohio), approx. $70. Water usage: 3.8 gal. Water exchange judged fair. Tank is insulated to reduce sweating during warm, humid weather.

BRIGGS CONSERVER 6280 (Briggs, Tampa, Fla.), $73. Water usage: 3.4 gal. Water exchange and ability to handle floating waste judged poor.

SEARS Cat. No. 49435 (Sears, Roebuck), $70 plus shipping. Water usage: 4.9 gal. Water exchange and ability to handle floating waste judged poor.

The home's water system

6
Saving energy on a small scale

It was inevitable that the concern over energy conservation would create a market for devices that—in theory, at least—make it easy to save energy and money. Would you like to cut the cost of running lights and electrical appliances? Just put a gadget next to the electric meter to suppress surges of current. Are you concerned about the amount of electricity you use? Meter the usage so you can figure out where to cut back. Is hot water costing you too much? Add a timer to the tank that will turn off the heater for part of the day. Do you want to lower your heating bills? Decorate a room with a gadget that will suck hot air from the ceiling and draw it down to the floor. Would you like to shrink your natural gas bills? Then turn off the range-top pilot lights and light the burners by hand each time you use them.

There are devices on the market that are supposed to do all of those things. They do function just as their manufacturers say they will—but there's often a catch. Most of them won't be of much help to you in saving energy in your home.

Some gadgets to avoid

A costly—and dubious—device

In the spring of 1977 we spotted an advertisement in the *New York Times* for the *Kill-A-Watt*, a $100 device that promised to "save up to 28 percent on electric bills." It sounded like a pretty potent weapon in the battle to save energy, so we tried to buy one. Our shopper's check was returned uncashed, however—with good reason, as we later learned.

Shortly after the *Times* ad appeared, the chairman of the New York Public Service Commission warned consumers "not to waste their money" on *Kill-A-Watt*. Then a Colorado resident wrote to Consumers Union asking about a similar device called *Powerguard*.

Kill-A-Watt, *Powerguard*, and other such devices are known as "transient surge suppressors." They're designed to hold down sudden surges of electricity in a power line. Surges up to several thousand volts do occur, but they last for only a thousandth of a second or so.

Utility companies and government agencies in at least five states have tried to defuse the selling of surge suppressors in recent years, charging that they are worthless as household energy-savers. (Such devices are used to protect utility power lines and are built into some appliances. They provide protection for electrical circuitry, not energy saving.) As one utility official put it, surges are so brief that "the additional power attributable to them is infinitesimally small and is not measured by electric meters."

That doesn't stop the promoters of surge suppressors, however. "I think there's something wrong with their [the utility companies'] meters," complained the head of the firm that marketed *Kill-A-Watt* in New York. (He also indicated that the adverse publicity had put him out of business.) "There can be some saving," the president of another surge-suppressor company told CU, "but no one can agree on the amount."

Predictably, manufacturers and utilities both have tests to support their positions, but, based on the test data we've seen, we think it's unlikely that a surge suppressor would be an effective energy-saver.

The New Jersey attorney general shares that view. In a strong attack on surge suppressors, he filed fraud charges late in 1976 against the manufacturer and several distributors of the *Powerguard*. The defendants admitted no wrongdoing but did agree to refrain from making any claims about the *Powerguard*'s energy-saving capabilities in advertisements, sales approaches, sales manuals, and the like. What's more, the agreement stipulated that retail contracts and distributorship agreements would from then on include the following warning: "There is no scientific proof that the use of this product will result in appreciable reduction in electrical consumption."

Well said.

An electricity 'speedometer'

If you knew how fast you were using electricity, presumably you might

79

feel compelled to slow down the rate of consumption. And if you had the household equivalent of a speedometer—something to measure the rate of electricity consumption—it would, presumably, be a useful aid to conservation.

That's the rationale for the *Fitch Energy Monitor* (Fitch Creations, Inc., Chapel Hill, N.C.). The display unit is meant to be installed in a wall —perhaps in the kitchen or next to a thermostat. Low-voltage wiring connects the *Monitor* to two "current transformers" mounted in the house's main electric panel. The unit carried a $125 list price in mid-1978.

Numbers on the *Energy Monitor*'s face display moment-by-moment usage in dollars and cents per hour rather than kilowatts; the unit can be set to show usage at your local electric rate.

Like a car speedometer, the *Energy Monitor* is useful only when you watch it. The device itself won't reduce electricity consumption, nor will it keep a running total of the cost of electricity. It simply reminds you how much money it costs to operate lights and appliances at any given moment. It's up to you to find ways to slow down the rate of consumption and thus lower your monthly utility bill. And the *Energy Monitor* may not be much help in deciding where or how to save.

Heaters, stoves, refrigerators, freezers, and other appliances that change temperatures use most of the electrical energy in a home. However, they generally cycle on and off by themselves, which will affect the *Energy Monitor*'s readings and give you a confusing picture of electric consumption.

Suppose, for example, the *Energy Monitor* says you're using 40 cents per hour worth of electricity while running the central air conditioning and household appliances. "Too expensive," you say, so you shut off the air conditioner—only to see the *Energy Monitor* read 41 cents. Does that mean your attempt to save energy backfired? Not at all. An appliance cycling on at that moment would account for the increase in consumption. Turning off the air conditioner might have saved 20 cents worth of electricity per hour, but you couldn't tell that from the *Monitor*.

The device has another drawback, we found: Since it computes costs on the basis of dollars per hour, it can distort the cost of electricity. Suppose you use an electric fry pan to make a pot roast. Let's say that the fry pan is rated at 1000 watts, that the kitchen has two 100-watt lights, and (for simplicity's sake) that you pay 10 cents per kilowatt-hour for electricity. The lights will use a steady 2 cents worth of electricity per hour, but the fry pan will cycle on and off to maintain the proper cooking temperature. If the pan is actually heating for only 12 minutes per hour, it too will consume 2 cents worth of energy each hour. But that's not what the *Energy Monitor* will tell you. To be sure, the device will show 2 cents when the lights alone are on. But it will report usage at 12 cents when the pan is heating. That's because it will report the pan's hourly rate of consumption as if the pan were on for the full hour, not its actual usage.

A household cost-of-energy meter could be useful. A recent study indicated that people can save energy if they can obtain consistent, believable information about the way they use it. But meters that provide this information will be useful only if certain conditions are met: They must give accurate, realistic readings of average energy costs for appliances that cycle on and off; they must be capable of evaluating the rate of energy consumption of a specific appliance.

In CU's judgment, the *Energy Monitor*'s digital display doesn't provide the right kind of information. And $125 (plus installation by a licensed electrician) is a lot to pay for a device of questionable usefulness.

"Electricity Miser" isn't very stingy

If an electric water heater operating around the clock costs, say, $450 a year to run, it should be possible to save $150 a year by shutting off the heater for eight hours a day. That, at least, is the theory behind the *Electricity Miser* (Micro Lambda, Inc., Winter Park, Fla.), a device that turns an electric water heater on and off every day at specified times.

We bought a *Miser* to test (it sold for $50 in March 1977) and found that, properly wired into an electric water heater's circuit, it will indeed turn a water heater on and off twice a day at preset times. Unfortunately, that probably won't save you much money.

Electric water heaters are extremely efficient, so there's not much you can do to reduce the cost of heating the water in the first place. Any saving would have to come out of the cost of storing the heated water. What's more, electric water heaters are shut down virtually all the time that hot water is being stored. They cycle "on" only for relatively brief periods to keep the water hot. Our test unit, for example, stored hot water with "on" periods of about twelve minutes and "off" cycles of roughly five hours each. The average cost of keeping our tankful of water hot: 18 cents a day, or about $67 a year (at 3.8 cents per kwh). Costs will vary somewhat, depending on how hot your water is, the room temperature around the water heater, and the cost of electricity in your area. The rest of the annual cost comes from heating cold water to replace the hot water you use.

You could save a few pennies by shutting the heater off for eight hours a day just before the tank is drained of hot water—something that might occur if you did several laundry loads in succession. That would save 6 cents a day *at most*, or nearly $23 a year, on our test unit. But running your heater this way means you would be without hot water not only for eight hours but also for the two hours or so it takes to heat a tank of cold water. That could be very inconvenient. Of course, you could reduce the "off" cycle to get hot water earlier, but that would also reduce your already small saving.

It won't help at all to shut down the heater with the tank full of hot water. The cost of recovering the heat lost during an eight-hour "off" cycle will just about cancel any saving you make during storage.

In CU's judgment, any significant reduction in energy costs due to this device would be as a result of reduced availability of hot water—a sort of mechanical rationing.

In our judgment, you'd be much better off if you followed the advice we give in Chapter 5: Add insulation to your heater; lower the heater's thermostat setting, thereby cutting down the amount of electricity needed to heat the water; or reduce the amount of hot water you use in the first place.

Heat circulators

Since hot air rises, it's logical to assume that the air in a room will be warmer at the ceiling than at the floor. People don't spend much time on the ceiling, though, so the heat up there isn't doing anyone very much good. But if the hot air from the upper part of a room could be moved down near the floor, it would equalize the room temperature. The result: The heating system would need to run less often, thereby saving all the fuel it took to overheat the air at the ceiling.

That's the rationale behind two heat circulating devices CU has tested. The *Nautilus Heat Recycler* (Nautilus Div., Broan Mfg. Co., Hartford, Wis.), $42, and the *Thermocycler*, (Western Magnum Corp., Hermosa Beach, Calif.), $50 plus shipping (prices as of September 1978). Both devices consist of a plastic base containing a motorized fan, plus duct sections which, when assembled, reach from floor to ceiling. Extra duct sections are available to accommodate rooms that have high ceilings; existing duct sections can be trimmed to fit rooms with low ceilings.

The heat circulators work—to the extent that the fans will pull air from the ceiling down to the floor at a rate of 10 to 15 cubic feet of air per minute. But we doubt that either device will lower your heating bills.

The *Thermocycler*'s instructions imply that a "typical" room can have a temperature difference of 30°F or more between ceiling and floor, and both devices claim to reduce the difference to about 5°. Based on our tests, though, we think a 30° difference is a gross exaggeration. We measured the temperatures in several rooms at the homes of CU staffers and friends of staffers. None of the rooms we checked had ceiling-to-floor temperature differences any greater than 5°.

We set up the heat reclaimers in those rooms anyway, just to see if they could move a noticeable amount of heat. They couldn't. The occupants of those rooms were unable to perceive any difference, nor could we measure any.

If we could have found a room with a 10° temperature difference, the heat circulators would have moved the equivalent of 110 to 160 Btu of heat per hour from ceiling to floor. But 160 Btu isn't much heat. In monetary terms, 160 Btu corresponds to about 0.2 cents of electric heat, or about 0.04 cents of gas heat.

And even if a room had a 30° temperature difference— which we judge to be extremely unlikely under normal conditions—the *Heat Recycler* or the *Thermocycler* would only match the heat output of a 150-watt electric space heater.

In CU's judgment, these heat circulators make poor energy-saving investments. A small electric fan can move much more air than either the *Heat Recycler* or the *Thermocycler*, and for a much lower initial cost. Note, too, that a room with large ceiling-to-floor temperature differences is likely to be a room that's poorly insulated or drafty. Insulation, caulking, weather stripping—or even a set of draperies—would be more effective than a heat recirculator in improving the comfort of that room.

Igniters for gas ranges

Let's say you're already saving gas by turning down your thermostat in the winter and your water heater all year round. Now you're thinking of turning off the pilot lights on your gas range and lighting the burners with matches—or with one of the igniting gadgets that campers use. Is it worth the trouble and inconvenience? That depends.

You will save gas. But if you're expecting a significant saving, forget it. For one thing, you should turn off only the range-top pilots. (Most oven-broilers have an ignition system that can't easily be turned on and off manually.) Furthermore, pilot lights are efficient sources of heat, and keeping them turned off in the wintertime could actually raise your heating bill a few pennies a month.

Even in warm weather, you won't save much by shutting off the pilots. With typical gas rates, you may cut your gas bill by 20 to 40 cents a month, depending on how your pilots are set. Of course, if you have air conditioning, it won't have to work quite as hard if the pilot lights are out. Assuming a kitchen that is air conditioned eight hours a day, you could figure on cutting another 20 to

40 cents a month from your electric bill.

Shutting off a pilot light is not a difficult job. Note, however, that any tampering with a gas range involves some hazard. Paying a service technician to shut off the pilots probably wouldn't be worth the expense. And so, if you decide to do the job yourself, keep in mind the following: Each pilot has a screw that controls the flow of gas. To shut the pilot off, the screw should be turned clockwise with a screwdriver as far as it will go, but don't force it. Be sure the gas is fully off by applying a drop of soapy water to the pilot orifice and watching for bubbles.

Once the pilot lights are shut off, you'll have to light the burners by hand. You can do that with matches, an old kitchen practice. Storing and using matches in the kitchen involve hazards that can be avoided, but as our tests showed, not all igniters are absolutely danger-free either.

To judge their comparative convenience and safety in the kitchen, CU gathered twelve such igniters ranging in price from $2 to $12 (as of February 1978). We tested three general types, all easily hand-held and weighing well under a pound.

Piezoelectric. Six of the models tested have piezoelectric crystals, which produce a spark when they're struck or bent by a triggering device. We judged most such models to be especially easy to use, although they make a noise that some people may find objectionable. They also have no parts that require periodic replacement.

Sparker. Three of the igniters we tested use a flint—the type used in cigarette lighters—to produce a shower of sparks. Such models require a new flint from time to time, but flints are readily available for a few cents apiece.

Glow plug. Three of the models we tested rely on batteries to heat a shielded filament, or glow plug; the hot filament ignites the gas. Two of those models use a pair of C or D cells. (A pair of alkaline C or D cells costs about $1.50.) The third glow-plug model, the *Star Lite Universal Gas Igniter*, requires a battery that we found difficult to buy locally. And for each sample of that model we bought, the battery that came with it was exhausted. (Extra batteries are available from the manufacturer for $1.50 plus shipping.)

On all three igniters of this type, the glow plugs themselves may have to be replaced sooner or later. Acquiring spares from the manufacturing source through the mails may take a couple of weeks (and cost about 50¢ each).

The glow-plug-type igniters could light liquified petroleum (LP) gas satisfactorily but were relatively slow to ignite natural gas. The other two varieties of igniter worked well on both types of gas.

Performance and safety

Our most important tests were to see how easily each igniter could light a gas burner. Engineering evaluations were supplemented by the judgments of staff panelists, who tried various models in our laboratory. Another group of panelists tried samples at home and used them with their own ranges.

All the igniters proved capable of lighting gas burners, but ease of use was very much a matter of personal preference. Some panelists said they would prefer to use matches instead. Other panelists said they found igniters were convenient to use. But every igniter was liked by at least one test panelist—and disliked by at least one other panelist.

In durability tests, we dropped the igniters three feet onto a vinyl-covered floor. We dropped each model ten times and noted any damage after each drop. Some models are noted in the Ratings as being more likely than most to sustain impact damage.

We also placed the tip of each igniter in a gas flame for one minute, simulating a situation that could occur if the igniter were accidentally left on a range top. Eight models suffered melting or other heat damage.

We checked each piezoelectric model for shock hazard by holding the tip against the skin of volunteer staff members and firing away. In all cases, they could barely feel it. Also in the interest of safety, we asked volunteers to jab their fingers against the tips of the glow-plug models. Burns, we concluded, were very unlikely. The outside of the glow plug doesn't get hot, and the holes in the glow plug are too small to permit even a child's finger to reach the hot filament.

The sparks from a flint-type igniter weren't judged hazardous to one's skin—but they could be a hazard to one's eyes. They could also be a fire hazard; we were able to ignite facial tissues with them. It would be unwise to use flint-type igniters where children might mistake them for toys.

Note that both natural and liquified petroleum (LP) gas—the fuels commonly used in gas ranges—are highly explosive and should be treated with plenty of respect regardless of which igniter you use. If you turn off the range pilot lights, be certain that all members of the household know it. Don't turn on the burner until you have the igniter in place, ready to use. If the burner doesn't light within a few seconds, turn it off and air out the area. Don't turn on the burner at all if you smell gas; find the source of the leak before you strike a spark.

Recommendations

The piezoelectric igniters have an important edge in convenience. They have no parts to replace, and they require no fuel. The sparker-type models, as a class, are the cheapest to buy. But they need a new flint every once in a while. And if they're misused, their hot sparks can be a hazard. Glow-plug igniters were slow to ignite natural gas, and they require new batteries every now and then.

If you consider buying one of these igniters, you'll find the best selection at stores that carry camping equipment or in catalogues that are aimed at the camping and scientific markets.

Ratings: Igniters for gas ranges

Listed, except as noted, in order of estimated overall quality. Prices are list as of February 1978.

Brand and Model	Price	Type	Comments
NTK HANDY LIGHTER (National Instrument Inc., 4119 Fordleigh Road, Baltimore 21215)	$9.50 plus shipping	Piezoelectric	Damaged in drop test but remained operable.
DATOR GAS LIGHTER (Terraillon Corp., Central Islip, N.Y.)	$11.00	Piezoelectric	Damaged slightly in drop test but remained operable. Rendered inoperable in burner-flame test. Also available, as Cat. No. 505, from Discovery House, 17241 Murphy Ave., Irvine, Calif. 92715; $11 plus shipping.

■ *The following four models were judged approximately equal in overall quality. Listed in order of increasing price.*

Brand and Model	Price	Type	Comments
TASCO SHOOT-A-LITE (Turner and Seymour Mfg. Co., Torrington, Conn.)	$2.19	Sparker	Not recommended in homes where children might consider it a toy.
COGHLAN'S CAMP STOVE LIGHTER (Coghlan's Ltd., Winnipeg, Canada)	$3.65	Sparker	Quieter than most. Not recommended in homes where children might consider it a toy. Supplied with 3 spare flints.
LANZI MATCHLESS GAS LIGHTER (Lanzi of America Inc., NYC)	$3.95	Glow-plug	Damaged in drop test but remained operable. Batteries not supplied, but does come with spare glow plug.
VOLTA BY MAGICLICK MODEL I (D. G. Vermace Corp., Rockville, Md.)	$9.99	Piezoelectric	Damaged slightly in drop test but remained operable. Rendered inoperable in burner-flame test.

■ *The following three models were judged approximately equal in overall quality. Listed in order of increasing price.*

Brand and Model	Price	Type	Comments
WONDER UNIVERSAL GAS IGNITERS (Wonder Corp. of America, Stamford, Conn.)	$4.00	Glow-plug	Damaged slightly in drop test but remained operable. Rendered inoperable in burner-flame test. Batteries not supplied, but comes with spare glow plug.
SPARK GUN II (Vernitron Piezoelectric Div., Bedford, Ohio)	$5.95	Piezoelectric	Noisier than most. Damaged in burner-flame test but remained operable.
PRIMUS SOLID STATE SAFETY IGNITER (Century Tool and Mfg. Co., Cherry Valley, Ill.)	$7.99	Piezoelectric	Essentially similar to *Spark Gun II*, preceding. Also available, as Cat. No. 72282, from Sears, Roebuck; $5.95 plus shipping.

■ *The following model was judged lower in overall quality than those preceding.*

Brand and Model	Price	Type	Comments
FUEGO SPARASCINTILLE (Universal, Firenze, Italy)	$12.00 plus shipping	Piezoelectric	Quieter than most. Damaged in burner-flame test but remained operable (available in this country as Cat. No. 61081, from Edmund Scientific, 1777 Edscorp Bldg., Barrington, NJ 08007).

■ *The following two models were judged approximately equal in overall quality. Listed in order of increasing price.*

Brand and Model	Price	Type	Comments
PRIMUS CAMPERS FLINT IGNITER (Century Tool and Mfg. Co.)	$3.32	Sparker	Rendered inoperable in burner-flame test; sample failed during home-use test. Not recommended in homes where children might consider it a toy. Supplied with 3 spare flints.
STAR LITE UNIVERSAL GAS IGNITER (Wonder Corp. of America)	$4.50	Glow-plug	Rendered inoperable in burner-flame test. Battery supplied in each tested sample was exhausted as received; replacement batteries may be hard to obtain locally.

7
If you must seek professional help

Unless you're an extremely unhandy person, you can handle many energy-saving home improvements—caulking, weather stripping, even some types of insulation—yourself. And if you're a deft handler of tools and materials, you can do a fair amount of remodeling without outside help. Still, there are some jobs that you'll probably want to leave to professional contractors—roofing, siding, or structural changes to the house, for instance. Many local codes *require* professionals to do wiring and plumbing, or to maintain the heating and cooling system. In all, homeowners paid more than $30 billion for home improvements in 1977—but not all of that money was well spent.

The home improvement industry is a chronic source of consumer problems, including shoddy work, jobs left unfinished, and contractors who damage more property than they improve. Nationwide, home repairs have consistently ranked second to automobiles as a source of complaints, according to a Federal survey of local consumer protection agencies. In 1975, the last year the survey was made, home repairs accounted for 10 percent of all complaints. In California, the board that licenses contractors had received twice as many complaints about home improvement contractors in 1977 as it had the previous year.

The problems vary in kind and in size. One homeowner, who lives in suburban Port Chester, New York, has had some relatively small but typical problems with contractors over the years. "We hired a sort of general handyman to finish a playroom in the basement," he told Consumers Union. "He hired another guy to install a gas heater, and we had no end of trouble getting the man back to adjust it. The contractor who put up new siding for us did a decent job, but his idea of cleanup was different from ours. He must have left a bushel of stuff behind."

The wise consumer need not be totally helpless in the home improvement market. If you need to hire a contractor, follow these steps in choosing a contractor and in negotiating the contract.

1. Choose a contractor

Get names of contractors from friends, neighbors, people at local home centers, or your utility company. Call in at least three contractors. Prepare yourself for the contractor's initial sales calls by writing down a rough set of specifications for the job you have in mind. List the work to be done, the kinds of materials you'd like to use, and so on. You should expect to alter and refine those specifications in the course of discussing the work with the contractors. But writing down a description of the work can help you decide what you *really* want a contractor to do, and thus help you resist a sales pitch for extra work.

Don't expect to close the deal on the contractor's first visit. Discuss the work you want done, go over your rough specifications, and take note of any modifications or suggestions the contractor makes. As one remodeler told CU, "This is a time to pick the contractor's brains, not just to shop for price."

The contractor may give you a very rough cost estimate on the first visit. If the preliminary price seems reasonable, ask for a precise estimate—both for the amount of money the job will cost and the amount of time it will take to do the work. It's also essential to get the names of previous customers. (A useful practice is to look for jobs similar to the work you have planned.) Even though a contractor isn't likely to give you the name of a dissatisfied customer, a check of references is the only effective way to judge a contractor.

Visit those homes, look over the work, and talk with the homeowners. You should ask if the job was started and completed on time, and if the actual cost exceeded the estimate. (If it did, find out why.) Find out if the family is pleased with the job, and whether the contractor has been willing to fix things that weren't done right the first time. Ask, too, if the contractor stayed around to supervise the workers, or if the contractor's main interest was in collecting the fee.

Once you've checked the contractor's past customers, contact the licensing bureau (if licenses are required where you live) or the consumer protection office in your area. Those agencies are not likely to recommend one contractor over another, but you should be able to learn if any complaints have been filed against a contractor, the nature of those complaints, and how they were resolved. While one or two complaints shouldn't alarm you, a string of similar problems should make you hesitate to hire that contractor.

If the contractor passes muster, then you're ready to sit down and put your agreement in writing. Go over the job specifications carefully; be sure you understand what the contractor will do and when it will be done. Then discuss the financing, the schedule of payments, and other provisions that should be written into the contract.

2. Get it in writing

A written contract is essential for expensive work. It's also important even for small home improvement jobs, because problems can easily arise on simple or inexpensive projects. The contractor may well have a preprinted form ready for your signature, but you should consider it only a starting point for negotiations. An analysis of several such forms, which was prepared for CU in mid-1977 by the National Consumer Law Center (NCLC), shows that those contracts have one aspect in common: They leave a lot to be desired from the homeowner's point of view.

Nearly all states have laws covering home improvement contracts in one way or another. Typically, those laws govern financing by including home improvements in consumer credit, truth-in-lending, or retail installment-sales statutes. However, fewer than one-third of the states have laws directed specifically at home improvement contractors or contracts. Some cities and counties have their own laws, which are often stricter than state laws. It's impossible to catalogue all the state and local laws here; if you need specific information, you should consult a consumer protection agency, local licensing bureau, the state attorney general, or a lawyer.

And when it comes time to negotiate a contract, be sure you consider the following important points.

Everything in writing. The contract should include—in writing—everything you've discussed with the contractor. A typical clause would say, "This instrument sets forth the entire contract between the parties and may be modified only by a written instrument executed by both parties." But before you sign a contract with that kind of clause, be sure the contract does have everything in black and white. If the contractor sweetens the sales pitch by offering extras that you want, see that they are included in the job specifications; otherwise, you might not get them. This clause also protects you if the contractor tries to add on delivery charges or other costs once work has begun.

Complete job specifications. A former contractor, who now works for the California board that licenses contractors, told CU: "I used to spell out everything in my contracts—even the size of the nails I'd use. It protected me as well as the homeowner." That much detail might be carrying things too far, but the principle is correct. The contract should be specific. For example: "Mineral wool insulation, rated R-19, to be blown into place between joists in attic floor." That's much better than specifications that say merely, "insulate attic." The contract should also specify brand names, colors, grades, styles, and model numbers for appliances and materials. If an architect's or engineer's drawings are required, be sure they're attached to the contract form and cited in the specifications.

Starting and completion dates. Both are essential, since they tell you when the work will take place—and, in some cases, they tell the contractor when to expect payment. Yet when the NCLC did its analysis, only four states (California, Florida, Maryland, and Wisconsin) and the District of Columbia had laws requiring that home improvement contracts specify starting and completion dates.

The contract should allow for reasonable delay beyond the control of the contractor, however (such as a spell of bad weather that keeps roofers from doing their job), and most contractors will insist on a clause that gives them some leeway. But a contract that allows for delays "due to fire, strikes, war, riots or other civil disturbances, governmental regulations or prohibitions, material or labor shortages, accidents, lockouts, force majeure, acts of God, adverse weather conditions, or any other cause or condition beyond the control of the contractor" excuses almost every kind of foot-dragging.

You can try to keep a contractor on schedule by including in the contract a sentence that says "all time limits in the contract are of the essence of the contract." You should note that this clause also obligates you to pay the contractor on schedule if the work is proceeding without delay. Another way to keep work delays to a minimum is to insert a clause allowing you to withhold final payment if the work slows up for no apparent reason. A hold-back clause can help you avoid other problems as well.

Hold-back clause. A roofing and siding contractor in suburban Westchester County, New York, told CU: "A contractor is going to fight like hell to get his money when the job's complete." Still, you should insist on making the final payment 30 days or so after the contractor finishes the work. That allows you to live with the improvements—and gives the contractor an excellent incentive to come back to fix anything that wasn't done right the first time. A hold-back clause can also protect you against other problems, such as unreasonable delays or liens against your property. (Liens are discussed in more detail below.)

A strong hold-back clause would say: "Final payment shall be due ___ business days after completion of work by contractor. Final payment may be withheld on account of defective work that is not remedied; claims filed; failure of the contractor to make payments properly to subcontractors or for labor, materials, or equipment; or unsatisfactory prosecution of the work by the contractor." (The last phrase, "unsatisfactory prosecution of the work," is intended to cover unreasonable delays.)

Modifications. One contract the NCLC looked at said, "I have read the above contract. I agree to pay for any additional work not stated in the above contract." Avoid that kind of language at all costs. It gives the contractor the right to charge you for work you didn't want and may not need. The contract should make clear that you and the contractor must agree on changes in the job specifications—and the cost of those changes—before any extra work can be started. (Keep in mind that asking for changes once the work has begun can cost a lot more money than you might think.) A suitable clause would say: "This contract can be modified only if the homeowner and the contractor sign a later agreement which sets forth the changes agreed to. If there are any work modifications, the resulting costs or credits to the homeowner will be included in that agreement."

Schedule of payments. Most state laws that cover payment schedules say only that the schedule shall be written into the contract. California's home improvement law is more explicit. It generally limits down payments to $100 or 1 percent of the contract price, whichever is greater; it also specifies that additional payments will reflect the cost of work actually done. If you can, incorporate that principle into your contract, negotiating a schedule that paces the payment to the work. "Never let the contractor get ahead of you," as one official put it. For example, if you're having the attic insulated and finished, you might give the contractor a small down payment, with the balance to be paid in four installments, as follows: the first when materials are delivered, the second when the insulation is installed, the third when the attic needs only a coat of paint to be fully finished, and the final payment *after* the job is completed to your satisfaction.

If the contractor is arranging financing for the improvements, the contract must conform to the Federal Truth-in-Lending laws. Among other things, Truth-in-Lending gives you the right to cancel the contract without penalty at least three business days after you sign it, if your house is being used as loan collateral. The law also requires that the contract spell out the interest rate in terms of the annual percentage rate (APR), the cash price plus the finance charge, and the amount of each payment.

Permits and variances. You may encounter contract language that says, "Buyer will identify boundary lines and be responsible for obtaining all necessary permits and zoning variations before commencement of work." It's better, we think, to give that task to the contractor. A suitable clause could say: "The contractor shall secure all permits, fees, and licenses necessary for the execution of the work. Further, the contractor shall give all notices and comply with all laws, ordinances, rules, regulations, and orders of any public authority bearing on the performance of the work."

Protection against liens. Just because you've paid the contractor doesn't mean that the money has been passed on to subcontractors or suppliers. If a contractor fails to pay suppliers, they can slap a lien (called a *mechanic's* or *materialman's* lien) on your house. In effect, the lien gives suppliers the right to take your property (or some of it, at least) as payment. Some states require home improvement contracts to include a warning about such liens. Mere notification is better than nothing, but you should try to get a contract that offers some protection as well. One way to do that is to hold up the final payment until the contractor offers evidence that no liens will be filed. Such a clause might say: "Final payment shall not be due until the contractor has delivered to the homeowner a complete release of all liens arising out of the contract, or receipts in full covering all labor, materials, and equipment for which a lien could be filed." A second option is to require the contractor to post a bond that would protect you against any liens. Homeowners have a right to demand that kind of bond in Hawaii and Louisiana, the two states with laws specifically covering mechanic's liens in home improvement agreements.

Liability coverage. According to the NCLC's survey, six states—Florida, Maine, Michigan, New Jersey, Pennsylvania, and Wisconsin—require contractors to carry insurance to cover liability, workers' compensation claims, or both. Whether required by law or not, it's advisable to deal with a contractor who carries adequate insurance. The contractor should offer proof of insurance, and the contract should specify that you're protected if claims should arise.

Warranty on the work. A contractor should be willing to back up the quality of the work in writing, by including a warranty in the contract. Some of the contracts the NCLC examined, however, included no warranties, while others offered only the vague assurance that "Contractor will do all of said work in a good, workmanlike manner." A stronger clause would say: "The contractor shall remedy any defects which appear during the progress of the work. Contractor warrants the work to be performed under this contract to be free from defects in material and workmanship for a period of ___ years from the date of completion. This provision applies to work done by subcontractors as well as to work done by the contractor's employees."

Several contractors we spoke with said homeowners should expect at least a one-year warranty on the work. Still, the duration of the warranty will depend on the nature of the work and your ability to negotiate with the contractor. Manufacturers of shingles and siding, for example, generally warranty their products for fifteen years or more. A contractor should provide a commensurate warranty on the installation of those materials.

Be sure, too, that the contractor gives you the manufacturers' written warranties that accompany fixtures, appliances, or other products.

Cleanup. If the contractor's form contract says, "Rubbish removal is homeowner's responsibility," have that clause changed. Insist on a clause that puts the burden of clean-

86   If you must seek professional help

ing up on the contractor. Such a clause often requires the contractor to leave the premises in "broom-clean condition."

Credits and returns. Some of the contracts the NCLC examined included clauses that read: "Any surplus materials remain the property of the contractor. No credit is due the homeowner on returns." It's better, we think, to have a clause that reads, "The surplus material that can be returned to the supplier will be credited to the homeowner." If it's not going to be used, you shouldn't have to pay for it.

Cancellation rights. Some states and cities have laws that give you a cooling-off period (similar to the provisions of the Federal Truth-in-Lending laws) that allows you a few days to review the contract and, if you wish, cancel it without penalty. If you're unsure of the law in your area, contact the local consumer protection agency or your state attorney general. If a cooling-off period is required, be sure the contract includes it.

Some contracts may also contain a "liquidated-damages" provision—in effect, a penalty clause if you decide to cancel after a cooling-off period expires. One such provision says, "Homeowner agrees that in event of cancellation of this contract before work is started, homeowner shall pay to contractor on demand 25 percent of the contract price as its stipulated damages for the breach." In other words, if you signed a contract for a $4000 job and canceled four days later (after the cooling-off period had lapsed), it would cost you $1000 to back out. A provision that's much less damaging, from your point of view, would say, "The contractor is entitled to 5 percent of the cash price, but no more than $100, if the homeowner cancels this contract more than three business days after it was signed, but before materials had been delivered or work had started." Liquidated-damages provisions are illegal in Michigan. Florida, Pennsylvania, and Wisconsin put ceilings on the amount of damages a contractor can demand. Again, be sure to find out what local law says before signing a contract with a liquidated-damages provision.

Keep in mind that a contractor can sue for actual damages if, at some point, you fail to meet your contractual obligations.

3. Read, then sign and stay alert

Read all documents carefully; you may want an attorney to review the contract and any other forms before you sign them. In any event, do not sign a "certificate of completion" (or a document by any other name that says the work has been completed to your satisfaction) until the work has actually been finished and you have inspected it carefully. In some states, including California and Texas, it is illegal for a contractor to have a certificate of completion signed in advance. In Florida, the certificate of completion includes a release of all mechanic's liens.

Taking the time to find a reputable contractor and including a hold-back clause in the contract will help ensure that the contractor finishes the work on time and does the job properly. Still, there's always the risk that the contractor won't follow the specifications called for in the contract. The contractor may also cut corners, even though the workers appear to be doing their job correctly. Those shortcomings might not be revealed for weeks, or months—long after the contractor has been paid in full.

Granted, it's impractical to watch every move the work crew makes. But if the workers do something that doesn't look right, clear up the problem right away; don't wait until the job's completed to raise questions or lodge complaints. You might also try one remodeling expert's method for keeping contractors on their toes: Take pictures of the work.

8

Government response to conservation

The Carter Administration's National Energy Act is not the Federal Government's first energy conservation effort. Two measures—the Energy Policy and Conservation Act, enacted in December 1975, and the Energy Conservation and Production Act, enacted in August 1976—established a number of Federal programs. Those that affect consumers directly include appliance efficiency standards, rate-reform demonstration projects for utility companies, and mandatory fuel economy standards for automobiles. The acts also authorized the Federal Government to oversee and help finance voluntary conservation programs in the states. According to a Department of Energy report issued in December 1977, those state programs alone are expected to cut the nation's energy usage by 6.7 percent in 1980.

The National Energy Act, as proposed, would enhance those existing efforts. It includes two sections intended to encourage saving energy in the home: one offering tax credits to homeowners who make energy-saving home improvements or who invest in solar energy equipment; another requiring utilities to help homeowners save energy, by publicizing energy conservation programs, by helping homeowners find contractors to install insulation and other products, or by arranging financing for those improvements.

In addition to the incentive programs, the National Energy Act included provisions that would affect the price of oil and natural gas for the next few years. Political wrangling over those sections of the Act has been intense, to say the least. As a result, Congress had not yet approved the National Energy Act in August 1978, when this book went to press. It's anybody's guess when the Act will actually take effect or exactly what provisions it will contain.

Nevertheless, the Federal Government already has several grant and loan programs in operation, most designed to help low-income families pay for insulation, storm windows, and other products.

The information that follows summarizes those Federal programs, as well as a small but important number of the energy conservation laws enacted at the state level since 1975.*

Federal conservation programs

Department of Housing and Urban Development (HUD)

Title I Property Improvement Loan Insurance Program

Allows banks, savings and loans, credit unions, and other qualified lenders to make loans, at an interest rate of 12 percent, for fifteen years for home improvements. Maximum loan: $15,000. To qualify, persons must meet lender's criteria. For more information, contact a loan officer at your bank, savings and loan association, or any other FHA-approved lending institution.

Community Development Block Grant Programs

Nearly 1500 localities have budgeted a total of $500 million for property rehabilitation. Aid can be in the form of direct grants, direct loans, loan subsidies, or rebates to property owners. Maximum amount of aid: varies. Programs generally targeted to low-income persons who live in designated neighborhood areas. For more information, contact a regional or area HUD office (listed in the telephone directory). HUD also publishes a "Directory of Localities with Community Development Block Grant Property Rehabilitation Financing Activities." It's available at local HUD offices or from HUD, Publications Service Center, Room B-237, 451 7th Street, N.W., Washington, D.C. 20410.

*The summaries that follow were drawn primarily from information supplied to Consumers Union in the spring of 1978 by various Federal agencies and by state governors and energy conservation offices. We have also relied on a catalogue of state energy conservation laws compiled by the National Conference of State Legislatures. Wherever possible, we have included addresses for agencies that administer the programs we describe. Readers should contact those agencies directly for detailed information about specific programs.

Section 312 Rehabilitation Loan Program

Some three hundred localities administer such programs, which provide direct loans to certain individuals at 3 percent interest for twenty years. Maximum amount of loan: $27,000 per housing unit. To qualify, properties must be located within Federally designated urban renewal, Concentrated Code Enforcement, or Community Development Block Grant areas. For more information, contact: HUD, Office of Public Affairs, Research and Production, Room 9243, Washington, D.C. 20410.

Farmers Home Administration (FmHA)

Section 502 Weatherization Loans

In one part of this program, participating utility cooperatives, such as the Rural Electrification Administration, make loans to co-op members at 8¼ percent interest for five years. Maximum amount of loan: $1500. To qualify, borrowers must live in rural areas and have low or moderate income. For more information, contact the local utility cooperative.

In a second part of the program, persons not served by a utility co-op can apply directly to an FmHA County Supervisor for a weatherization loan. Amount loaned will vary. To qualify, borrower's needs must exceed $1500. Other eligibility criteria described above also apply for these loans. For more information, contact the FmHA (listed in the telephone directory under United States Government, Department of Agriculture, FmHA) or the FmHA, 14th and Independence Avenues, N.W., Washington, D.C. 20250.

Section 504 Program

This program is designed to help families with very low incomes to remove safety or health hazards or repair a substandard house. Outright grants are available to the low-income elderly. Loans at 1 percent interest for twenty years are available to others. Maximum amount of loan or grant: $5000 per family. For more information, contact the FmHA, as noted above.

Department of Energy (DOE)

Weatherization Program

All states except Hawaii have these grant-in-aid programs, which are addressed to low-income persons, the elderly, and the disabled. Individual state agencies distribute funds according to criteria approved by the DOE. Maximum individual grant: $800 per family for energy conservation materials. For more information, contact the Office of Economic Opportunity for your state (list begins page 95).

Community Services Administration (CSA)

Weatherization Program

Similar to the DOE grant program, above, in many respects. Maximum individual grant: $400 per family for energy-saving materials. For more information, contact the CSA office for your region (list begins page 97).

State conservation programs

The information that follows summarizes some of the state laws designed to conserve energy. Specifically:
- *Incentive programs*, which cover tax credits, loan programs, or other inducements to invest in energy-saving products.
- *Utility rate reform*, which includes special rate schedules for the poor or the elderly, new rates designed to promote conservation, and so on. (A number of legislatures have gone only so far as to authorize studies of rate reform; we have omitted them from this summary. In addition, we have omitted rate reforms that apply only to a single utility.)
- *Building codes and standards*, which include conservation guidelines added to building codes, as well as standards for solar energy equipment, insulation, and air conditioners and other appliances. Rather than include specific provisions from each state's code, we have, for the most part, simply noted those states that have adopted energy-efficiency standards. If you, or a contractor or architect you've hired, need more information, contact the local building inspector or the state energy office.

Alabama

Incentives
- Income tax exemption equal to cost of converting from gas or electric heat to wood heat.

Building codes and standards
- State's building commission to develop thermal-efficiency standards for new buildings.

Alaska

No applicable laws.

Arizona

Incentives
- Income tax credit of 25 percent (with $100 maximum) of the cost of certain types of insulating and ventilating equipment; credit available until December 31, 1984.
- Income tax credit of 35 percent (with $1000 maximum) of the cost and installation of solar heating and cooling equipment; maximum amount of credit decreases by 5 percent per year until 1984, when it is scheduled to be repealed entirely.
- Solar energy devices exempted from property, sales, and use taxes.
- Cost of solar energy equipment can be amortized over thirty-six months when reporting income for state tax purposes.

Building codes and standards
- State's corporation commission to

develop specifications for the certification of "intermittent ignition" devices as an alternative to standing pilot lights. Bans sale of new "residential-type" gas appliances equipped with pilot lights twenty-four months after alternative means have been certified. Water heaters exempted from this law.

Arkansas

Incentives

• Income tax deduction equal to 100 percent of the cost of purchasing and installing energy-saving equipment, including insulation, storm windows and doors, solar energy equipment, certain kinds of ventilation equipment.
• Arkansas Power & Light, state's largest private utility, offers free "energy audits" (evaluations) and program to arrange loans to customers for energy-saving improvements, with loans to be repaid with monthly utility bills.

Utility rate reform

• Authorizes state-regulated utilities to engage in conservation programs, which include: alternative rate structures, use of equipment that can interrupt service, use of "renewable" resources, home insulation. Utilities permitted to increase rates when costs are incurred for such programs.

California

Incentives

• Income tax credit of 55 percent (up to $3000) of the cost of purchasing and installing solar energy equipment. Cost of insulation and water-saving devices can be included if installed in conjunction with solar energy system. Similar incentives offered to owners of multi-family dwellings. Credit applies to system installed between January 1, 1977, and December 31, 1980.
• Gas and electric utilities in state operating home-insulation programs. Some utilities will do actual installation and arrange financing; others will refer customers to contractors or help customers obtain estimates from qualified contractors. Certain utilities offer loans at 8 percent interest for five years to finance insulation; maximum amount of loan: $500 for single-family homes, $2500 for multiple-family dwellings.

Utility rate reform

• State's public utilities commission to designate "lifeline" amounts of gas and electricity for residential customers (amounts that satisfy minimum needs for essential uses, such as heating, lighting, and cooking). Rates for lifeline service cannot exceed rates in effect on January 1, 1976, and cannot be increased until average rates have increased 25 percent over 1976 levels.

Building codes and standards

• Energy Resources Conservation and Development Commission has established guidelines and criteria for solar energy equipment eligible for tax credit. Commission also to prescribe interim standards governing the safety of insulation sold in the state.
• Statewide energy conservation standards in effect, which cover insulation, windows, and heating and cooling equipment.
• Efficiency standards established for refrigerators, air conditioners, space heaters, water heaters, and plumbing fittings.

Colorado

Incentives

• State's housing finance authority empowered to grant loans to low- and moderate-income families for energy-saving home improvements.
• Allows income tax deduction equal to cost of installation, construction, remodeling, or purchase of solar, wind, or geothermal energy equipment.
• Solar energy systems assessed at lower rate than rest of property.
• Property tax reassessment delayed for five years for homes more than thirty years old on which conservation improvements have been made.

Building codes and standards

• Minimum statewide thermal-efficiency standards in effect, as of October 1, 1977, for new residential construction and renovation. Standards set specific R-values for insulation and require double-glazing for windows and weather stripping for doors. Building permit will not be issued unless standards are met.

Connecticut

Incentives

• Towns authorized to grant property tax exemption for installation of solar or wind energy equipment. Exemption limited to difference between assessed valuation of property that has solar equipment, and property that has conventional portion of heating/cooling system. Applies to new buildings or additions constructed between October 1, 1976, and October 1, 1991; exemption allowed for fifteen years following construction.
• Solar collectors purchased after October 1, 1977, exempted from sales tax.
• University of Connecticut Cooperative Extension Service offers information, workshops, and seminars on energy-saving products and techniques.

Building codes and standards

• Commissioner of Planning and Energy to establish standards for solar energy equipment.
• Conservation standards incorporated into state's building code.

Delaware

No applicable laws.

District of Columbia

No applicable laws.

Florida

Building codes and standards

• Local governments required to include energy-efficiency standards in building codes.

Georgia

Incentives

• Provides sales tax refunds for solar energy equipment.
• Localities authorized to exempt solar energy equipment from *ad valorem* property taxes.

90   Government response to conservation

Building codes and standards
- State code for energy conservation in new buildings includes thermal-efficiency and lighting-efficiency standards.

Hawaii

Incentives
- Income tax credit of 10 percent of cost of device for solar energy equipment. Applies to devices in service between December 31, 1974, and December 31, 1981. Credit may be carried forward if it exceeds taxpayer's liability.
- That portion of building devoted to "alternate energy improvements" exempt from property taxes. Applies to improvements that are made between June 30, 1976, and December 31, 1981.

Building codes and standards
- Each county's building code to include energy-efficiency standards.

Idaho

Incentives
- Income tax deduction equal to cost of purchase and installation of solar, wind, or geothermal energy equipment. Taxpayers can claim 40 percent of amount in first year, 20 percent per year for three years thereafter. Maximum deduction: $5000 per year.
- Income tax deduction equal to amount paid for installation of new insulation, weather stripping, storm doors, and/or storm windows in existing homes. No deduction for replacing existing insulation.

Building codes and standards
- State's optional building code supplemented with energy conservation provisions. City of Boise has separate energy conservation code for new construction.

Illinois

Incentives
- Provides property tax relief for solar energy equipment.
- Utility companies to provide loans for insulation and other energy-saving home improvements, generally at 18 percent annual interest.

Indiana

Incentives
- Allows property tax deduction for solar energy equipment. Deduction equal to value of property with equipment, minus value of property without equipment.

Building codes and standards
- State's administrative building council has adopted new lighting- and thermal-efficiency standards.

Iowa

Incentives
- Solar energy equipment exempt from property taxes for five years.

Building codes and standards
- State code modified to include performance standards for certain heating and cooling equipment, lighting standards, and insulation levels.

Kansas

Incentives
- Income tax credit of 25 percent (with $1000 maximum) for installation of solar energy equipment in homes. Credit can be carried forward for three years if amount of credit exceeds tax liability.
- Personal income tax deduction of 50 percent (with $500 maximum) for cost of labor and materials used to insulate home; insulation must meet FHA standards.
- Five-year rebate equal to 35 percent of total annual property taxes paid on building equipped with solar energy system that supplies 70 percent of building's heating and cooling needs.

Kentucky

No applicable laws.

Louisiana

No applicable laws.

Maine

Incentives
- Division of Community Services authorized to administer winterization program, with priority given to the following: low-income elderly, low-income disabled persons, other low-income groups.
- Solar energy equipment exempted from property taxes for five years from date of installation. Exemption available until January 1, 1983.
- Provides refunds of sales or use taxes paid on solar energy equipment. Refunds available until January 1, 1983.

Maryland

Incentives
- Cities and counties allowed to grant property tax credits for installation of solar energy equipment. Credits may be granted for a maximum of three years.
- Installation of solar energy equipment shall not bring on an increase in property tax assessments.

Massachusetts

Incentives
- Solar or wind energy equipment allowed property tax exemption on value that equipment adds to property. Exemption allowed for ten years following installation.

Building codes and standards
- State's building code includes requirements for insulation and other energy conservation measures for new buildings and major renovations. Code also specifies that insulation must conform to existing product standards for thermal resistance and fire safety.

Utility rate reform
- State's private utility companies required to adopt "peak load" rate structures, which reflect the costs of providing power at various times of the day and during different seasons. New rates to be optional at first, later mandatory.

Michigan

Incentives
- Property, sales, and use tax exemptions for installation of solar energy equipment. Exemptions available until January 1, 1985.
- State housing development authority to administer grants and loans to individuals who wish to purchase energy conservation materials.

State conservation programs 91

Minnesota

Incentives
- State's housing finance agency to make loans to low- and moderate-income families for energy-saving improvements.
- Property tax exemption for solar and wind energy systems, and for agriculturally derived methane energy systems installed prior to 1984.
- Several utility companies offer household energy audits, various types of home insulation programs.

Building codes and standards
- Statewide building code, which includes conservation standards, now mandatory. Code includes standards of performance for solar energy equipment; sellers are required to disclose the extent to which their equipment meets those standards.
- Commissioner of Administration to promulgate minimum energy-efficiency standards for existing residential buildings.
- State energy agency to promulgate rules covering quality and product safety specifications for insulation. Insulation offered for sale to be subject to continuing inspection and follow up by approved laboratories. Insulation that presents a "clear and present danger by the nature of its composition" to be banned from sale.
- Sale of room air conditioners with Energy Efficiency Ratio (EER) of less than 7 banned after January 1, 1978.
- Sellers of homes required to provide "energy disclosure statements" to buyers after October 1, 1979.

Mississippi

No applicable laws.

Missouri

No applicable laws.

Montana

Incentives
- Tax credit of up to $250 for installation of solar or other alternate energy equipment. Credit can be claimed until 1982.
- Property tax deduction of up to $1800 for energy-saving improvements or installation of "alternate energy source." Does not apply to improvements financed by government or private grants.
- Two utility companies, in conjunction with state energy office, conducting home energy audit in 1978; audit will tell homeowners estimated saving through insulation, storm windows, and other measures.

Building codes and standards
- Model energy-saving code which includes requirements for insulation and other energy conservation measures for new construction.

Nebraska

No applicable laws.

Nevada

Incentives
- Allowance against property tax for solar, wind, or other alternate energy device; allowance equal to difference between assessed value of property with system and value without system. Maximum allowance: $2000.
- State's major electric utility companies conducting home energy audits and arranging financing for homeowners who wish to install insulation.

Utility rate reform
- State's public service commission has "flattened" electric and gas utility rates, so that the cost of a basic unit of fuel stays constant as usage increases.

Building codes and standards
- State's public works department has promulgated energy conservation standards for new buildings. Standards include requirements for insulation and other measures.

New Hampshire

Building codes and standards
- Public buildings must be built to meet energy conservation standards. Governor's council on energy promoting use of those standards in other new construction.

New Jersey

Incentives
- Gas and electric utility companies offering loans for adding insulation, attic fans, or energy-saving thermostats. Maximum amount of loan: $500. No interest charged if loan repaid in ninety days; otherwise, loans granted for up to three years, at 1 percent per month.
- Many fuel oil companies in state arranging for financing and installation of insulation. Payment plans vary; aim is to have combined payment for fuel and loan not to exceed normal fuel bills.
- State's mortgage finance agency has arranged for some state banks to offer loans, at 7 percent interest for up to twelve years, for energy-saving home improvements. Program limited to families who meet income criteria. Minimum monthly payment: $10.
- Local community action agencies will insulate homes of low-income families free of charge. Priority in this program given the elderly and the disabled.
- Property tax exemption equal to assessed value of solar energy equipment.
- Solar energy systems exempt from state sales tax.

Utility rate reform
- Board of public utilities authorized to establish "lifeline" rates for senior citizens.
- Seasonal electric and gas rates established; rate schedules "flattened," so that cost of a basic unit of fuel remains constant as usage increases.

Building codes and standards
- State's energy conservation program includes standards for efficient operation of heat pumps, air conditioners, and oil-fired boilers; thermal-efficiency and lighting-efficiency standards for new and renovated buildings.
- State's gas utility companies to devise plans to replace pilot lights on existing gas furnaces and other appliances.

New Mexico

Incentives
- Income tax credit of 25 percent (with $1000 maximum) for installa-

tion of solar equipment. If credit exceeds liability, taxpayer receives a refund.

Building codes and standards
- Uniform building code includes provisions for energy conservation.

New York

Incentives
- State's electric and gas utilities mandated to perform energy audits for a nominal fee; utilities to arrange financing for insulation and other conservation measures, such as caulking, weather stripping, and energy-saving thermostats. Measures must pay for themselves through lower fuel bills within seven years and meet criteria established by state's Public Service Commission. Maximum loan: $1500 for single-family home, $2500 for two-family home, $3000 for three-family home. Interest rate: varies between roughly 9 and 10 percent, depending on utility company. Utilities required to maintain list of qualified contractors; equipment can be installed by homeowners, tenants, or contractors.
- Solar and wind energy systems exempt from property taxes for fifteen years; applies to exemption applications that are filed before July 1, 1988.

Building codes and standards
- Energy-efficiency standards established for room air conditioners and water heaters. Appliances not meeting standards cannot be sold. Refrigerators, freezers, and dishwashers required to have "power saver switch" that turns off heating element.
- Six utility companies offering loans to customers who wish to install insulation. Maximum amount of loans varies from $300 up; interest rates vary from 10 to 12 percent per year. Repayment periods range from thirty-six to sixty months.

Building codes and standards
- Statewide building code includes requirements for insulation and other energy conservation measures for new buildings and major renovations.

North Carolina

Incentives
- Personal tax credit of 25 percent (with $100 maximum) for the cost of installing insulation, storm windows, and storm doors on buildings constructed before January 1, 1977. Credit available in 1977 and 1978.
- Individual tax credit of 25 percent (with $1000 maximum) for installation of solar energy equipment that meets Federal performance criteria. Credit can be carried forward for up to three years if it exceeds tax liability.
- Buildings with solar energy equipment to be assessed for property tax as if they had conventional heating and cooling equipment; special assessment effective from January 1, 1978, to December 1, 1985.
- State's housing finance agency to guarantee conservation loans (up to $1200 per individual) to low-income persons.

Building codes and standards
- State's building code includes standards for insulation, requirements for caulking and weather stripping, and efficiency standards for water heaters. Provisions apply to houses and apartment buildings up to three stories high built after January 1, 1975.
- State's secretary of revenue to adopt rules and regulations for insulation, storm windows, and storm doors installed under tax-credit program. Products must have useful life of at least three years and meet other minimum standards.
- Contracts for installation of insulation must include provisions showing compliance with state building code requirements. Provides for local inspection of insulation. Program is subject to review by legislature in 1979.
- No utility hookup or occupancy to be allowed in buildings constructed after January 1, 1978, until building meets minimum standards for insulation in new construction.

North Dakota

Incentives
- Income tax credit of 5 percent per year, for two years, for the actual cost of purchase and installation of solar or wind energy equipment.
- Solar energy equipment exempt from property taxes for five years following installation.
- State's energy office, in conjunction with some private utility companies and rural electrical cooperatives, offering free energy audits. Montana-Dakota Utilities and the electrical cooperatives also have agreements with lending institutions to help homeowners arrange financing for home insulation.

Building codes and standards
- Statewide energy conservation standards supplement local building codes.

Ohio

Incentives
- Utility companies required to provide lists of approved insulation contractors and lenders to homeowners who wish to make energy-saving home improvements.
- Monthly credit of 25 percent (with $87.50 maximum) on utility bills available to low-income people. Credit available from December through April. State's Department of Taxation pays utilities.

Building codes and standards
- State's Board of Building Standards to set conservation standards for new one-, two-, and three-family dwellings.
- Board to set thermal-efficiency and safety standards for certain weatherization materials and heat pumps.
- Pilot lights in gas appliances banned after January 1, 1980; ban does not apply to water heaters.

Oklahoma

Incentives
- Residential tax credit of 25 percent (with $2000 maximum) for cost of solar energy equipment. Credit can be carried forward for up to five years if it exceeds tax liability.

Building codes and standards
- State's energy department to develop standards for solar energy

equipment manufactured, sold, or installed in the state. Manufacturers and sellers of solar energy equipment required to disclose test results and extent to which equipment meets or exceeds Federal standards for solar energy equipment.

Oregon

Incentives
• Investor-owned utilities, publicly owned utilities, and major fuel oil dealers to provide weatherization services to customers. Services to include information, inspection, installation of energy-saving materials, and financing. Excludes mobile-home dwellers, but includes some tenants.
• Personal income tax credit of 25 percent (with $125 maximum) for the cost of energy-saving materials installed between October 4, 1977, and January 1, 1985. Credit can be carried forward for up to five years if it exceeds tax liability. Improvements must meet conservation standards in state building code; persons receiving other weatherization aid not eligible for credit.
• Tax credit of 25 percent (with $1000 maximum) for homeowners who install solar, wind, or geothermal energy equipment. Equipment must meet state performance criteria and be certified by state. Credit can be carried forward for up to five years if it exceeds tax liability.
• Added value of solar energy equipment exempted from *ad valorem* property taxes. Applies to installation made between January 1, 1976, and January 1, 1998.
• Loans of up to $3000 available to veterans who install solar, wind, or geothermal energy equipment that provides at least 10 percent of home's energy requirements.
• Homes built before July 1, 1974, and purchased after October 1, 1977, must be weatherized as a condition of receiving veteran's loan; cost of weatherization can be added to principal of loan.
• Home weatherization refund program, for low-income elderly persons, provides up to $300 in aid per household. Persons receiving other weatherization aid are not eligible for refund.
• $50 annual refund for fuel and utility rate relief available to taxpayers at least sixty years old and with household income less than $5000.

Building codes and standards
• State Department of Commerce, in consultation with state Energy Conservation Board, to establish standards for insulation, storm windows, weather stripping, and other energy-saving items.
• Energy Conservation Board to adopt voluntary energy-efficiency rating system for single-family houses. State Department of Energy has responsibility for publicizing rating system and encouraging its use by real estate agents and other sellers.
• Department of Energy to establish performance criteria for solar, wind, and geothermal energy equipment.

Pennsylvania

No applicable laws.

Rhode Island

Incentives
• Solar heating and cooling equipment that meet Federal performance criteria to be assessed at no more than the value of conventional systems.
• Governor's energy office and Rhode Island Citizens Energy Conservation Corp. (RICEC) administering program of free energy audits; RICEC will also arrange for contractors to make energy-saving home improvements, with RICEC inspecting work upon completion. Some banks will arrange loans at preferred interest rates for homeowners who wish to make energy-saving home improvements.

Building codes and standards
• State building code amended to include energy conservation provisions for new and renovated buildings.

South Carolina

No applicable laws.

South Dakota

Incentives
• Solar, wind, and geothermal energy systems entitled to property tax credit. Credit equal to assessed value of property with the system, minus value of property without it, but not less than cost of system. Full credit available for five years, when amount of credit is reduced.

Tennessee

Incentives
• Property tax exemption for solar or wind energy equipment.

Building codes and standards
• New uniform energy-efficiency code sets minimum standards for new and renovated buildings.

Texas

Incentives
• Legislature authorized to exempt solar or wind energy equipment from sales tax.
• Several utility companies offer energy audits and will arrange financing for homeowners who wish to install insulation.

Utah

Incentives
• State's largest gas utility company will help homeowners who wish to install insulation to find a contractor; cost of work added to customer's utility bill.

Building codes and standards
• Energy conservation building code extended to cover any building requiring a building permit from any political subdivision. Code is effective January 1, 1978-December 31, 1979, and is to be repromulgated every three years. Local governments permitted to reject state code after any three-year period, if local code adopted.

Vermont

Incentives
• Income tax credit of 25 percent (with $1000 maximum) for installation of "renewable energy system."
• Towns authorized to offer property tax exemption for solar, wind, or

other "alternate" energy equipment.
• State's housing finance agency authorized to make low-interest loans to low- and moderate-income persons for energy-saving improvements, including insulation and storm windows.

Virginia

Incentives
• Property tax exemption for solar energy equipment, at the option of local governments.
• Housing development authority to establish loan program for low- and moderate-income families for the purchase and installation of energy-saving improvements including alternate energy equipment.

Building codes and standards
• State's energy code includes minimum R-values for insulation.

Washington

Incentives
• Solar energy systems that meet Federal standards are exempted from property taxes for seven years from the filing of a claim. Exemption offered until December 31, 1981.

Building codes and standards
• Minimum insulation levels established for new residential buildings.

West Virginia

No applicable laws.

Wisconsin

Incentives
• Income tax credit for alternate energy equipment; credit determined as percentage of cost of equipment, with maximum percentage declining each year until 1984.

Building codes and standards
• State to establish performance standards for solar, wind, and other alternate energy equipment.
• State's building code includes energy conservation standards for one- and two-family dwellings.

Wyoming

No applicable laws.

State offices of economic opportunity

(For information concerning DOE Weatherization Program, page 89.)

Alabama
Alabama Energy Management Board
Alabama Development Office
State Capitol
Montgomery, Alabama 36130

Alaska
Department of Community and
 Regional Affairs
Division of Community and
Rural Development
619 Warehouse Avenue
Anchorage, Alaska 99506

Arizona
Department of Economic Security
Bureau of Special Programs
111 West Osborn
Phoenix, Arizona 85015

Arkansas
Department of Local Services
Division of Community Services
971 First National Bank Building
Little Rock, Arkansas 72201

California
Office of Economic Opportunity
555 Capitol Mall, Room 325
Sacramento, California 95814

Colorado
Colorado Office of Human Resources
1550 Lincoln Street
Denver, Colorado 80203

Connecticut
Department of Community Affairs
1179 Main Street
P.O. Box 786
Hartford, Connecticut 06101

Delaware
Office of Economic Opportunity
820 North French Street, 4th Floor
Wilmington, Delaware 19801

District of Columbia
D.C. Department of Housing and
 Community Development
Office of Policy, Planning, and
 Evaluation
1325 G Street, N.W.
Washington, D.C. 20005

Florida
Department of Community Affairs
Division of Community Services
2571 Executive Center Circle East
Tallahassee, Florida 32301

Georgia
Office of Energy Resources
270 Washington Street, S.W.
Atlanta, Georgia 30334

Idaho
Office of Economic Opportunity
State House
Boise, Idaho 83720

Illinois
Office of Manpower and
 Human Development
Energy Conservation Unit
623 East Monroe
Springfield, Illinois 62706

Indiana
Office of Community Services
 Administration
20 North Meridian
Guaranty Building, 2nd Floor
Indianapolis, Indiana 46204

Iowa
Office of Economic Opportunity
Office for Planning and Programming
523 East 12th Street
Des Moines, Iowa 50319

Kansas
Office of Economic Opportunity
Social and Rehabilitation Services
535 Kansas Avenue, Room 1006
Topeka, Kansas 66603

Kentucky
Department for Human Resources
Planning Branch (SEOO)
275 East Main, 6th Floor West
Frankfort, Kentucky 40601

Louisiana
Department of Urban and
    Community Affairs
300 Louisiana Avenue
Baton Rouge, Louisiana 70802

Maine
State of Maine
Division of Community Services
State House
193 State Street
Augusta, Maine 04333

Maryland
Maryland Office of
    Economic Opportunity
1100 North Eutaw Street, Room 615
Baltimore, Maryland 21201

Massachusetts
Department of Community Affairs
Division of Social and
    Economic Opportunity
10 Tremont Street, 6th Floor
Boston, Massachusetts 02108

Michigan
Department of Commerce
Energy Administration
Law Building, 4th Floor
Lansing, Michigan 48913

Minnesota
Governor's Manpower Office
Division of Economic Opportunity
690 American Center Building
150 East Kellogg Boulevard
St. Paul, Minnesota 55101

Mississippi
Mississippi Governor's Office of
    Human Resources and
    Community Services
Barefield Complex, Suite 407
455 North Lamar
Jackson, Mississippi 39201

Missouri
Department of Natural
    Resources and Energy
P.O. Box 176
Jefferson City, Missouri 65101

Montana
Department of Community Affairs
Capitol Station
Helena, Montana 59601

Nebraska
Nebraska Energy Office
P.O. Box 95805
Lincoln, Nebraska 68509

Nevada
Office of Community Services
210 West Telegraph, Room 205
Capitol Complex
Carson City, Nevada 89701

New Hampshire
Division of Human Resources
Office of the Governor
15 North Main Street
Concord, New Hampshire 03301

New Jersey
Office of Economic Opportunity
363 West State Street
P.O. Box 2768
Trenton, New Jersey 08625

New Mexico
Office of the Governor
Community Affairs Bureau
Room 104 A, P.O. Box 2348
Pera Building
Sante Fe, New Mexico 87503

New York
New York Department of State
Division of Economic Opportunity
162 Washington Avenue
Albany, New York 12231

North Carolina
Department of Commerce
Energy Division
P.O. Box 25249
Raleigh, North Carolina 27611

North Dakota
Division of Economic Opportunity
State Capitol Building
Bismarck, North Dakota 58501

Ohio
Department of Economic and
    Community Development
P.O. Box 1001
30 East Broad Street
Columbus, Ohio 43216

Oklahoma
Department of Economic and
    Community Affairs
5500 North Western Avenue
Oklahoma City, Oklahoma 73118

Oregon
Economic Opportunity Programs
State Economic Opportunity Office
772 Commercial Street, S.E.
Salem, Oregon 97210

Pennsylvania
Bureau of Human Resources
530 South Office Building
P.O. Box 155
Harrisburg, Pennsylvania 17120

Rhode Island
State of Rhode Island
Department of Community Affairs
150 Washington Street
Providence, Rhode Island 02903

South Carolina
South Carolina Office of
    Economic Opportunity
Governor's Office
1321 Lady Street, Suite 311
Columbia, South Carolina 29201

South Dakota
State Economic Opportunity Office
Capitol Building
Pierre, South Dakota 57501

Tennessee
Community Services Administration
444 James Robertson Parkway
Nashville, Tennessee 37219

Texas
State of Texas
Department of Community Affairs
P.O. Box 13166
Capitol Station
Austin, Texas 78711

Utah
State of Utah
Department of Community Affairs
110 State Capitol
Salt Lake City, Utah 84114

Vermont
Vermont Economic
 Opportunity Office
Agency of Human Services
118 Main Street
Montpelier, Vermont 05602

Virginia
Commonwealth of Virginia
State Housing Office
6 North Sixth Street
Richmond, Virginia 23219

Washington
Washington State Economic
 Opportunity Office
400 Capitol Center Federal Building
Olympia, Washington 98504

West Virginia
West Virginia State Economic
 Opportunity Office
State Capitol Building, Room 144
Charleston, West Virginia 25305

Wisconsin
Office of Economic Opportunity
123 W. Washington Avenue,
 8th Floor
Madison, Wisconsin 53703

Wyoming
Department of Health and
 Social Services
SD PASS/WCSA
Room 361 Hathaway Office Building
Cheyenne, Wyoming 82002

Regional community services administration offices

(For information concerning CSA Weatherization Program, page 89.)

Region 1: Connecticut, Maine, Massachusetts, New Hampshire, Rhode Island, Vermont
Community Services Administration
E-400, John F. Kennedy
 Federal Building
Boston, Massachusetts 02203

Region 2: New Jersey, New York, Puerto Rico, Virgin Islands
Community Services Administration
26 Federal Plaza, 32nd Floor
New York, New York 10007

Region 3: Delaware, District of Columbia, Maryland, Pennsylvania, Virginia, West Virginia
Community Services Administration
3535 Market Street, Gateway Bldg.
Philadelphia, Pennsylvania 19104

Region 4: Alabama, Florida, Georgia, Kentucky, Mississippi, North Carolina, South Carolina, Tennessee
Community Services Administration
101 Marietta Street, N.W.
Atlanta, Georgia 30303

Region 5: Illinois, Indiana, Michigan, Minnesota, Ohio, Wisconsin
Community Services Administration
300 South Wacker Drive
 24th Floor
Chicago, Illinois 60606

Region 6: Arkansas, Louisiana, New Mexico, Oklahoma, Texas
Community Services Administration
1200 Main Street
Dallas, Texas 75202

Region 7: Iowa, Kansas, Missouri, Nebraska
Community Services Administration
911 Walnut Street
Kansas City, Missouri 64106

Region 8: Colorado, Montana, North Dakota, South Dakota, Utah, Wyoming
Community Services Administration
Federal Building, 1961 Stout Street
Denver, Colorado 80294

Region 9: Arizona, California, Hawaii, Nevada
Community Services Administration
450 Golden Gate Avenue, Box 36008
San Francisco, California 94102

Region 10: Alaska, Idaho, Oregon, Washington
Community Services Administration
1321 Second Avenue
Seattle, Washington 98101

State energy offices

Alabama
Alabama Energy Management
 Board
Alabama Development Office
3734 Atlanta Highway
Montgomery, Alabama 36130

Alaska
Alaska Department of Commerce
 and Economic Development
Division of Energy and Power
 Development
338 Denali Street
Anchorage, Alaska 99501

Arizona
Arizona Programs Office
Office of Economic Planning and
 Development
Executive Tower, Room 505
1700 West Washington
Phoenix, Arizona 85007

Arkansas
Arkansas Energy Conservation
 and Policy Office
960 Plaza West Building
Little Rock, Arkansas 72205

California
California Energy Resources
 Conservation and Development
 Commission
1111 Howe Avenue
Sacramento, California 95852

Colorado
Colorado Office of Energy
 Conservation
1410 Grant Street, B-104
Denver, Colorado 80203

Connecticut
Connecticut Office of Policy
 and Management
340 Capitol Avenue
Hartford, Connecticut 06115

Delaware
Delaware Office of Management,
 Budget, and Planning
Townsend Building
P.O. Box 1401, 3rd Floor
Dover, Delaware 19901

District of Columbia
Washington, D.C., Municipal
 Planning Office
District Building
Washington, D.C. 20004

Florida
Florida State Energy Office
310 Bryant Building
Tallahassee, Florida 32304

Georgia
Georgia Office of Energy Resources
270 Washington Street, S.W.
Atlanta, Georgia 30334

Hawaii
Hawaii State Energy Office
Department of Planning and
 Economic Development
P.O. Box 2359
Honolulu, Hawaii 96804

Idaho
Idaho Office of Energy
State House
Boise, Idaho 83720

Illinois
Illinois Department of Business
 Division of Energy
 and Economic Development
222 South College Street
Springfield, Illinois 62706

Indiana
Indiana Department of Commerce
 Energy Group
115 North Pennsylvania Street
Indianapolis, Indiana 46204

Iowa
Iowa Energy Policy Council
215 East 7th Street
Des Moines, Iowa 50319

Kansas
State of Kansas Energy Office
503 Kansas Avenue, Room 241
Topeka, Kansas 66603

Kentucky
Kentucky Department of Energy
Capitol Plaza Office Tower, 9th Floor
Frankfort, Kentucky 40601

Louisiana
Louisiana Department of Natural
 Resources
P.O. Box 44156
Baton Rouge, Louisiana 70804

Maine
Maine Office of Energy Resources
55 Capitol Street
Augusta, Maine 04330

Maryland
Maryland Energy Policy Office
301 West Preston Street
Baltimore, Maryland 21201

Massachusetts
Massachusetts Energy Policy Office
73 Tremont Street
Boston, Massachusetts 02108

Michigan
Michigan Energy Administration
Michigan Department of Commerce
Law Building, 4th Floor
Lansing, Michigan 48913

Minnesota
Minnesota Energy Agency
740 American Center Building
160 East Kellogg Boulevard
St. Paul, Minnesota 55101

Mississippi
Mississippi Fuel and Energy
 Management Commission
Woolfolk State Office Building,
 Room 1307
Jackson, Mississippi 39202

Missouri
Missouri Energy Program
Department of Natural Resources
P.O. Box 176
Jefferson City, Missouri 65101

Montana
Montana Energy Office
c/o Lieutenant Governor's Office
Capitol Station
Helena, Montana 59601

Nebraska
Nebraska Energy Office
P.O. Box 95085
Lincoln, Nebraska 68509

Nevada
Nevada Department of Energy
1050 East William, Suite 405
Carson City, Nevada 89710

New Hampshire
New Hampshire Governor's Council
 on Energy
26 Pleasant Street
Concord, New Hampshire 03301

New Jersey
New Jersey Department of Energy
1100 Raymond Boulevard
Newark, New Jersey 07102

New Mexico
New Mexico Energy Resources
 Board
P.O. Box 2770
Santa Fe, New Mexico 87501

New York
New York State Energy Office
Agency Building No. 2
Empire State Plaza
Albany, New York 12223

North Carolina
North Carolina Department of
 Commerce Energy Division
430 North Salisbury Street
Raleigh, North Carolina 27611

North Dakota
North Dakota Office of Energy Management and Conservation
1533 North 12th Street
Bismarck, North Dakota 58501

Ohio
Ohio Department of Energy
30 East Broad Street, 34th Floor
Columbus, Ohio 43215

Oklahoma
Oklahoma Department of Energy
4400 North Lincoln Boulevard, Suite 251
Oklahoma City, Oklahoma 73105

Oregon
Oregon Department of Energy
528 Cottage Street, N.E.
Salem, Oregon 97310

Pennsylvania
Pennsylvania Governor's Energy Council
P.O. Box 1323
Harrisburg, Pennsylvania 17120

Rhode Island
Rhode Island Governor's Energy Office
80 Dean Street
Providence, Rhode Island 02903

South Carolina
South Carolina Energy Management Office
Edgar A. Brown Building
1205 Pendleton Street
Columbia, South Carolina 29201

South Dakota
South Dakota Office of Energy Policy
State Capitol
Pierre, South Dakota 57501

Tennessee
Tennessee Energy Authority
Capitol Hill Building, Suite 250
Nashville, Tennessee 37219

Texas
Texas Governor's Office
c/o Administrative Assistant for Energy Resources
7703 North Lamar, #512
Austin, Texas 78752

Utah
Utah Energy Office
455 East 400 South, Suite 303
Salt Lake City, Utah 89111

Vermont
Vermont State Energy Office
Pavilion Office Building
Montpelier, Vermont 05602

Virginia
Virginia Energy Office
823 East Main Street
Richmond, Virginia 23219

Washington
Washington State Energy Office
400 East Union, 1st Floor
Olympia, Washington 98504

West Virginia
Fuel and Energy Division
West Virginia Governor's Office of Economic and Community Development
1262½ Greenbrier Street
Charleston, West Virginia 25311

Wisconsin
Wisconsin Office of State Planning and Energy
1 West Wilson Street
Madison, Wisconsin 53702

Wyoming
Wyoming Energy Conservation Office
Capitol Hill Office Building
Cheyenne, Wyoming 82002

Index

A

Air conditioners
  condition of, 10–11
  Cooling-Load Estimate Form, 67
  Cost Calculator, 66
  filter cleaning, 15
  oversizing, 11
Air conditioning
  alternatives to, 57–60
  effect of insulation on, 57–59
  temperature and humidity
    factors, 57–60
Air leakage, 9, 10, 17, 18, 23, 26, 27, 28, 30
  saving table for windows, 31
American Gas Association, 54–55, 56
American National Standards
  Institute, 54–55
American Society of Heating,
  Refrigerating, and Air-Conditioning
  Engineers (ASHRAE), 11, 27
Attic fans, whole-house, see Fans,
  whole-house attic

B

British thermal unit (Btu), explanation
  of, 8

C

Caulking compounds, 17–22
  Ratings, 21–22
  tips on working with, 13, 19, 20
Cellulose insulation
  advice for installation, 39
  Federal flammability standard, 38
CertainTeed Corp., 32
Chevron Research Company, 17
Chevron USA, 17
"Chimney robbers," see Flue heat
  recovery devices
Clothes dryers, cleaning of lint screen, 15
Combustion efficiency (C.E.), 47–49
  saving table, 47
Commerce, Department of, 50
Community Services Administration, 89
  offices, addresses of regional, 97
Conduction, 9, 26–27, 28
  heat saving table for windows, 30

Conservation measures, estimated
    savings from
  as based on average costs, 12
  furnace maintenance, 47
  home insulation, 36–37
  lowering thermostat, 41
  water heater adjustments, 69–70
  weather stripping, 28–29, 31
  windows (storm and thermal), 27–31
Conservation measures,
  overview, 13–16
Conservation programs
  summaries of Federal, 88–89
  summaries of state, 89–95
Consumer Product Safety
  Commission, 38–39, 55
Consumers Union Ratings,
  explanation of, 12–13
Contractor, selection of, 84–85
Contracts, home improvement, 85–87
Cooling, ways to reduce cost, 59–60
Cooling-Load Estimate Form for Room
  Air Conditioners, 67

D

Damper, flue, see Flue dampers
Degree-days
  explanation of, 10
  zone charts, 29–31, 37
Direct venting of furnaces, 49
"Directory of Localities with Community
  Development Block Grant Property
  Rehabilitation Financing
  Activities," 88
Dryers, clothes, cleaning of lint screen, 15
Ducts, heating, insulation of, 14

E

Economic opportunity, addresses of
  state offices, 95–97
Electricity Miser, 80
Energy, Department of, 8–9, 55, 88, 89
Energy Conservation and Protection
  Act, 88
Energy Efficiency Ratio (EER), 11, 58, 66
Energy offices, addresses of state, 97–99
Energy Policy and Conservation Act, 88
Exhaust fans, 9, 15

F

Fans, exhaust, 9, 15
Fans, whole-house attic, 14, 60–65
  fire hazards, 63–64
  Ratings, 64–65
  shutters, 61–62, 65
  timers, 61, 65
Farmers Home Administration, 10, 33, 89
Federal conservation programs,
  summaries of, 88–89
Federal Housing Administration, 10, 32
Fire hazards associated with
  cellulose insulation, 38–39
  whole-house attic fans, 63–64
Fireplace damper, closing, 15
Fitch Energy Monitor, 80
Flue dampers, 14, 53–56
  safety aspects of, 54–55
  testing of, 55–56
Flue heat recovery devices, 14, 49–53
  Ratings, 53
Fuel costs, nation-wide averages, 12
Furnaces
  direct venting of, 49
  filters, cleaning of, 15
  flue dampers, 14, 53–56
  flue heat recovery devices, 14, 49–53
  heat loss from, 40, 47, 49–51, 53
  ignition systems for, 49
  maintenance of, 10–11
  oversizing, 11
  Ratings, flue heat recovery
    devices, 53

G

Gas ranges, see Ranges, gas
Gaskets, refrigerator and freezer,
  tightness of, 15

H

"Handbook of Fundamentals,"
  ASHRAE, 27
Heat circulators, 81
Heat flow, 9–11
Heat loss
  air leakage, 9, 10, 17, 18, 23, 26, 27,
    28, 30

101

conduction, 9
   from chimneys, 9, 40, 47, 49–51
   from fan, kitchen exhaust, 9
   from furnace, 40, 49–51
   from windows, 23, 26–27, 28, 30
Heater, water
   explanation of energy use in, 7
   insulation for, 14, 69–70
   savings from conservation measures, 12, 68–70
   shut-off devices, 80–81
   storage costs, hot water, table, 70
Homefoamers, The, 32
Hot water pipes, insulation of, 14, 70
Housing and Urban Development, Department of, 33, 88
Humidity, 11, 58

I

Igniters for gas ranges, 81–83
   Ratings, 83
Ignition systems for furnaces, 49
Instruments for measuring Combustion Efficiency, 47
Insulation, 12, 13, 32–39
   and air-conditioning costs, 57–59
   cellulose, 38–39
   for hot water pipes, 14, 70
   for water heater, 14, 69–70
   saving calculator, 36–37

K

Kill-A-Watt, 79
Kilowatt-hour (kwh), explanation of, 8

L

Lamb, David, 33
Laundry appliances, 15, 16
Loan programs, Federal, 88–89

M

Michigan Consolidated Gas Co., 33
Minimum Property Standards, 10
Money saved from conservation measures, *see* Conservation measures, estimated savings from
Monitors, electricity, 79–80
Multi-temperature thermostats, *see* Thermostats, energy-saving

N

National Association of Home Builders, 33
National Bureau of Standards, 17, 59
National Conference of State Legislatures, 88
National Consumer Law Center, 85–87
National Energy Act, 88
National Energy Plan, 7
National Oceanic and Atmospheric Administration, 29, 58

Nautilus Heat Recycler, 81
New Jersey attorney general, 79
New York Public Service Commission, 79

O

Oak Ridge National Laboratory, 41
Owens-Corning, 32–33

P

Payback period, 12, 33–34
Pilot lights, furnace, 49
Pilot lights, igniters for range tops, 15, 81–83
   Ratings, 83
Pipes, water, insulation for, 14, 70
Powerguard, 79
Predicasts, Inc., 7

R

R-value
   as applied to air conditioning, 58
   as applied to insulation, 32–33
   as applied to storm windows, 26–27
   explanation of, 10
Ranges, gas, igniters for, 81–83
   Ratings, 83
Refrigerator, cleaning of condenser coils, 15
Replacement windows, *see* Thermal windows
Rooms, closing off, 15

S

Save-Fuel Corporation, 54
Savings, money, from conservation measures, *see* Conservation measures, estimated savings from
Seasonal efficiency, 47–49
Setback thermostats, *see* Thermostats, energy-saving
Showers, water-saving devices for, 70–73
   flow restrictor, Ratings, 72
   shower head Ratings, 72–73
   shut-off controls, 71
Shutters for whole-house attic fans, 61–62
   Listings, 65
Solar energy, CU's test projects on, 12
State conservation programs, summaries of, 89–95
State offices of economic opportunity, 95–97
State offices of energy, 97–99
Storm windows, 13, 26–31
Stoves, *see* Ranges
Surge suppressors, 79

T

Tax credits, 32, 88, 89, 90, 91, 92, 93, 94, 95

Temperature
   effect on cooling, 57–60
   effect on heat flow, 9–10, 27, 57
   stack, of furnaces, 49–50
Tennessee Valley Authority, 33
Thermal windows, 26–29
Thermocycler, 81
Thermometer, stack, for measuring combustion efficiency, 47
Thermostats
   devices for setting back, 43–44
   energy-saving, 40–46
   Listings, 45–46
   lowering of heating system, 13, 40
   lowering of water heater, 14, 68–69
Timers for whole-house attic fans, 61, 65
"Tips for Energy Savers," 11–12
Toilets, tank-type
   reducing water consumption, 74–75
   water-saving devices for, 75–76
   Ratings, water-saving devices, 76–77
Toilets, water-saving, 76
   Ratings, 78
Truth-in-Lending laws, 86

U

U-value, explanation of, 10
Underwriters Laboratories, 54, 55, 56
United States Congress, 7, 38, 88
Utilities, role in conservation, 88

W

Washington Suburban Sanitary Commission, 68
Water heater
   conservation measures for, 12, 68–70
   explanation of energy use, 7
   insulation for, 14, 69–70
   lowering thermostat on, 14, 68–69
   storage costs, hot water, table, 70
   timer for, 80–81
Water pipes, insulating, 14, 70
Water Resources Council, 68
Water-saving devices, 15, 70–78
   for showers, 15, 70–73
   for toilets, 15, 74–78
Weather factors affecting cooling needs, 57–60
Weather stripping, 13, 23–25, 27, 28–29, 31
   Ratings for durability, 25
Weatherization programs, Federal, 89
Window shades, 16
Windows, 26–31
Woolfolk, Charles, 54–55
Work sheets
   Air-Conditioning Cost Calculator, 66
   Cooling-Load Estimate Form for Room Air Conditioners, 67
   Insulation Saving Calculator, 36–37
   Window Saving Calculator, 28–29

Paperbounds from Consumer Reports Books

Consumer Reports Money-Saving Guide to Energy in the Home. CU's energy-saving strategies with product Ratings. 1978. $3

James Beard's Theory & Practice of Good Cooking. Basic techniques plus many recipes. 1977. CU printing, 1978. $6.75

Child Health Encyclopedia. A comprehensive guide for parents. 1975. CU printing, 1978. $7.50

Consumers Union Reviews Classical Recordings. Consumer Reports' reviews with updated comments, basic discography. 1978. $5

Access. The guide to a better life for disabled Americans. 1978. CU edition, $5.50

Ulcers. What they are; who's likely to get them—and why; which treatments work best. 1978. CU edition, $5

Guide to Used Cars. CU's reports and Ratings for 1974-77 cars; repair records, good and bad bets for 1972-77 cars. 1978. $5.50

You and Your Aging Parent. A guide to understanding emotional, physical, and financial needs. 1976. CU printing, 1978. $3.75

The Consumers Union Report on Life Insurance. CU's guide to planning and buying the protection you need. 1977. $3

Funerals: Consumers' Last Rights. CU's practical advice on conventional funerals and some low-cost alternatives. 1977. $5.50

Guide to Consumer Services. CU's advice on selected financial and professional services. 1977. $3.50

You Are Not Alone. Guide to emotional problems, mental illness, and getting professional help. 1976. CU edition, $5.50

The Medicine Show. CU's guide to some everyday health problems and products. 1974; updated 1976. $3.50

Licit and Illicit Drugs. CU's award-winning report on drugs, users, laws, policies, attitudes. 1972. $4

TO ORDER: Send payment, including 50¢ per book for postage/handling, together with your name and address to Dept. EN78, Consumer Reports Books, Orangeburg, N.Y. 10962. Please allow 4 to 6 weeks for shipment. NOTE: Consumers Union publications may not be used for any commercial purpose.